WORDS

5TH EDITION

SPELLING,

PRONUNCIATION,

DEFINITION,

AND APPLICATION

GREGG PUBLISHING DIVISION
McGraw-Hill Book Company, Inc.
New York
Chicago
Dallas
Corte Madera, Calif.
Toronto
London

Doris H. Crank, Ed.D.
Illinois State Normal University

Floyd L. Crank, Ph.D.
University of Illinois

Mary E. Connelly, B.S., M.Ed.
Boston University

E. Lillian Hutchinson
Consulting Editor

WORDS—

Spelling, Pronunciation, Definition, and Application   Fifth Edition

1 2 3 4 5 6 7 8 9 0   KP-62   9 8 7 6 5 4 3 2
13444
Library of Congress Catalog Card No. 60-15862

PUBLISHED BY GREGG PUBLISHING DIVISION
McGraw-Hill Book Company, Inc.
Printed in the United States of America

PREFACE

A thought that cannot be expressed is a total loss. Words —well chosen and correctly used, orally or in writing—are the magic elements from which our thoughts can be formed into expressions. With the "right" words at our command, we can say and write—we can communicate what we are thinking to others with greater clarity and confidence. This revision of WORDS has been designed to fill the need for a plan of functional vocabulary development—including spelling, pronunciation, definition, and application— that would enable the student to cope with the growing demands of modern personal and business life for quick and effective communications.

The approach used in WORDS, Fifth Edition, is based on the latest research findings; and this approach results in a most satisfactory blending of quality as well as quantity goals in the instructional process. The presentation starts with the assumption that each student in the course has already developed a spelling vocabulary of unknown quality. Consequently, the first step that the book undertakes in Section One is to find out where each student stands in spelling ability.

In the balance of Section One of the book, the student is taught how to recognize and how to correct his present spelling difficulties. Once he has gained a solid footing, the student is ready to expand his vocabulary; and in Section Two he is given what he needs for personal growth in three areas: general vocabulary, general business vocabulary, and specialized business vocabulary. The careful planning of the sequence of presentation permits progress on the basis of a solid preparatory foundation. The student can move along as rapidly as he is able and can concentrate on words that he does not already know or that he does not use effectively.

The presentation of WORDS, Fifth Edition, is designed to afford maximum flexibility to accommodate wide ranges in student ability, all kinds of classroom conditions, and any type of scheduling problem. For example, a teacher who is limited to a short lesson period a day in a rather brief course may start the instruction directly with Section Two. Classes of mature adults might also be handled in this way. The teacher who has a little more time may concentrate on Section Two in class and hold the students responsible for mastery of Section One. Of course, other variations can be worked out as circumstances warrant; but most teachers will want to cover the entire book right straight through.

Remember, WORDS, Fifth Edition, was written with full and frank awareness that many students of business subjects have serious deficiencies in spelling. If uncorrected, these deficiencies will seriously impair the students' chances of business success and will invite criticism of business teaching methods. The instructor who is also frank to recognize that the problem affords little room for compromise will be happy to find that WORDS, Fifth Edition, makes every instructional minute count. The approach, the methods, the plan—all help the teacher to get at the root of the students' difficulties, to take corrective action, and to build up to new levels of skill competency. By following this course, the teacher will be doing everything that can be done to obtain the best results with the time and resources available; and those results—superior results—will prove the effort very much worthwhile, thanks to a truly significant degree of individualization of instruction. No time is wasted on spelling "frills" and word oddities. The emphasis is concentrated on a functional vocabulary that is important in everyday activities.

Here is an outline of the major segments of the book:
Section One: Taking Stock of Words You Know
    Part 1 Words Spelled According to Sound and Meaning
    Part 2 Words Spelled According to Rules and Words Requiring Special Care
Section Two: Learning to Spell New Words
    Part 1 The Four-Step Approach
    Part 2 Words for Your General Vocabulary
    Part 3 New Words for Your General Business Vocabulary
    Part 4 Words for Your Specialized Business Vocabulary

Each unit in Section Two consists of four daily lessons and then a check-up lesson. The treatment of each word in the typical lesson includes its spelling, phonetic spelling, syllabication, and definition. The teaching plan calls for immediate practical application and recurring review. Complete instructions will permit the student to do a great deal of the work independently or with only a minimum of supervision.

Getting acquainted with the new presentation will be a simple matter for the instructor who uses the highly informative manual and key that is furnished by the publisher upon adoption of the text. A set of objective tests is available, also.

The system of indicating pronunciation in this text is used by permission, from Webster's New Collegiate Dictionary, copyright 1960 by G. & C. Merriam Co., publishers of the Merriam-Webster Dictionaries.

DORIS H. CRANK
FLOYD L. CRANK
MARY E. CONNELLY

CONTENTS

SECTION ONE

TAKING STOCK OF WORDS YOU KNOW

PART 1 Words Spelled According to Sound and Meaning

PART 2 Words Spelled According to Rules and Words Requiring Special Care

PART ①

WORDS SPELLED ACCORDING TO SOUND AND MEANING

How do you rate as a speller?

If you are like most people, you will have to admit that your spelling skill can be improved. Even good spellers find that occasional periods of refresher training and review help them become consistently accurate spellers. Even though you have been learning to spell since you were in the second or third grade, if you are like most people there is still much that you can learn about words and word usage.

If you expect to hold a responsible job in a business office, you must be a good speller. You have no alternative. Everyone in an office—the typist, the secretary, the file clerk, the mail clerk, the supervisor—must communicate with other office workers hundreds of times each day. A large part of business communication is written, and this material must be clear and accurate. Correct spelling and precise word usage are two important aspects of clear communication.

If your spelling skill needs considerable improvement, this book will help you to learn how to spell correctly. If you are a good speller, you can brush up on what you already know and "pin down" those tricky words that still cause you trouble. The best way to start with your spelling improvement is to find out how you rate as a speller. The material in this book can then be used to meet your individual needs.

Pretest. Your instructor will now give you a spelling test consisting of 100 words that are commonly misspelled in business communications. Listen carefully to the instructions and do your very best. Your answers will help to reveal your spelling weaknesses.

A **Personal Program of Spelling Improvement.** Well, how did you make out on the pretest? Was it "rough going" in spots? If so, don't be discouraged. The list is not an easy one—it contains many spelling traps for the unwary. These traps are the causes of most spelling errors. Fortunately, experts have been able to identify the common spelling traps. You should begin your spelling-improvement program by finding out how and why spelling errors are made. After you have studied some of the causes of spelling errors, you will be asked to analyze the errors that you made on the pretest. You can then work out the details of your personal program of spelling improvement.

Spotting Sound Errors

Lesson 1 Omission of Silent Letters

When spelling unfamiliar words by sound, it is easy to omit the silent letters. For example, the word *build* might be misspelled as *bild*, and the same mistake might be carried over into the spelling of derivatives, such as *builder* (as *bilder*) and *building* (as *bilding*). If you are aware that silent letters occur in many words, you will be on the lookout for this spelling trap.

Practice. Test your ability to recognize silent letters. Copy each of the following words; then draw a circle around the silent letter or letters in each word.

coupon	consign	employee	knitted
gauge	bouquet	guidance	salmon
leisure	foreign	subpoena	respite
mortgage	subtle	colleague	debt
routine	tourist	hustle	jostle

Lesson 2 Mispronunciation or Slovenly Enunciation

Spelling a word according to sound becomes doubly hazardous if you do not know the correct pronunciation of the word. A person who pronounces the word *athlete* as "ath-a-lete" instead of "ath'lete" probably will misspell the word as *athalete*. There are many words that present spelling traps because certain syllables within the words are either mispronounced or not enunciated distinctly. As a part of your spelling-improvement program, you will wish to make sure that you are not misspelling words because of mispronunciation or poor enunciation. The following exercise contains a list of words that illustrate the necessity of correct pronunciation and precise enunciation.

Practice. Copy each of the following words; then draw a circle around the letter or the syllable that a person might mispronounce or fail to enunciate clearly.

finally	reconnoiter	affidavit	genuine
inauguration	preponderance	manual	accompaniment
congenial	laboratory	artistically	mischievous
ingenious	chocolate	luxurious	ordinance
co-operative	hosiery	maintenance	supervisory

Lesson 3 Poor Auditory Discrimination

Another common spelling pitfall, especially when spelling by sound, involves the choice of the wrong vowel to represent an elusive sound—misspelling the word *despair* as *dispair*, the word *bulletin* as *bullatin*, and the word *warrant* as *warrent*, for example. The choice of the wrong vowel to represent an elusive sound occurs frequently (1) in word beginnings, when there is a tendency to slur the initial vowel sounds—*discribe* for *describe;* (2) in the middle of words, when a vowel becomes a one-letter syllable or part of a two-letter syllable—*manditory* for *mandatory;* and (3) in word endings, when there is a tendency to slur the final vowel sound—*tourest* for *tourist*. The following exercise contains a list of words that illustrate the necessity for selecting the correct vowels to represent elusive sounds.

Practice. Copy each of the following words; then draw a circle around the letter or syllable for which a person might select the wrong vowel to represent an elusive sound.

verbatim	dignified	ridicule	maritime
vanity	applicant	authorize	formidable
dissipate	discipline	versatile	dominant
bulletin	incorporate	aspirant	merchandise
decimal	offensive	fundamental	advertiser

Lesson 4 Faulty Syllabication

Other spelling mistakes occur when a person tries to spell by sound without knowing the correct syllabication of the word. For instance, *accommodate* is frequently misspelled because it is erroneously divided according to sound, as "ac-com-o-date," instead of according to syllables, as "ac-com-mo-date." Learning how words are divided according to syllables is a dependable way of improving your spelling. The following exercise provides practice in correct syllabication.

Practice. The following words often are divided into syllables incorrectly. The part of the word that causes frequent trouble is italicized. Copy each word. Indicate by a slash mark (/) where the correct syllabic divisions should occur in each word, being particularly careful when dividing the italicized areas.

accommo-date	piti-ful	recon-cili-a-tion	eli-gi-ble
par-allel	strenu-ous	toler-ant	mis-cellane-ous
dissatis-fac-tion	con-gratu-la-tions	linen	affili-ate
fa-cili-ty	u-tili-ty	in-ference	reference
dis-crimina-tion	vac-illate	in-deli-ble	accomplish-ment

Lesson 5 Substitution of Wrong Letters to Represent Sounds

A person may know the correct pronunciation and syllabication of a word and may enunciate the syllables correctly, but he may still choose the wrong letter to represent one of the necessary sounds. For example, the word *absence* is sometimes erroneously spelled as *absense* and at other times as *absents*. In fact, errors of this type are not limited to single-letter substitutions. English is a tricky language, and many of its sounds cause confusion in spelling. The word *proceed*, for example, frequently is misspelled as *procede*. The following exercise contains other common words in which spelling errors of this type frequently occur.

Practice. Copy each of the following words; then draw a circle around the letter or letters for which a person might substitute incorrect letters.

arraign	survey	urgency	alphabetic
pamphlet	tangible	conveyance	tragedy
analyze	generosity	decide	vicinity
fragile	plateau	decipher	technique
scheme	advertising	procedure	specimen

Lesson 6 Incorrect Prefixes and Suffixes

A number of spelling errors may also be attributed to the use of the incorrect form of a prefix or suffix. The word *endure* may be misspelled as *indure*. Note that the *cal* ending in the word *critical* is spelled differently from the ending in the word *article*. The following exercise provides practice in identifying prefixes and suffixes that may cause spelling errors.

Practice. Copy each of the following words, selecting the correct prefix or suffix from the choices given in parentheses beside the root word.

(des, dis) -cription	criti- (cal, cle)
(per, pre, pro) -paid	warr- (ant, ent)
(em, im) -ployee	respons- (able, ible)
(des, dis) -satisfaction	allow- (ance, ence)
(per, pre, pro) -ceed	specta- (cal, cle)
(per, pre, pro) -spiration	indispens- (able, ible)
(em, im) -barrass	accord- (ance, ence)
(des, dis) -crimination	depend- (ant, ent)
(des, dis) -cussion	exten- (sion, tion)
(per, pre, pro) -rogative	resump- (sion, tion)

Lesson 7 Addition of Letters

Spelling errors are sometimes made because unnecessary letters are used to construct the words. For example, an unnecessary *d* may be used to spell the word *legible*, or an unnecessary *l* may be used to spell the word *until*. The words in the following exercise illustrate other instances when spelling errors are made by the addition of unnecessary letters.

Practice. One word in each of the following pairs of words is incorrectly spelled because it contains an unnecessary letter. Select the correct words and copy them on a separate sheet of paper.

cancel, cancell
fiscall, fiscal
vetoe, veto
excell, excel
controll, control
incur, incurr

counsel, counsell
protocol, protocoll
musick, music
embargoe, embargo
legible, ledgible
colossall, colossal

concur, concurr
gratis, gratiss
sellfish, selfish
propell, propel
tresspass, trespass
stratedgy, strategy

Spotting Meaning Errors

Lesson 8 Confusion of Homonyms

Certain words in the English language are pronounced alike but have different meanings. Such words are known as "homonyms." The equivalent of a spelling error occurs when the wrong word is chosen for the meaning desired. For example, the word *there*, meaning "location," represents a spelling error when it is used instead of *their* to indicate possession. The following exercise provides practice in choosing the correct homonym.
Practice. For each homonym given here, write a sentence using the word correctly.

stationery
stationary
residents
residence

marshal
martial
their
there

lessen
lesson
miner
minor

elusive
illusive

Lesson 9 Confusion of Words That Sound Somewhat Alike

Some words sound *somewhat* alike but have very different meanings. Again, a misspelling results when a similar-sounding, but incorrect, word is chosen for the meaning intended. For instance, you might use *accept*, meaning "to receive" or "to agree to," when you should use *except* to express exclusion or rejection. The following practice will help you identify words of this type.
Practice.
1. Copy the following pairs of similar words; then underscore the part of each word that distinguishes it from the other word of the pair.

collision, collusion
liable, libel
morale, moral
absurd, absorb
personal, personnel
co-operation, corporation

addition, edition
respectfully, respectively
formerly, formally
premises, promises
lightening, lightning
pastor, pasture
persecute, prosecute

practicable, practical
prophecy, prophesy
realty, reality
statue, statute
receipt, recipe
desert, dessert

2. Use each word in the following five pairs of similar words correctly in a sentence.

personal, personnel	**persecute, prosecute**	**realty, reality**
respectfully, respectively	**prophecy, prophesy**	

Analysis of Pretest Errors

You now have seen that many spelling errors can be traced to mistakes in the pronunciation of words or to mistakes in the meaning of words. Armed with this knowledge, you can analyze your own spelling errors, including those that you made on the pretest, and identify the reasons for your mistakes. Once you know what your spelling problems are, you can concentrate on the specific skills that will help you attack and overcome your spelling difficulties.

To help you analyze the errors that you made on the pretest, draw up an analysis form similar to the one shown here. In the column headed "Test Word," write the words that you misspelled on the pretest. As you write each word, place a check (√) in the column that indicates the reason for misspelling the word. For example, if you misspelled the word *federal* as *fedral*, write the correct spelling of the word in the column at the left. Then place a check (√) in the column headed "Slovenly Enunciation," since you misspelled the word because you failed to enunciate all the syllables clearly. When you have completed the error analysis, check with your teacher to make certain that you analyzed the errors correctly.

Error-Analysis Chart

Test Word	Silent-Letter Omission	Mispronunciation or Slovenly Enunciation	Poor Auditory Discrimination	Faulty Syllabication	Substitution	Incorrect Prefixes or Suffixes	Addition of Letters	Confusion of Homonyms	Confusion of Words That Sound Somewhat Alike

Attacking Sound Errors

Once you know what your spelling problems are, the next step is to learn what to do to correct them. You are now ready to develop specific skills to help you attack and correct some of your spelling difficulties.

Lesson 10 Finding Words in the Dictionary

Suppose your error-analysis chart (page 7) reveals a spelling mistake traceable to mispronunciation, such as spelling the word *definite* as *defanite*. What steps can you take to eliminate this spelling difficulty?

If you are wondering what is wrong with your spelling, *defanite*, your first step should be to look up the word in your dictionary. Here is how to proceed:

1. Using the alphabetical thumb index, open the dictionary to the first letter of the word you seek.
2. Using the guide words at the top of the pages, locate the page that includes your word.
3. Locate the word alphabetically on the page.

---

deficiency judgment 217 de

deficiency judgment. *Law.* A judgment for the balance of a debt after the security has been realized and the proceeds applied to payment.
de·fi′cient (dĕ·fĭsh′ĕnt), *adj.* [L. *deficiens, -entis,* pres. part. of *deficere* to be wanting. See DEFECT.] Lacking in some quality necessary for completeness; defective. — *n.* One that is deficient. — -**ly,** *adv.*
def′i·cit (dĕf′ĭ·sĭt), *n.* [Lit., it is wanting, 3d pers. pres. indic. of L. *deficere.*] Deficiency in amount, as of income.
‖**de fi′de** (dē fī′dē). [L.] Literally, of the faith; specif., *R.C.Ch.,* designating a revealed truth taught by the Church.
de·fi′er (dĕ·fī′ẽr), *n.* One who defies.
def′i·lade′ (dĕf′ĭ·lād′), *v. t. & i. Fort.* To arrange (fortifications) so as to protect the lines from frontal or enfilading fire and the interior of the works from plunging or reverse fire. — *n. Mil.* Act or process of defilading.
de·file′ (dĕ·fīl′), *v. t.* [Influenced by *foul* and by *file* to foul, but orig. fr. OF. *defouler* to trample, crush, fr. *de-* + *fouler* to trample.] **1.** To make filthy; to befoul. **2.** *Archaic.* To ravish; to violate. **3.** To make ceremonially unclean; to pollute. **4.** To tarnish, as reputation; to dishonor. — **Syn.** See CONTAMINATE. — **de·file′ment,** *n.* — **de·fil′er** (-fīl′ẽr), *n.*
de·file′, *v. t. & i.* [F. *défiler,* fr. *dé-* (fr. L. *de*) + *file* a row or line.] To march off in a line, file by file; to file off.
de·file′ (dĕ·fīl′; dē′fīl), *n.* Any narrow passage or gorge.
de·fine′ (dĕ·fīn′), *v.t.* [OF. *definer, definir,* fr. L. *definire* to limit, define, fr. *de* + *finire* to limit, end, fr. *finis* limit.] **1.** To mark the limits or boundaries of; to make distinct or fix in outline or character. **2.** To describe, expound, or interpret; to explain; hence, to determine the precise signification of; to discover and set forth the meaning of, as a word. **3.** To set apart in a class by identifying marks; to distinguish. — **de·fin′a·ble** (-fīn′à·b'l), *adj.* — **de·fin′er** (-fīn′ẽr), *n.*
def′i·nite (dĕf′ĭ·nĭt), *adj.* [L. *definitus,* past part. of *definire.* See DEFINE.] **1.** Having distinct or certain limits; limited; fixed. **2.** Clear and unmistakable in meaning; precise in detail; explicit. **3.** Limiting; determining; as, the *definite* article. — **Syn.** See EXPLICIT. — **Ant.** Indefinite. — **def′i·nite·ly,** *adv.* — **def′i·nite·ness,** *n.*
definite article. *Gram.* The article *the,* which is used to designate a particular person or thing.
def′i·ni′tion (dĕf′ĭ·nĭsh′ŭn), *n.* **1.** Explanation of the meaning or

de·for·ma′tion (dē′fôr·mā′shŭn) state of being deformed; disfigu Alteration of form or shape; a
de·formed′ (dĕ·fôrmd′), *adj.* **form′ed·ly** (-fôr′mĕd·lĭ; 30),
de·form′i·ty (-fôr′mĭ·tĭ), *n.; n* formed; disfigurement. **2.** De thetic flaw or defect. **3.** A d
de·fraud′ (dĕ·frôd′), *v. t.* [L.: fr. *fraus, fraudis,* fraud.] property, by deceit. — **Syn.** dā′shŭn), *n.* — **de·fraud′er,** *n*
de·fray′ (dĕ·frā′), *v. t.* [F. *d* expense.] **1.** To pay, or to pr To bear the expenses of. — **de·** **fray′er,** *n.* — **de·fray′ment,**
de·frock′ (dĕ·frŏk′), *v. t.* To
de·frost′ (dĕ·frŏst′), *v. t.* To
de·frost′er (-frŏs′tẽr), *n.* A frost or ice; specif., one for a v
deft (dĕft), *adj.* [ME. *defte.* ity; quick and neat in actio **Ant.** Awkward. — **deft′ly,** ac
de·funct′ (dĕ·fŭngkt′), *adj.* acquit oneself of, finish, depar deceased. — **Syn.** See DEAD.
de·fy′ (dĕ·fī′), *v. t.; -FIED* (-fī deriv. of L. *dis-* + *fidus* faith bat. **2.** To challenge to perf dare. **3.** To set at nought; a attempts at; as, to *defy* descr *défi,* fr. the v.] *Slang.* A cha
‖**dé′ga·gé′** (dā′gà′zhā′), *adj.* Free; at ease; unconstrained.
de·gas′ (dē·găs′), *v. t.; DE·GA* To free from gas.
de Gaull′ist (dē gōl′ĭst). A fol War II, one of the Fighting F

Once you have located the word, check the spelling letter by letter, as follows:

1. Be sure that you read the letters in their correct order.
2. Do not insert letters that are not there.
3. Do not leave out letters that belong in the word.
4. If more than one spelling is given, choose the preferred (the first) spelling.
5. Be on guard against words that may be spelled or pronounced very much like the one you are checking.

Practice. For practice in locating and checking dictionary entries, look up each of the following words. On a sheet of paper, copy each word, supplying the missing letters.

ackn-------ment
capit-----tion
concen----tion
corp----tion
docu----

ente----ise
frau----ent
partn-----ip
seni---ity
synd----te

Lesson **11** Learning Pronunciation by Phonetics (According to Sound)

Verifying the spelling of the word will only show you *where* you made the mistake. This procedure has little if any lasting value in preventing the repetition of the error later on because you have not yet reached the source of your trouble. Unless you know and remember that *definite* is pronounced "definite" and not "defanite," you will make the same mistake the next time you try to spell the word by sound. How, then, can you learn the correct pronunciation of a word so that you can use the spelling-by-sound method and use it accurately when you next encounter the same word? Again, the answer is to be found in the dictionary.

Each entry in the dictionary is printed in bold-faced type. Immediately following the entry, the word is respelled phonetically; that is, according to speech sounds. The phonetic spelling of the word is your key to its correct pronunciation. For example, *definite* is respelled phonetically as "dĕf′ĭ·nĭt." The phonetic symbols indicate how each sound is to be made. In this case, *d* would be sounded as in *day*, *e* as in *end*, *f* as in *fill*, *i* as in *charity*, *n* as in *nod*, *i* as in *ill*, and *t* as in *to*. (See the illustration.) The accent mark at the end of the first syllable indicates that the principal stress should fall on that syllable. The centered period (·) at the end of the second syllable indicates that no stress is to be placed on that syllable. (Many longer words contain two accents, a primary and a secondary accent.) A lighter accent mark would indicate where a secondary, or lighter, stress should be placed: "ăp′á·rā′tŭs."

You will need to become skilled in interpreting phonetics if you really wish to learn how to pronounce words properly. In the special drills and lessons that follow, you are given plenty of practice in the phonetic approach to spelling improvement. Plan to take advantage of all these opportunities.

Practice. Copy each of the following words on a sheet of paper. Beside each word, write the phonetic spelling as it appears in the dictionary.

agenda
bankruptcy
clientele
depletion
expedite

integrity
monopoly
potential
recoup
surety

Merriam-Webster Pronunciation Key

Symbol	Example	Name	Symbol	Example	Name
ā	āle	long a	N	boN	
ȧ	chȧotic	half-long a		(French bon)	small-capital n
â	câre	circumflex a	ng	sing	
ă	ădd	short a	ō	ōld	long o
a̤	a̤ccount	italic short a	ȯ	ȯbey	half-long o
ä	ärm	two-dot a	ô	ôrb	circumflex o
à	àsk	one-dot a	ŏ	ŏdd	short o
a̤	sofȧ	italic one-dot a	ŏ̧	sŏ̧ft	short-circumflex o
b	but		o̤	cŏnnect	italic short o
ch	chair		oi	oil	
d	day		ōō	fōōd	long double o
du̇	verdu̇re	ligatured d-u	o͝o	fo͝ot	short double o
ē	ēve	long e	ou	out	
ḙ	hḙre	hooked long e	p	pen	
ė	ėvent	half-long e	r	rat	
ĕ	ĕnd	short e	s	sit	
ĕ̤	silĕ̤nt	italic short e	sh	she	
ẽ	makẽr	tilde e	t	to	
f	fill		th	thin	plain t-h: voiceless
g	go		t̶h̶	t̶h̶en	barred t-h: voiced
h	hat		tu̇	natu̇re	ligatured t-u
ī	īce	long i	ū	cūbe	long u
ĭ	ĭll	short i	u̇	u̇nite	half-long u
ĭ̤	charĭ̤ty	italic short i	û	ûrn	circumflex u
j	joke		ŭ	ŭp	short u
k	keep		ṳ̆	circṳ̆s	italic short u
к	=ch in German ich	small-capital k	ü	German grün	umlaut u
l	late		v	van	
m	man		w	win	
n	nod		y	yet	
			z	zone	
			zh	=z in azure	

Lesson 12 Learning to Syllabicate

If, because of faulty syllabication, you also misspell words such as *occasionally* and *recommend*, you will wish to pay special attention to the system used in the dictionary for marking the syllabic division in the vocabulary entry. Every entry of more than one syllable is divided. The end of each syllable is indicated by some mark, which may be a centered period (·), a heavy accent mark ('), or a light accent mark ('). In the bold-faced type, *recommend* appears as **rec'om·mend'**, indicating that the word has three syllables, with light stress on the first syllable, no stress on the second syllable, and principal stress on the last syllable.

rec'om·mend' (rĕk'ŏ·mĕnd'), *v. t.* [ML. *recommendare.*] **1.** To commit; to consign; entrust; — now usually *commend.* **2.** To praise; now specif., to make a commendatory statement concerning (a person or thing). **3.** To commend; to offer or suggest with favoring representations. **4.** To make acceptable; to attract favor to; as, his manners *recommended* him. **5.** To advise; counsel.

In addition to being an aid in spelling, knowledge of correct syllabication is necessary in order to divide a word properly at the end of a written line. (In type and in typewriting, however, certain division points are considered more attractive and more efficient than others. For the rules governing the choice, see page 212.)

However, it is the same story again. You cannot learn to syllabicate words for accurate spelling without a great deal of practice. Therefore, pay particular attention to the syllabication of every word that is presented in the lessons that follow.

Practice. Copy each of the following words on a sheet of paper. Then rewrite each, dividing it into syllables as shown in the dictionary.

Example: allocation   al'lo·ca'tion

arbitration	financier
barometer	guarantee
conciliation	inheritance
deductions	liquidation
efficiency	potential

Lesson 13 Mastering Attack Skills

Continued attention to pronunciation and syllabication will gradually sharpen your hearing—you will learn to hear all the sounds of the letters in a word (except, of course, the silent letters) and to hear them correctly. You will then be far less likely to make faulty substitutions, use incorrect prefixes and suffixes, slip in letters that do not belong, or be fooled by silent letters. For maximum results, don't forget that *you* must play the major role in the consistent practice that we are suggesting.

In addition to the steps outlined in Lesson 11, here are some logical steps to follow as you learn to overcome your spelling weaknesses. The first step, of course, is to look up the misspelled word in the dictionary. Then—

As you *Look* at or *See* the word—
1. Study its general appearance and distinguishing characteristics.
2. Look for familiar word beginnings and endings.

As you *Pronounce* or *Say* the word—
1. Learn the phonetic spelling, the accents, and the individual syllables.
2. Practice pronouncing the word aloud.
3. Think of the spelling for each syllable.

As you *Spell* the word—
1. Sound it to yourself.
2. Cover the word and spell it; then verify the spelling.

As you *Write* the word—
1. Sound the word to yourself.
2. Write the word neatly and legibly.
3. Verify the spelling; then write the word again.
4. Use the word in a sentence.

Practice. Follow the procedures outlined above to correct the sound-type errors that you made on your pretest.

Lesson 14 Review Practice—Omission of Silent Letters

1. Copy each of the following "silent-letter" words on a sheet of paper. After each word, write the phonetic spelling as it is shown in the dictionary.

answer	acknowledging	height	corps
campaign	friend	psychology	leisure
scientific	doubt	gauge	foreign
undoubtedly	column	exhaust	knowledge
muscle	forehead	guidance	mortgage

2. Practice pronouncing each "silent-letter" word listed above to make sure that you know how the word sounds when spoken correctly. Look for unusual letter combinations that represent a sound, as *sw* in *answer*.

3. As someone dictates each word to you, pronounce and spell the word; then give the silent letter or letters in the word.

4. Write the word that matches each of the following definitions:

   (a) To measure.
   (b) A military unit.
   (c) The upper part of the face.
   (d) Escape of waste gases.
   (e) Belonging to a country other than one's own.
   (f) Distance above a base.
   (g) Accurate, systematic, and exact.
   (h) Beyond question or doubt.
   (i) Body tissues that move various parts of the body.
   (j) The science of the mind.

Lesson 15 Review Practice—Mispronunciation or Slovenly Enunciation

1. Copy each of the following words on a sheet of paper. After each word, write the phonetic spelling as it is shown in the dictionary.

occasionally	library	chimney	disastrous
federal	administration	accrued	quantity
parliament	February	specifically	government
candidate	afterwards	continuous	laboratory
interesting	similar	handkerchief	maintenance

2. Underscore the parts of each word that might be mispronounced or that might not be enunciated clearly.
3. Pronounce each of the words aloud, being careful to enunciate clearly and to pronounce each syllable correctly.
4. Spell the words orally as they are dictated to you.
5. Write the word that matches each of the following definitions:

   (a) The second month.
   (b) A legislative body.
   (c) Bearing resemblance; of like characteristics.
   (d) Explicitly; definitely.
   (e) Place for scientific research.
   (f) Unlucky; unfortunate; calamitous.
   (g) Without ceasing; constant.
   (h) Control or regulation exercised over men and communities.
   (i) Means of support or sustenance.
   (j) Accumulated.

Lesson 16 Review Practice—Poor Auditory Discrimination

1. Copy each of the following words on a sheet of paper. After each word, write the phonetic spelling as it is shown in the dictionary.

doctor	absence	acquaintance	criticism
magnificent	estimate	ceremony	eligible
citizen	beautiful	dormitory	eliminate
definitely	marvelous	intelligence	definite
backward	abundance	comparative	legitimate

2. Underscore the parts of each word for which sounds are hard to discriminate.
3. Pronounce each of the words aloud, being careful to enunciate clearly and to pronounce each syllable correctly. Study the vowels in the word carefully.
4. Spell the words orally as they are dictated to you. As you spell each word, recall the precise sound of each vowel.
5. Write the word that matches each of the following definitions:

   (a) A plentiful supply.
   (b) Worthy of acceptance.
   (c) Grand in appearance.
   (d) Authorized or lawful.
   (e) The power of understanding.
   (f) To calculate; to assign a value to.
   (g) Involving the act of comparing.
   (h) Wonderful; exciting astonishment.
   (i) Severe judgment.
   (j) A sacred rite or observance.

Lesson 17 Review Practice—Faulty Syllabication

1. Copy each of the following words on a sheet of paper, dividing each word into correct syllables. After each word, write the phonetic spelling as given in the dictionary.

recommend   interrupt   accommodation   difference
military   consideration   questionnaire   accumulate
especially   literary   possession   brilliant
assistant   possibility   immediately   opportunity
appreciate   extraordinary   occasion   collateral

2. Pronounce each of the words aloud, being careful to sound each *individual* syllable clearly and completely. Recall the correct spelling of each syllable.
3. Spell the words aloud as they are dictated. As you spell, recall the sound of each syllable.
4. Write the word that matches each of the following definitions:

   (a) That which may occur.
   (b) Willingness to help others.
   (c) A connected series of inquiries.
   (d) To praise as desirable.
   (e) That which is pledged as security for a debt.
   (f) Ownership.
   (g) Sparkling or glittering.
   (h) To break continuity.
   (i) To increase or amass.
   (j) Unusual; out of the ordinary.

Lesson 18 Review Practice—Substitution of Wrong Letters to Represent Sounds

1. Copy each of the following words on a sheet of paper. After each word, write the phonetic spelling as it is shown in the dictionary.

recover   conscience   descend   adjourn   triumph
extreme   society   surprise   matinee   century
magazine   construction   bankruptcy   oxygen   concede
proceed   gesture   carburetor   suffice   hygiene

2. Underscore the parts of each word where substitution errors might occur.
3. Pronounce each word aloud, enunciating clearly and sounding each syllable correctly.
4. Spell the words aloud as they are dictated to you. As you spell, recall the "tricky" spots. Associate spelling and sound in your mind.
5. Write the word that matches each of the following definitions:

   (a) To rejoice over a victory.
   (b) A collective body of persons comprising a community.
   (c) An expressive motion or action.
   (d) State of being unable to pay just debts.
   (e) To continue or advance.
   (f) Entertainment held in the daytime.
   (g) The science that relates to the preservation of health.
   (h) To allow; to surrender.
   (i) Part of an internal-combustion engine.
   (j) To be satisfactory or adequate.

Lesson 19 Review Practice—Incorrect Prefixes and Suffixes

1. Copy each of the following words on a sheet of paper, dividing each word into correct syllables. After each word, write the phonetic spelling as given in the dictionary.

existence	procession	warrant	attendance
description	performance	permissible	preferred
despair	physician	erroneous	eligible
expression	permanent	dictionary	accessible
responsible	discussion	persuade	procedure

2. Draw a circle around the prefixes and suffixes in the words.

3. Pronounce each of the words aloud, being careful to enunciate precisely and to pronounce each prefix and each suffix correctly.

4. Spell the words aloud as they are dictated to you. As you spell, recall the vowels in the prefixes and the suffixes.

5. Write the word that matches each of the following definitions:

   (a) Incorrect, mistaken, or false. *erroneous*
   (b) Unchangeable; steadfast.
   (c) Dependable; involving trust or obligation.
   (d) Easy to reach or enter.
   (e) Consideration of a question in open debate.
   (f) To guarantee; to justify.
   (g) Suitable; qualified.
   (h) Allowable.
   (i) State of being.
   (j) To abandon all hope.

Lesson 20 Review Practice—Addition of Letters

1. Copy each of the following words on a sheet of paper. After each word, write the phonetic spelling as it is shown in the dictionary.

careful	ninth	already	selfish	sandwich
privilege	compel	grateful	useful	until
rebel (n.)	develop	embargo	allege	wholly
civil	among	welfare	colossal	gratis

2. Circle the parts of each word where letters might be incorrectly added.

3. Pronounce each of the words aloud, making sure that each syllable is enunciated clearly and pronounced correctly. As you sound each syllable, note its spelling.

4. Spell the words orally as they are dictated to you.

5. Write the word that matches each of the following definitions:

   (a) Immense, vast, huge.
   (b) Without charge.
   (c) To affirm, declare, or assert.
   (d) One who resists authority.
   (e) To grow, evolve, amplify.
   (f) Obliging, polite, respectful.
   (g) In the midst of.
   (h) Acting with caution.
   (i) To urge irresistibly.
   (j) The state of having good health and happiness.

Attacking Meaning Errors

If you are constantly stumped in the correct choice of homonyms, such as *principle* and *principal*, or by those "almost-alikes," such as *respectfully* and *respectively*, you need another plan of attack.

Lesson 21 Mastering Attack Skills

You must learn to associate the word with its correct meaning. Perhaps the meaning has never been exactly clear to you, or perhaps you acquired your difficulty a long time ago by repeating what someone else said incorrectly. In any case, the most effective approach is a fresh start—in which you actually find out exactly what each troublesome word means and how it should be used. Let's have another look at the dictionary.

prin′ci·pal (prĭn′sĭ·păl; -p′l), *adj.* [OF., fr. L. *principalis,* fr. *prin-ceps.*] Highest in rank, authority, or importance; chief; main. — *n.* 1. A leader, chief, or head. 2. a A capital sum placed at interest, due as a debt, or used as a fund; — disting. from *interest* or *profit.* b The main body of a decedent's estate, portion of estate, devise, or bequest; — disting. from *income.* 3. *Archaic.* A fundamental point; a prin-ciple. 4. *Arch. & Engin.* The construction which gives shape and strength to a roof, generally one of several trusses of timber or iron. 5. *Educ.* A presiding or chief executive officer of a college, or esp. *U. S.,* of a school or academy. 6. *Law.* a One who employs another to act for him. b One primarily liable on an obligation, as disting. from an *endorser, surety,* etc. c The chief actor in a crime, or an abettor present at it; — distinguished from an *accessory.* 7. *Music.* a In English organs, the chief open metallic stop, an octave above the open diapason. b [*cap.*] An octave or 4-foot organ stop; — used in com-pound names. c A fugue subject; — opposed to *answer.* — prin′ci-pal·ly, *adv.* — prin′ci·pal·ship′, *n.*

Used by permission, from Webster's New Collegiate Dictionary, copyright 1960 by G. & C. Merriam Co., pub-lishers of the Merriam-Webster Dictionaries.

The definition or meaning of the word immediately follows the phonetic spelling, part of speech, and derivation data. Read the definition carefully.

As you *Look* at the word—

1. Note the shape of the word and look for familiar parts.
2. Study the explanation and see if it fits the idea or ideas that you are trying to express. Look for precise meanings of the word.
3. When the word has several meanings, study *all* of them. The meanings may be quite divergent, such as the difference between meaning **1.**, "leader," and mean-ing **6.c**, "the chief actor in a crime," among the possible applications of the word *principal.*
4. Note the meanings that are closely related. Bold-faced letters (**a, b, c,** etc.) usually are used to group meanings that are related.
5. You can further enrich your vocabulary by studying the synonyms and anto-nyms that sometimes appear at the end of the dictionary entry. Synonyms are words with similar meanings. Antonyms are words of opposite meaning. For example, note the number of words that are synonymous with *business.*

busi'ness (bĭz'nĕs; -nĭs), *n.* [*busy* + *-ness.*] **1.** *Obs.* Busyness. **2.** One's rightful work or personal concern; as, attend to *business*; hence, justifiable reason for meddling or the like; as, he had no *business* to do that. **3.** One's particular, *esp.* one's regular, work, occupation, or employment. **4.** Affair; matter; as, it was a strange *business.* **5.** In the theater, the details in acting or in staging a play usually left to the discretion of actors or director. **6.** Mercantile pursuit or transactions; trade; commerce; as, he prefers *business* to law. **7.** A commercial or industrial enterprise; as, to sell one's *business.* **8.** Custom; patronage; as, to increase *business* by advertising.
Syn. (1) See WORK.
(2) **Business, commerce, trade, industry, traffic,** as here compared, mean a form of activity that has for its end the supplying of commodities. **Business,** often an inclusive term, specifically names the combined activities of those engaged in the purchase or sale of commodities or in related financial transactions; **commerce** and **trade,** of those engaged in the exchange and transportation of commodities; **industry,** of those producing commodities, especially by manufacturing, processing, etc., on so large a scale that problems of labor and capital are involved; **traffic,** of those engaged in the operation of public carriers, such as railroads, ships, bus lines, etc.

Used by permission, from Webster's New Collegiate Dictionary, copyright 1960 by G. & C. Merriam Co., publishers of the Merriam-Webster Dictionaries.

Once you have ascertained the correct meaning, you must take steps to fix this meaning in your mind.

As you *Pronounce* the word—

1. Study the phonetic spelling, the accents, and the syllables.
2. Check to see if the pronunciation or meaning changes according to the part of speech.
3. Look at the word that frequently is confused with the one you are studying. Sound both words, making sure that you hear any difference in sound.
   (a) For homonyms, learn the part of the word that is spelled differently.
   (b) For words that sound somewhat alike, learn to distinguish the similarities and differences.

As you *Spell* the word—

1. Recall the meaning.
2. Recall the differences or similarities in spelling.
3. Sound the word to yourself and associate sound and meaning.

As you *Copy* the word—

1. Sound the word as you write it.
2. Write the correct meaning.
3. Circle the differences between, or similarities to, other words.
4. Use the word in a practical sentence.
5. Make a deliberate effort to include the word in your speaking and especially in your written vocabulary.
6. Write three to five synonyms and antonyms for the word, if possible.

Practice. Follow the procedures outlined above to correct the meaning-type errors made on your pretest.

Lesson 22 Review Practice—Confusion of Homonyms

1. Copy each of the following pairs of words on a sheet of paper. After each word, write all the meanings given in the dictionary.

peace	presence	forth	wait
piece	presents	fourth	weight
capital	thrown	course	stationary
capitol	throne	coarse	stationery
birth	two	principle	led
berth	too	principal	lead
council	canvas	waist	compliment
counsel	canvass	waste	complement

2. Write the synonyms and antonyms that are listed for each word.
3. Say each word aloud to make sure you know the correct pronunciation. Copy the phonetic spelling for any word that is strange to you. Check to see if the pronunciation or meaning changes when the part of speech changes.
4. For each word, study the spelling and the meaning together. Write the words as your teacher dictates them.

Lesson 23 Review Practice—Confusion of Words That Sound Somewhat Alike

1. Copy each of the following groups of words on a sheet of paper. After each word, write all the meanings given in the dictionary.

colonel	whether	accede
colonial	weather	exceed
precede	affect	formally
proceed	effect	formerly
angle	personal	respectfully
angel	personnel	respectively
thorough	lose	choose
through	loose	chose
latter	quality	quiet
later	quantity	quite
attack	except	prominent
attach	expect	permanent
	accept	

2. Write the synonyms and antonyms that are listed for each word.
3. Say each word aloud to make sure you know the correct pronunciation. Write the phonetic spelling for any word that is strange to you. Check to see if the pronunciation or meaning changes when the part of speech changes.
4. For each word, study the spelling and the meaning together. Write the words as your teacher dictates them.

Progress Check

1. Your teacher will dictate a spelling test. Spell each word carefully, keeping in mind the "sound" and "meaning" traps that cause frequent misspellings.

2. Copy each of the following words, dividing each word into correct syllables:

military   accommodation
especially   possession
assistant   immediately
appreciate   occasion
consideration   difference

3. Copy each of the following words. Beside each word, write its phonetic spelling.

gauge   military
candidate   proceed
estimate

4. Copy each of the following words, supplying the missing letters in each word. The meanings are given to help you identify the words.

und-- - -edly	beyond question or doubt	ac- - - -late	to increase or amass
p- -man-nt	unchangeable; steadfast	compl-ment	to add to or to supplement
main- - -ance	means of support	conc- - -	to allow or to surrender
exist- - -e	state of being	co- -se	a period of instruction and study
specifi- - -ly	definitely; explicitly		
al- -ge	to affirm, declare, or assert	form- -ly	in a ceremonious manner
comp- - -son	the act of comparing	- -cept	to exclude or omit
coun- -l	to advise	-ffect	to influence or to act upon

PART ②

WORDS SPELLED ACCORDING TO RULES AND WORDS REQUIRING SPECIAL CARE

"Sound" and "meaning" are two of the types of errors frequently made in spelling. Other types of errors are those caused by failure to apply the rules of spelling, those due to carelessness, and those resulting from "demon" words.

This section of study is designed specifically to help you locate and analyze errors other than the sound and meaning types. Careful study on your part as you work through the accompanying exercises will give you a thorough orientation to all the types of spelling errors that people usually make.

Pretest. Your instructor will now give you a pretest of 100 words. These words will test your ability to apply rules, the care with which you write words, and your ability to spell demon words. Write the test as carefully as you can. Then check your spelling of the words. Keep either your test paper or a list of the words you misspelled —together with the way you misspelled them—to use for error analysis in a later lesson.

Spotting Rule Errors

Many spelling errors result from failure to apply established spelling rules. Rules are easy to forget unless they are used constantly. Seven spelling rules that seem to cause the most trouble are given in this part. The practice exercises accompanying the rules will enable you to spot the troublesome words more readily.

Lesson **24** Spelling Rules—I Before E

Let's see now, is it rec*ei*ve or rec*ie*ve? ch*ei*f or ch*ie*f? If you have to hesitate every time you encounter such words or—worse still—if you find yourself guessing most of the time, you surely need to brush up on the rule. You may recall learning the following rule as a verse when you were in elementary school. Here it is:

> *I* before *e*
> Except after *c*
> Or when sounded like *a*
> As in *neighbor* and *weigh*

Knowing this rule will enable you to arrive at the correct spelling of *most* "ie" words, but watch for these exceptions:

neither	leisure	forfeit
financier	efficient	height
seized	ancient	inveigle
either	foreign	sovereign
weird		society

Practice. Apply the rule given above by copying each of the following words, supplying the correct form of the "ie" combination for each word.

ch--f	f--ld	n--ce	fr--ght
conc--t	dec--t	r--gn	n--ther
--ght	h--r	l--sure	w--rd
anc--nt	f--rce	p--r	rel--ve
forf--t	h--ght	var--ty	s--ze

Lesson 25 Spelling Rules—Silent Final E

The silent final *e* can be troublesome because sometimes it is dropped and at other times it is retained when a suffix is added. If you find yourself in doubt as to when you should drop and when you should retain the silent final *e*, learning and applying the two common spelling rules given here will solve the problem for you.

1. Silent final *e* is usually *dropped* before a termination beginning with a vowel. This rule is illustrated by such words as:

enclose	enclosure	base	basic
guide	guidance	advise	advisory

This rule can be strictly applied in most cases, but again watch for the exceptions:

notice	noticeable	enforce	enforceable
manage	manageable	agree	agreeable
advantage	advantageous	peace	peaceable
outrage	outrageous	service	serviceable
dye	dyeing	change	changeable
mile	mileage	plebe	plebeian

2. Silent final *e* is usually *retained* before a termination beginning with a consonant, as shown by the following illustrations:

encourage	encouragement	false	falsehood
care	carefully	like	likeness

Again, be wary of exceptions:

truly	duly	acknowledgment	judgment
wholly	ninth	argument	

Practice. Apply the rules given above by copying on a separate sheet of paper the following words, combining the correct form of the suffix shown in parentheses.

measure (able)	desire (ous)	complete (ly)	change (able)
arrange (ment)	advantage (ous)	safe (ty)	use (age)
notice (able)	disgrace (ful)	abuse (ive)	congratulate (ory)
force (ible)	reconcile (able)	appraise (al)	enforce (able)
noise (less)	entire (ty)	mile (age)	obscure (ity)

Lesson 26 Spelling Rules—Final Consonants

Final consonants cause spelling problems because these consonants sometimes are doubled and at other times are not when a suffix is added. Violation of the final-consonant rule accounts for a high percentage of errors in spelling. Even though you may be a good speller, you probably should brush up on the rules that govern the final consonants.

1. When the termination begins with a vowel:
   a. DOUBLE the final consonant of the root word when it ends in a single consonant preceded by a single vowel IF—
   (1) The word has one syllable, or
   (2) The word is accented on the last syllable.

plan	planning	ship	shipped
com·pel′	compelling	oc·cur′	occurred

Note that this rule does not apply when a word ends in the following consonants: *c, h, j, q, w, x,* and *z.* The following words represent additional exceptions.

de·fer′	def′er·ence	
re·fer′	ref′er·ence	
in·fer′	in′fer·ence	
pre·fer′	pref′er·ence	pref′er·a·ble
trans·fer′	trans·fer′a·ble	
cha·grin′	cha·grined′	
gas	gas′e·ous	

   b. DO NOT DOUBLE the final consonant of the root word—
   (1) When the word is accented on any syllable except the last:

ben′e·fit	ben′e·fit·ed	dif′fer	dif′fer·ent
prof′it	prof′it·ed	cred′it	cred′it·ed

Learn these exceptions:

can′cel	cancellation
ques′tion	questionnaire
crys′tal	crystallize

   (2) When the word ends in more than one consonant:

perfo*rm*	performance	persi*st*	persistence
confi*rm*	confirming	depe*nd*	dependable

   (3) When the word ends in a single consonant preceded by more than one vowel:

app*ear*	appearance	eq*ual*	equalize
n*eed*	needy	obt*ain*	obtainable

2. When the termination begins with a consonant, DO NOT DOUBLE the final consonant of the root word.

develop	development	leader	leadership
royal	royalty	broad	broadcast

3. Words ending in a double consonant usually retain both consonants when a termination is added.

skill	skillful	embarrass	embarrassing
enroll	enrolling	install	installment

Practice. Test your skill in applying the rules governing the final consonant. On a separate sheet of paper, rewrite each of the following root words, adding to each word the suffix shown in parentheses:

expel (ing)	forfeit (ure)
budget (ing)	compel (ing)
consider (able)	excel (ence)
exist (ing)	lament (able)
suit (able)	infer (ence)
remit (ance)	occur (ence)
crystal (ize)	profit (ed)
lighten (ing)	assess (ing)
marvel (ous)	develop (ment)
transfer (able)	refer (ence)

Lesson 27 Spelling Rules—Final Y

Final *y* is another tricky letter in spelling because it is sometimes retained and at other times is changed from *y* to *i* before a termination. If you learn the two rules that control the final *y*, you should have no further spelling problems of this type.

1. When final *y* is preceded by a consonant, *change* the *y* to *i* before all terminations except those beginning with *i*.

beauty	beautiful	accompany	accompanying
easy	easily	copy	copying

2. When final *y* is preceded by a vowel, the *y* is usually *retained* before all terminations.

buy	buyer	enjoy	enjoyable
employ	employer	delay	delaying

Practice. On a separate sheet of paper, rewrite each of the following words, adding to each word the suffix given in parentheses.

reply (ing)	marry (age)
heavy (est)	horrify (ed)
justify (able)	victory (ous)
comply (ance)	convey (ance)
certify (cate)	supply (ing)

Lesson **28** Spelling Rules—Plurals

For most English nouns, the formation of plurals is fairly simple. In a few instances, however, forming the correct plurals may be difficult. Learn the following basic rules that govern the formation of plurals and you will have little trouble in using the correct forms.

1. *Regular Plurals*. The plurals of English nouns are regularly formed by adding *s* to the singular.

apartment	apartments	college	colleges
feature	features	bushel	bushels

2. *Plurals of Nouns Ending in S or Any Sound of S*. When the singular form of either a common or a proper noun ends with an *s* or an *s* sound (*ss*, *x*, *ch*, and *sh*), add *es* to the singular to form the plural.

chorus	choruses	dispatch	dispatches
dress	dresses	sash	sashes
annex	annexes	Mr. Evans	the Evanses

3. *Plurals of Nouns Ending in Y*.
   a. When a noun ends in *y* preceded by a consonant, the plural is formed by changing *y* to *i* and adding *es*.

authority	authorities	enemy	enemies
boundary	boundaries	luxury	luxuries
century	centuries	testimony	testimonies
cruelty	cruelties	vacancy	vacancies

   b. When a noun ends in *y* preceded by a vowel, the plural is formed by adding *s* to the singular.

holiday	holidays	weekday	weekdays
key	keys	alloy	alloys

Note: To form the plural of a proper noun that ends in *y*, always add *s* to the singular; for example, *the Levys* and *the Gildays*.

4. *Plurals of Nouns Ending in O*.
   a. The plurals of nouns ending in *o* usually are formed by adding *s* to the singular.

Eskimo	Eskimos	ratio	ratios
piano	pianos	tobacco	tobaccos

   b. The plurals of certain nouns ending in *o* are formed by adding *es* to the singular.

innuendo	innuendoes	embargo	embargoes
tomato	tomatoes	veto	vetoes
Negro	Negroes	potato	potatoes

Practice. (See end of Lesson 29.)

Lesson 29 Spelling Rules—Plurals (Continued)

5. *Plurals of Nouns Ending in I.* Nouns ending in *i* preferably form their plurals by adding *s* only.

rabbi	**rabbis**	**alibi**	**alibis**

6. *Plurals of Nouns Ending in F, Fe, Ff.* The plurals of most nouns ending in *f*, *fe*, and *ff* are formed by adding *s* to the singular.

belief	**beliefs**	**rebuff**	**rebuffs**
strife	**strifes**	**tariff**	**tariffs**

EXCEPTIONS to this rule include:

half	**halves**	**leaf**	**leaves**
wife	**wives**	**shelf**	**shelves**
life	**lives**	**ourself**	**ourselves**
knife	**knives**	**thief**	**thieves**
self	**selves**		

7. *Other Plurals.*

   a. Some nouns change form to make the plural:

foot	**feet**	**tooth**	**teeth**
mouse	**mice**	**woman**	**women**

   b. Plurals of compound words are formed in the following ways:
   (1) If the compound is a solid word, form the plural at the end.

stepchild	**stepchildren**	**storekeeper**	**storekeepers**
cookbook	**cookbooks**	**courthouse**	**courthouses**

   (2) If the compound is hyphenated or is made up of two words, the plural is added to the chief element (usually the noun).

lieutenant colonel	**lieutenant colonels**	**brother-in-law**	**brothers-in-law**
notary public	**notaries public**	**court-martial**	**courts-martial**

   (3) If neither element of the hyphenated compound is a noun, the plural is added to the last part of the compound.

go-between	**go-betweens**	**stop-off**	**stop-offs**

   c. Some nouns are rarely, if ever, used in the singular form.

annals	**auspices**	**statistics**	**specifications**
hysterics	**trousers**	**earnings**	**arrears**
athletics	**wages**	**scruples**	**acoustics**
goods	**headquarters**	**congratulations**	**logistics**

Practice. On a separate sheet of paper, write the plural for each of the following words. Consult the dictionary if necessary.

resident	thief	property	alibi
bonus	by-product	scruples	soprano
memorandum	businessman	container	trolley
accessory	shelf	ratio	arrears
Eskimo	embargo	bylaw	suffix

Lesson **30** Spelling Rules—Possessives

Possessives can prove troublesome unless you pause long enough to classify the root word and select the correct ending for the possessive form. The six basic rules given here are very necessary in your program of spelling improvement.

1. To form the possessive of *singular* nouns *not* ending in *s*, add an apostrophe followed by an *s*.

customer	customer's	world	world's
month	month's	Frank	Frank's

2. If a *singular* noun ends in *s* or an *s* sound, add an apostrophe and an *s* if a new syllable is formed in the pronunciation of the possessive.

boss	boss's	fox	fox's
class	class's	Jones	Jones's

If the addition of *s* would make an *s*-ending word hard to pronounce, the apostrophe only may be added.

hostess	hostess'	Frances	Frances'

3. The possessive of *regular plurals* is formed by adding only the apostrophe after the *s*.

lawyers	lawyers'	celebrities	celebrities'
sheriffs	sheriffs'	Negroes	Negroes'

4. The possessive of *irregular plurals* is formed by adding the apostrophe followed by an *s*.

freshmen	freshmen's	Englishwomen	Englishwomen's

5. The possessive forms of *personal pronouns* and of *who* do not require the apostrophe. Each pronoun has its own special possessive form.

I: my, mine	she: her, hers	they: their, theirs
you: your, yours	it: its	who: whose
he: his	we: our, ours	

6. The sign of the possessive is added at the end of a compound word.

somebody else's	secretary-treasurer's

Practice. On a separate sheet of paper, write the possessive form for each of the following words:

fox 's	witness '	it its	who whose
celebrities '	gentlemen 's	I my mine	he his
sister-in-law	she hers	they their	class '
school 's	anyone else 's	oxen 's	cashier 's
Thomas '	you your	Burns '	boys '

Lesson 31 Spelling Rules—Compound Words

Compound words are spelling problems because some are written as one solid word, others are two separate words, and still others are hyphenated. Check the following seven rules to brush up on accepted modern practice in the formation of compound words.

1. *Compound Adjectives.*

  a. When two or more words are used *before* a noun as a one-thought modifier, the modifier is hyphenated.

able-bodied man	self-addressed envelope
a house-to-house survey	long-lived family

  b. When a compound adjective follows a noun, usually it is not hyphenated.

man who is able bodied	records are up to date
survey taken house to house	remark was uncalled for

2. *Compound Verbs.* Most compound verbs, including those formed with prefixes, are written as solid words. All "under" and "over" compounds are written as solid words. Verbs that are built up from two or more words should be hyphenated.

prepay	overturn	dry-clean
postdated	underestimate	quick-freeze

3. *Compound Nouns.* Compound nouns are more frequently written as solid words or as two words than hyphenated.

Solid

airmail	copyholder	notebook	manpower
policyholder	summertime	postmark	background
armchair	breakup	homestead	lawsuit
livestock	letterhead	shorthand	salesmen

Two Words

copy writer	parcel post	balance sheet	income statement
bank note	half dollar	cross reference	real estate
piece goods	common sense	money order	day labor

Hyphenated

cure-all	go-between	son-in-law	take-off
tie-ins	co-worker	know-nothing	loud-speaker

4. *Compound Adverbs and Conjunctions.* When two or more words are combined and used as adverbs or conjunctions, the words almost always are written solid.

nevertheless	however	meanwhile	forever
moreover	throughout	meantime	elsewhere

5. *Special Compounds.* A number of foreign phrases are commonly used in business correspondence. Note that the following compounds are written as separate words:

per diem	ad valorem	per capita
per cent	per annum	pro rata

Practice. Each line of the columns below contains a series of words that, when properly combined, will make a compound word or expression. Form each of the compound words or expressions, referring to the rules or your dictionary whenever necessary.

bond	holder		
air	pump		
kilowatt	hour		
actor	manager		
law	suit		
business	man		
piece	goods		
car	mile		
cabinet	worker		
real	estate		
hard	wood		
horse	power	hour	
give	and	take	
man	of	war	
to	dry	clean	
clear	cut	distinction	
middle	aged	man	
first	class	condition	
bargain	priced	goods	
light	blue	letter	head
up	to	date	methods
remnant	five	yards	long
twelve	year	old	child
records	up	to	date

Lesson 32 Spelling Rules—Compound Words (Continued)

6. *Compound Numerals and Fractions.*
   a. Compound numerals from *twenty-one* to *ninety-nine* are hyphenated.

fifty-two	one hundred forty-seven
sixty-five	seven hundred eighty-six

   b. Fractions are hyphenated, the hyphen being placed between the numerator and the denominator unless one element or both already contain a hyphen.

one-eighth	ninety-six hundredths
seven-sixteenths	forty-four thirty-seconds

7. *Prefixes and Suffixes in Compound Words.* When the first element of a compound word is a prefix or the last element is a suffix, the compound usually is written solid. In such words as

confer	intolerant
detract	illegal

the prefix is joined to the remainder of the word. Suffixes are added in such words as

technician	fraudulent
excitement	corrective

Sometimes, however, the prefix or suffix is separated from the rest of the word by a hyphen. Learn the following simple rules to help you remember when to write a hyphen in words containing prefixes or suffixes.

a. The suffixes *less* and *like* usually combine with words to form solid compounds; however, if the combination results in the same letter (the *l*) three times in succession, the hyphen is used.

bell-like	shell-less	shell-like

b. The prefix *self* is almost always followed by a hyphen.

self-esteem	self-confidence

(*but* selfless, selfish, selfhood)

c. When the last letter of a prefix is the same as the first letter of the word to which it is being added, a hyphen is necessary.

co-operate	semi-independent
re-enter	pre-existing

d. The hyphen is necessary in some verbs beginning with the prefix *re*, in which *re* means "again," to distinguish them from identically spelled words of different meanings.

recount a story	re-count the vote
reform a criminal	re-form the mold
recover a loss	re-cover a chair
remark on his progress	re-mark the sales tags

e. When the second element is a capitalized word, a hyphen is inserted after the prefix.

pro-British	trans-Canadian	anti-American

f. Combinations with *vice*, *ex*, and *elect*, in connection with titles, are hyphenated.

ex-president	vice-chairman	senator-elect

Practice. Each line of the following columns contains a series of words that, when properly combined, will make a compound word or expression. Form the compound words or expressions correctly on a separate sheet of paper. Refer to the rules if necessary.

forty	four		
pro	American		
self	evident		
trans	African		
vice	principal		
self	contained		
ex	chairman		
semi	invalid		
president	elect		
skill	less		
re	establish		
two	thirds	majority	
re	cover	a	loss
re	view	the	slides
one	hundred	twenty	five
re	lay	the	brick
re	tire	the	wheel

Spotting Carelessness and Demon Errors

Lesson 33 Errors Due to Carelessness

Sometimes spelling errors are caused by failure to exercise care in writing the word. Under this heading we find the spelling errors that fall into the "Of course I knew better but . . . " category. This is where haste and poor handwriting take their biggest toll. Letters may be dropped, scrawled, or even reversed in writing. The following examples show the wide range of possible errors that may be prevented if more care is exercised:

vacuum written hastily as *vacuim* (failure to complete upstroke to form final "u")

dilemma written hastily with second "m" omitted (dilema) or with second "m" written as an "n" (dilemna)

privilege written as *privilige* because the writer failed to open and round out upstroke for third vowel

irrelevant written as *irrevelant* due to careless transposition of letters

administration written as *admistration* because the writer carelessly overlooked an important syllable

Practice. On a separate sheet of paper, copy each of the following words. Draw a circle around the part or parts of each word that might be misspelled because of carelessness. Beside each word, indicate the error that would be made.

quantitative	remuneration	museum
illegible	unanimity	permanent
cardiac	meeting	qualitative
	necessary	

Lesson **34** Errors Caused by Word Demons

Adding to the woes of persons who would improve their spelling ability are certain demon words in the language that represent unique spelling problems or exceptions to common rules. For example, *install* frequently is misspelled with only one *l* instead of two *l*'s. Other words in the demon category appear below, with examples of the possible misspellings shown in parentheses:

se*i*ze (s*ie*ze)   super*se*de (super*ce*de)
ch*ie*f (ch*ei*f)   pani*cky* (pani*cy*)

Practice. Copy each of the following words on a separate sheet of paper. Draw a circle around the part of each word that presents unusual spelling difficulties.

sacrilegious   codicil   consensus
nuclear   facsimile   vacillate
Baton Rouge   inoculate   souvenir
       disseminate

Analysis of Pretest Errors

You now have seen that many spelling errors can be traced to causes other than sound or meaning. You have learned that errors also can be due to carelessness in writing, to inability to spell demon words, and to failure to apply rules. With this additional knowledge, you can analyze all the spelling errors that you make—including those that you made on the pretest—and identify the reasons for your mistakes.

Error-Analysis Chart

Test Word	Careless-ness	Demons	I before E	Silent Final E	Final Consonants	Final Y	Plurals	Posses-sives	Compound Words

To help you analyze the errors that you made on the pretest for "other" types of errors, draw up an analysis form similar to the one shown above. In the column headed "Test Word," write the words that you misspelled on the pretest. As you write each word, place a check (√) in the column that indicates the reason for misspelling the word.

For example, if you misspelled the word *occurred* as *occured*, write the correct spelling of the word in the column at the left. Then place a check (√) in the column headed "Final Consonants," since you misspelled the word because you failed to double the final consonant. When you have completed the error analysis, consult your teacher to make certain that you analyzed the errors correctly.

Attacking Rule Errors and Other Difficulties

The success of your spelling-improvement program in overcoming other spelling errors will depend entirely on yourself. Your continuing awareness of the types of mistakes that you are inclined to make; your consistent and concentrated attention to rules and suggestions; and your critical periodic appraisal of results are the factors that will make the "big difference." The corrective procedures and exercises that follow are designed to give you still more directed practice, so that everything will stay fresh and clear in your mind. Every skill demands practice, and spelling is no exception.

Lesson 35 Review Practice—Spelling Rules

1. *I Before E.* Copy each of the following words, supplying the correct "ie" combination; then write, beside each word, the portion of the "ie" rule that applies to the word.

notor--ty	dec--tful	r--n	sover--gn
conc--ted	sl--gh	conc--vable	effic--ntly
h--nous	forf--ture	recip--nt	l--sure
inv--gle	consc--ntious	len--nt	l--u
repr--ve	--ghty	al--nate	m--n

2. *Silent Final E.* Some form of the word endings given in the italicized column headings below may be added to the words in the column. Select the correct word ending in each case and list the resulting words on a separate sheet of paper.

ible *able*	*ance* *ence*	*ory* *ary* *ery*	*ure*	*ous* *ious*
excite	precede	advise	foreclose	grieve
use	interfere	supervise	erase	desire
manage	observe	scene	enclose	advantage
sale	guide	imagine	disclose	outrage
notice	persevere	congratulate	seize	continue
like	continue	statute	expose	injure
change	grieve	regulate	please	space
force	insure	mandate	legislate	fame

ing	*ful*	*ment*	*ly*
dye	use	commence	extreme
file	disgrace	retire	severe
compute	care	replace	whole
refine	hate	advance	entire
pursue	force	disburse	large
advise	purpose	arrange	precise
feature	hope	manage	true
describe	bale	engage	close

Lesson 36 Review Practice—Spelling Rules

1. *Final Consonants.* Some form of the word endings given in the italicized column headings below may be added to the words in the column. Select the correct word ending in each case and list the resulting words on a separate sheet of paper.

ed	able ible	ing	ent ant	age	ance ence	or er	al
repair	tax	enroll	claim	short	allow	retain	renew
defer	obtain	adjoin	insist	bag	admit	job	option
concert	control	plan	correspond	pass	clear	remind	acquit
limit	deduct	furnish	repel	cart	persist	counsel	rent
ship	profit	open	recur	lug	defer	ship	mechanic

en ion ian	ary ery ory	ous eous	ize	ty ity	ation	ment
less	honor	gas	crystal	prior	inform	align
strength	direct	hazard	material	penal	tax	enroll
civil	custom	humor	equal	mental	cancel	assign
rebel	slip	prosper	standard	plural	commend	amend
forbid	second	marvel	circular	vital	confirm	develop

2. *Final Y.* On a separate sheet of paper, copy each of the words below. Then, proceeding across the columns, form as many additional words as possible by joining to the root word the word endings suggested in the column headings. (See *enjoy* as an example.)

	ed	ing	ment	ous	ful	ence ance	ible able	age
enjoy	enjoyed	enjoying	enjoyment	---	---	---	enjoyable	---
accompany								
carry								
convey								
comply								
certify								
injury								
victory								
beauty								
marry								
duty								
pity								
justify								
employ								

Lesson 37 Review Practice—Spelling Rules

1. *Plurals.*

   a. Copy each of the following words. Beside each word, write the rule that determines how the plural is formed.

employees	annexes	mementoes
possibilities	corps	rebuffs
valleys	journeys	courtesies
cities	sopranos	rabbis
major generals	daughters-in-law	teeth
annals	commodities	storehouses
sashes	roofs	statistics
potatoes	wives	
carriers	tie-ins	

   b. For each of the following words, write the correct plural form.

boss	alto
mouse	alloy
thief	knife
cargo	alibi
shelf	security
roof	tariff
drop-off	medley
window	arrears
brush	dispatch
opportunity	shield

   c. Write the correct plural for each word shown in parentheses.
   1. By a special process, the (alloy) are mixed with other (metal) to make a usable product.
   2. The (dress) were (luxury) that brought (rebuff) from the male (element) of the (family).
   3. All the (child) will help decorate the (shelf) to carry out a theme of (Eskimo).
   4. (Passer-by) could see the signs written on the (wall) of the house.
   5. The (chorus) were comprised of (soprano), (alto), (tenor), and (bass).

2. *Possessives.* Supply the correct form for each word in parentheses. Do you know the difference between the possessive form and the contraction form?
   a. The next step is (you).
   b. The recommendation is (she).
   c. (It) too late to ask the mailing department for (it) report now.
   d. (They) windshield is made of shatterproof glass; (our) is not.
   e. That dilapidated car of (they) is an eyesore; (there) no reason why they should not buy a new one.
   f. (It) difficult to tell (who) fault this is.
   g. (Who) been reading my (*Who Who*)?
   h. (It) most unfair to blame him for (somebody else) mistake.
   i. A (week) service under the (boss) direction satisfies the (men) requirements.
   j. At the (lawyer) meeting, the (secretary-treasurer) report was read by (Mr. James) brother.

Lesson **38** Review Practice—Spelling Rules

Compound Words. Listed below is a group of common expressions using compound words. On a separate sheet of paper, copy the italicized word or words and write the rules that govern the forms of the compounds.

a. *postage-free* envelope
b. *afternoon* sun
c. package sent *free of charge*
d. *undergo* surgery
e. *withdraw* the motion
f. single *proprietorship*
g. *top-stitch* the collar
h. *last-minute* rush
i. *overestimate* the budget
j. *quick-frozen* meat

k. *re-elect* the senator
l. *Ninety-five* were correct
m. *illegal* operation
n. *re-count* the votes
o. *vice-president* in charge of operations
p. *three-fourths* full
q. *self-evaluation* scale
r. *trans-Canadian* flight

Lesson **39** Attacking Carelessness Errors

When your error analysis shows that you are making spelling errors because of carelessness, you must begin to spend more time and concentrate more on the tasks that require written work. The general procedures for attacking errors of a careless nature are:

1. Find the word in the dictionary.
2. Observe the general shape and appearance of the letter combinations.
3. Check the spelling letter by letter.
4. Study the accents and the phonetic spelling.
5. Study carefully the sequence of syllables and the way each syllable is spelled.
6. Pronounce the word correctly and enunciate the syllables clearly.
7. Do not confuse the word with a similar word of different meaning.
8. Sound each syllable as you write the word.
9. Form letters carefully and legibly as you write.

Practice. Locate each of the following words in the dictionary. Copy the words on a sheet of paper, separating each word into correct syllables. As you write each word, note the sequence of letters. Beside each word, write its phonetic spelling. Form your letters carefully as you write.

aluminum	familiarity	strategy	irresponsible
denomination	buoyant	inconvenient	tentative
manual	bankruptcy	predominant	indelible
facilitate	registration	eligible	decipher
civilian	perseverance	integral	proportionate

Lesson **40** Attacking Demon Errors

Spelling errors caused by demon words require a rather special attack procedure. The demon word may contain no clues as to its correct spelling. A plan of attack for such errors must be based on concentration techniques and memory aids. The person who has trouble with demon words should attack the spelling errors in the following manner:

1. Find the word in the dictionary. Look at the general shape and appearance of the letter combinations.
2. Sound the syllables according to the phonetic spelling and the accents.
3. Study carefully the syllables that have particularly difficult letter combinations.
4. As you write the word, underscore the troublesome parts.
5. Try to find a device that will help you remember letter combinations. Example: Deb*ris is* p*i*led h*i*gh.

Practice. Locate each of the following words in the dictionary. Copy the words on a sheet of paper, dividing them into correct syllables. Beside each word, write the phonetic spelling and indicate the memory aid that will help you learn to spell the word.

irrelevant	desiccate	corroborate	encore
debris	cancellation	exhilaration	debut
inveigle	heinous	reconnoiter	indict
innocuous	exorbitant	inexhaustible	drudgery
indebtedness	epitome	synonym	exemplary

Progress Check

1. Your teacher will dictate a spelling test. Spell each word carefully, keep in mind the rules, and write each word neatly and legibly. The list of words will show if you need additional practice in attacking various types of spelling errors.
2. On a separate sheet of paper, write the word or words that belong in the blank spaces in the following sentences.
   a. ____ before ____, except after ____;
      or when sounded like ____, as in ____ and ____.
   b. Silent final *e* is usually dropped before a termination beginning with a ____.
   c. Silent final *e* is usually retained before a termination beginning with a ____.
   d. When adding a suffix—
      (1) To a one-syllable word that ends in a single consonant preceded by a single vowel, ____ the final consonant.
      (2) To a word that ends in two or more consonants, ____ the final consonant.
      (3) To a word that is accented on the last syllable—if the word ends in a single consonant preceded by a single vowel—____ the final consonant.
      (4) To a word that is accented on any syllable except the last, ____ the final consonant.
      (5) To a word ending in a single consonant preceded by two or more vowels, ____ the final consonant.
   e. When the final *y* is preceded by a consonant, ____ before all terminations except those beginning with ____.
   f. When final *y* is preceded by a vowel, ____ before all terminations.
   g. When the singular form of a noun ends in *s* or an *s* sound, ____ to the singular to form the plural.
   h. When a noun ends in *y* preceded by a consonant, form the plural by ____.
   i. When a noun ends in *y* preceded by a vowel, form the plural by ____.
   j. Most nouns ending in *f, fe, ff* form plurals by ____.
   k. To form the possessive of a singular noun not ending in *s*, add ____.

l. To form the possessive of a singular noun ending in *s*, usually add _____.

m. To form the possessive of regular plurals, add _____.

n. To form the possessive of irregular plurals, add _____.

o. The sign of the possessive for a compound word is added _____.

p. All "over" and "under" compound verbs are written as _____.

q. Combinations with _____, _____, and _____, in connection with titles, are hyphenated.

r. When the last letter of a prefix is the same as the first letter of the word to which it is being added, _____.

s. When the second element of a word is capitalized, _____.

t. The prefix *self* is almost always _____.

3. Copy each of the following words, making whatever corrections are necessary in their spelling.

niether *neither*	consensus *consensus*	referrence *reference*
anceint *ancient*	noticable *noticeable*	preferrence *preference*
foriegn *foreign*	managable *manageable*	transferrable *transferable*
financeir *financier*	advantageous ✓	allowance ✓
forfeit ✓	enforcable *enforceable*	cancelation *cancellation*
either ✓	changable *changeable*	questionaire *questionnaire*
crystalize *crystallize*	renumeration ✓	musuem ✓
confirmming *confirming*	annexs *annexes*	pianoes
appearrance *appearance*	dispatchs *dispatches*	tomatos
obtainable ✓	centurys *centuries*	lifes
beautyful *beautiful*	alloys ✓	thiefs
accompaning *accompanying*	vacancys *vacancies*	tooths

4. Give examples of the following exceptions to spelling rules:

a. Six exceptions to the "*i* before *e*" rule.

b. Eight exceptions to the rule about dropping the silent final *e*.

c. Five exceptions to the rule for doubling final consonants.

d. Two exceptions to the rule for not doubling final consonants when suffixes are added.

SECTION TWO

LEARNING TO SPELL NEW WORDS

PART 1 The Four-Step Approach

PART 2 Words for Your General Vocabulary

PART 3 New Words for Your General Business Vocabulary

PART 4 Words for Your Specialized Business Vocabulary

PART 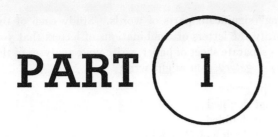 1

THE FOUR-STEP APPROACH

Your newly acquired system of error analysis and your attack skills will help you to overcome difficulties in spelling the words that you already know. You have a solid foundation in spelling. Now you need an effective method for mastering the spelling of words that you have been hesitant about and new words that you should learn to use in order to enrich your vocabulary. The method that can do the job has been reduced to an easy-to-remember, four-step routine:

See
Say
Spell
Write

This routine—if you really know how to use it—is the key to learning new words. Study carefully the suggestions that follow so that you may rapidly master this four-step routine. Once you have mastered it, you will be able to apply it directly to avoid specific types of errors that could be made in spelling new words.

Step 1: Seeing the Word

SEE: Don't be fooled by the apparent simplicity of the word. Seeing means much more than a hasty glance. You need to know how to look and what to look for when you encounter a new word.

1. Look up the new word in the dictionary.
2. Give yourself time to concentrate on the word.
3. Try to "see" the word in your mind. Get acquainted with the shape and placement of the prominent features of the word as a whole.
4. Study the parts of the word, noting the parts that are familiar to you because of other words that you know. These might include:
   a. Familiar short words joined to form larger, different words:
      afternoon, however.
   b. Familiar word beginnings:
      *dis*like, *un*wanted.
   c. Familiar word endings: part*ed*, sift*ing*.
   d. Familiar double letters: le*tt*er, te*ll*er.

Practice. Test your skill at "seeing" significant parts of words. Study each of the following words separately and identify the letters or combinations of letters that you will need to remember in each. On a separate sheet of paper, write your analyses of the words. For example, for the word *derogatory*, you might write

de	is the prefix
r	is not doubled
g	is not doubled
a	is the single-vowel syllable
ory	is the suffix

discerning	undoubtedly	acquit	preferably
candidate	psychiatry	grimy	principle
occasion	inexplicable	continuous	hindrance
parallel	exorbitant	ridiculous	accessible
letterhead	dentifrice	standard	financier

Step 2: Saying the Word

SAY: Mastering the correct sound of the word is a major part of the battle in avoiding those sound-type spelling errors. The trick is to learn the correct way to say the word before the incorrect pronunciation or syllabication has a chance to register in your mind.
1. Look up the word in the dictionary.
2. Study the phonetic spelling, the accents, and the syllables.
3. Note the silent letters; for example, *p*seudo (sū′ dō).
4. Watch for an unusual spelling of a sound: de*bt*or (dĕt′ẽr).
5. Practice pronouncing the word until the "sound" becomes easy and natural for you.
6. Associate spelling and sound in your mind.
7. If necessary, invent memory devices to remember difficult words: station*e*ry, meaning pap*e*r; princip*le*, meaning ru*le*.

Practice. This exercise will give you practice in analyzing words and so will help you master the correct sounds.

Look up each word in the dictionary.

Copy the phonetic spelling, syllables, and accents.

Pronounce each word aloud, syllable by syllable, enunciating precisely.

Call out the trouble spots: silent letters, unusual spelling of sounds, prefixes, suffixes, single-letter syllables, etc.

discerning	undoubtedly	acquit	preferably
candidate	psychiatry	grimy	principle
occasion	inexplicable	continuous	hindrance
parallel	exorbitant	ridiculous	accessible
letterhead	dentifrice	standard	financier

Steps 3 and 4: Spelling and Writing the Word

SPELL: Now that you have studied the word and fixed it in your mind:
1. Look at the printed word.
2. Cover the word or close your eyes and spell it.
3. Verify the correctness of your spelling.
4. Repeat this procedure until you feel confident about the spelling.

WRITE: The whole purpose of knowing how to spell is to permit you to write your thoughts. This is why your ability to write and to use the word correctly is the final true test of spelling accuracy.

1. Write the word neatly and legibly.
2. Sound the word as you write it.
3. Compare the word that you wrote with the one that you had hoped to write.
4. If your spelling is correct, cover the word and write it again. If your spelling is incorrect, determine the correct spelling and write the word again.
5. Use the word in a sentence.
6. Use the word appropriately as frequently as you can whenever you have occasion to express thoughts in writing.

Practice. Practice spelling and writing the words listed here.

1. Cover the words as you spell them, or spell as someone dictates to you.
2. Verify the spelling.
3. Write the words on a sheet of paper.
4. Use each word in a sentence.

discerning	undoubtedly	acquit	preferably
candidate	psychiatry	grimy	principle
occasion	inexplicable	continuous	hindrance
parallel	exorbitant	ridiculous	accessible
letterhead	dentifrice	standard	financier

Summary and Review

Summary Exercise—for See, Say, Spell, and Write routine.

For each of the following words, practice your skills of seeing, saying, spelling, and writing, as you learn to spell them.

1. Inspect each word, analyzing it in terms of the letters and combinations of letters you wish to remember.
2. Look up the phonetic spelling, the syllables, and the accents for each word, noting peculiar sounds or omissions of sounds. Learn to say the word correctly.
3. Cover the word with a card (or finger) and spell it without looking. Then remove the card and verify the spelling.
4. Write the word on a separate sheet of paper; then check to see that you spelled it correctly.
5. Use the word in a sentence.

accelerate	gratuitously	nebulous	salient
consensus	homogeneous	obliterate	tenable
disseminate	irrevocable	panacea	ultimate
expedient	lucrative	qualitative	vacillate
feasible	meritorious	rectify	waybill

You will use the SEE, SAY, SPELL, and WRITE routine as you learn to spell the words presented in the lessons that follow.

PART ②

WORDS FOR YOUR GENERAL VOCABULARY

Your general vocabulary includes words that you need and use every day in your personal and business activities. Obviously, you need to know how to say, spell, and use these words correctly if you wish to communicate your thoughts and ideas to others.

This part of the text is divided into eight units. Each unit is devoted to the study of words that represent a specific type of potential spelling error. For example, Unit 1 covers certain sound-type words. Each unit contains five lessons. The first four lessons are regular daily lessons; the fifth is a check-up lesson.

The daily lesson is organized around the following major features:

1. *Preview:* The purpose of the preview test is to find out how many of the words you can already spell correctly. You can then concentrate your efforts on the words that you cannot spell or that you do not know the meaning of.

2. *Checking Performance:* Your preview test is checked right away so that any errors can be located without delay.

3. *Error Analysis:* Next, you examine every error and identify it according to known common types of errors.

4. *Attack Procedures:* With specific types of errors in mind, you apply the correct remedial techniques set forth in Section One.

5. *Learning to Spell New Words:* If the preview list contains any words that you did not attempt to write because you did not know them, you will now use the SEE, SAY, SPELL, and WRITE routine to learn them. Thus, you will not only be learning to spell, but you will also be expanding your vocabulary.

The periodic check-up lesson contains the following elements:

1. *Unit Test:* This test is comprised of words chosen from the preceding four daily lessons.

2. *Proofreading Test:* This test calls on you to make a practical application of your newly acquired spelling skills.
3. *Cumulative Test:* The real test of a good speller is his ability to remember the correct spelling of words long after the lesson is over. This test is introduced at the end of Unit 2 to provide an automatic review of words previously studied.
4. *Checking Your Tests:* All three tests are checked to determine your spelling efficiency.
5. *Error Analysis:* Any errors made in the spelling tests are identified by type so that remedial measures can be taken.
6. *Review:* Here you apply the correct attack skills to eliminate your remaining errors once and for all.
7. *Retest:* Knowing for sure that your mastery of the words is complete is bound to be a source of keen personal satisfaction to you. The retest gives you a chance to prove that you have really licked your problems.

Unit 1 Sound Words

Sound is the key to the correct spelling of the words in this unit. Spend a few moments reviewing "Spotting Sound Errors," beginning on page 3, and then begin your study of Lessons 1-4 of this unit, applying the following procedures.

Preview. Your teacher will dictate a list of 75 general-vocabulary words. Number a sheet of paper from 1 to 75. Spell as many of the words as you can, but attempt only the words that you are quite sure you know how to spell. If you do not know the spelling of a word, place a question mark (?) beside the number.

Checking Performance. Compare your spellings with the words given in the appropriate lesson. Place an *X* beside each word that you misspelled. To the right of a misspelled or omitted word, write the correct spelling.

Error Analysis. Classify the errors that you made by noting the type of error beside each word that you misspelled. For instance, if an error was caused by faulty syllabication, write "faulty syllabication" beside the word. Refer to Section One if you have forgotten the types of errors.

Attack Procedures. Attack procedures for sound-type errors were presented in Section One, beginning on page 7. Review the corrective techniques recommended for each type of error.

Learning to Spell New Words. The pretest words that you did not know how to spell now appear on your answer sheet preceded by a question mark. Use a separate sheet of paper to practice those words, following the SEE, SAY, SPELL, and WRITE routine (see pages 39-41). Hand in the drill paper to your instructor.

Lesson 1

1. accept	ăk·sĕpt′	ac-cept	To receive with favor; to approve.
2. account	ă·kount′	ac-count	A reckoning, computation, or record.
3. across	à·krŏs′	a-cross	On the opposite side; crosswise.
4. admissible	ăd·mĭs′ĭ·b'l	ad-mis-si-ble	Worthy of being admitted; acceptable.
5. advance	ăd·văns′	ad-vance	To promote; to move forward.
6. affairs	ă·fârs′	af-fairs	Things to be done; matters; concerns.
7. afraid	à·frād′	a-fraid	Filled with fear or apprehension.
8. against	à·gĕnst′	a-gainst	In opposition to; in contact with.
9. allowed	ă·loud′	al-lowed	Permitted; approved of.
10. already	ôl·rĕd′ĭ	al-read-y	Previously.
11. although	ôl·thō′	al-though	Even if; in spite of the fact that.
12. among	à·mŭng′	a-mong	In company with; in the midst of.
13. amount	à·mount′	a-mount	Sum, quantity, or total.
14. animal	ăn′ĭ·măl	an-i-mal	One of the lower animals; a beast.
15. answer	ăn′sēr	an-swer	A reply; a solution to a problem.
16. arrive	ă·rīv′	ar-rive	To come; to reach a place.
17. arriving	ă·rīv′ĭng	ar-riv-ing	Reaching a point or place.
18. article	är′tĭ·k'l	ar-ti-cle	A thing of a particular type or kind; a composition or writing.
19. attack	ă·tăk′	at-tack	*v.* To assault, assail, or bombard. *n.* An assault; an offensive action.
20. attention	ă·tĕn′shŭn	at-ten-tion	Notice; observant care; concentration.
21. beautiful	bū′tĭ·fōol	beau-ti-ful	Full of beauty; having qualities that constitute beauty.
22. beauty	bū′tĭ	beau-ty	Physical, moral, or spiritual loveliness.
23. business	bĭz′nĕs	busi-ness	One's regular work; trade; industry.
24. carries	kăr′ĭz	car-ries	Bears; conveys; transports.
25. city	sĭt′ĭ	cit-y	An important town.
►			
26. college	kŏl′ĕj	col-lege	An institution for study and instruction, higher than the secondary school.
27. common	kŏm′ŭn	com-mon	Ordinary; familiar; popular.
28. control	kŏn·trōl′	con-trol	To exercise restraining power over.
29. controllable	kŏn·trōl′à·b'l	con-trol-la-ble	Having qualities that permit the exercise of guiding or restraining power.
30. daughter	dô′tēr	daugh-ter	A female child.
31. decide	dē·sīd′	de-cide	To determine; to settle; to rule; to resolve.
32. difference	dĭf′ēr·ĕns	dif-fer-ence	State of being different; variation.
33. different	dĭf′ēr·ĕnt	dif-fer-ent	Unlike; not the same.
34. divide	dĭ·vīd′	di-vide	To separate; to sever.
35. doctor	dŏk′tēr	doc-tor	One licensed to practice medicine; one holding an advanced academic degree.
36. dollar	dŏl′ēr	dol-lar	The monetary unit of the United States.
37. during	dūr′ĭng	dur-ing	Throughout the course of; in the time of.
38. effort	ĕf′ērt	ef-fort	Exertion; pains; trouble.

39.	enemies	ĕn′ĕ·mĭz	en-e-mies	Foes.
40.	enemy	ĕn′ĕ·mĭ	en-e-my	One hostile to another; a foe.
41.	enjoy	ĕn·joi′	en-joy	To have the benefit of; to get satisfaction from experiencing.
42.	especially	ĕs·pĕsh′ăl·ĭ	es-pe-cial-ly	Not generally; specially.
43.	exercise	ĕk′sĕr·sīz	ex-er-cise	To use; to drill; to put into practice.
44.	explain	ĕks·plān′	ex-plain	To make plain or clear; to expound.
45.	families	făm′ĭ·lĭz	fam-i-lies	Groups of parents and children.
46.	family	făm′ĭ·lĭ	fam-i-ly	A household; a group of immediate kin.
47.	famous	fā′mŭs	fa-mous	Celebrated in fame; renowned.
48.	finally	fī′năl·ĭ	fi-nal-ly	Lastly; at last; at the end.
49.	finished	fĭn′ĭsht	fin-ished	Completed; concluded.
50.	force	fōrs	force	Power; strength.

▶

51.	forwarded	fôr′wĕrd·ĕd	for-ward-ed	Sent forward; sent on.
52.	forwarding	fôr′wĕrd·ĭng	for-ward-ing	Sending on or ahead.
53.	general	jĕn′ĕr·ăl	gen-er-al	Not special or concrete; not precise.
54.	happened	hăp′ĕnd	hap-pened	Occurred by chance.
55.	honor	ŏn′ĕr	hon-or	Respect; homage; reverence.
56.	husband	hŭz′bănd	hus-band	A man who has a wife.
57.	important	ĭm·pôr′tănt	im-por-tant	Significant; having consequence; weighty.
58.	include	ĭn·klōōd′	in-clude	To enclose; to contain; to involve.
59.	interested	ĭn′tĕr·ĕs·tĕd	in-ter-est-ed	Having a share or concern in a project.
60.	iron	ī′ĕrn	i-ron	*n.* A metallic element widely used in making steel. *v.* To press wrinkles out of material.
61.	issuance	ĭsh′ū·ăns	is-su-ance	Act of issuing or giving out.
62.	journal	jûr′năl	jour-nal	A periodical publication; a diary.
63.	kitchen	kĭch′ĕn	kitch-en	A room used for cooking.
64.	labor	lā′bĕr	la-bor	Physical or mental toil; work.
65.	later	lāt′ĕr	lat-er	At a subsequent time.
66.	lead	lĕd	lead	A heavy, pliable metal.
67.	manner	măn′ĕr	man-ner	A way of acting; behavior.
68.	mention	mĕn′shŭn	men-tion	To specify by name.
69.	mentioned	mĕn′shŭnd	men-tioned	Specified by name.
70.	minute	mĭn′ĭt	min-ute	The sixtieth part of an hour.
71.	notice	nō′tĭs	no-tice	Announcement; observation.
72.	pair	pâr	pair	Two things of a kind.
73.	peace	pēs	peace	A state of quiet or tranquillity.
74.	practice	prăk′tĭs	prac-tice	To do, perform, carry on, or exercise.
75.	proved	prōōvd	proved	Established; made certain; verified.

Lesson 2

1.	according	ă·kôr′dĭng	ac-cord-ing	Agreeing; conforming.
2.	affidavit	ăf′ĭ·dā′vĭt	af-fi-da-vit	A sworn statement in writing, usually made under oath.

3. agree	á·grē′	a-gree	To concede; to admit.
4. always	ôl′wăz	al-ways	At all times.
5. another	ă·nŭth′ẽr	an-oth-er	Being one more in addition.
6. battle	băt′′l	bat-tle	A general encounter between armies or enemies.
7. believing	bĕ·lēv′ĭng	be-liev-ing	Having faith or confidence.
8. between	bĕ·twēn′	be-tween	In the space or interval that separates.
9. beyond	bĕ·yŏnd′	be-yond	Farther away; over there.
10. board	bōrd	board	A piece of sawed lumber.
11. brought	brôt	brought	Past tense and past participle of *bring*.
12. build	bĭld	build	To erect; to construct.
13. circle	sûr′k′l	cir-cle	A closed plane curve.
14. contents	kŏn′tĕnts	con-tents	That which is contained.
15. course	kōrs	course	Direction of progress; method of procedure.
16. double	dŭb′′l	dou-ble	Twofold; coupled.
17. escape	ĕs·kāp′	es-cape	To get away.
18. evening	ēv′nĭng	eve-ning	The close of the day.
19. every	ĕv′ẽr·ĭ	ev-er-y	Each, without exception; complete.
20. everything	ĕv′ẽr·ĭ·thĭng′	ev-er-y-thing	Every object or every fact.
21. experience	ĕks·pẽr′ĭ·ĕns	ex-pe-ri-ence	Knowledge or skill derived from some past activity.
22. hoping	hōp′ĭng	hop-ing	Trusting; relying; anticipating.
23. hurry	hûr′ĭ	hur-ry	To move with great haste.
24. laid	lād	laid	Past tense and past participle of *lay*.
25. laugh ▶	läf	laugh	To show mirth; to express with laughter.
26. losing	lōōz′ĭng	los-ing	Suffering loss; failing to win.
27. losses	lŏs′ĕz	loss-es	Decreases in amounts or degrees.
28. material	má·tẽr′ĭ·ăl	ma-te-ri-al	That of which anything is composed or may be constructed.
29. middle	mĭd′′l	mid-dle	A central point or portion.
30. million	mĭl′yŭn	mil-lion	The number of ten hundred thousand.
31. modern	mŏd′ẽrn	mod-ern	Characteristic of the present or recent time.
32. moment	mō′mĕnt	mo-ment	An instant.
33. native	nā′tĭv	na-tive	Born or originated in a particular place.
34. necessary	nĕs′ĕ·sĕr′ĭ	nec-es-sar-y	Indispensable; absolutely essential.
35. neighbor	nā′bẽr	neigh-bor	A person who lives near another.
36. neither	nē′thẽr	nei-ther	Not either.
37. offer	ŏf′ẽr	of-fer	*v.* To present; to propose. *n.* A proposal; a bid.
38. offered	ŏf′ẽrd	of-fered	Presented; tendered; proffered.
39. office	ŏf′ĭs	of-fice	A place in an establishment where clerical work is done.
40. officer	ŏf′ĭ·sẽr	of-fi-cer	One who holds an office.
41. offices	ŏf′ĭs·ĭz	of-fi-ces	Places where clerical work is done.
42. pagination	păj′ĭ·nā′shŭn	pag-i-na-tion	Page numbering.

43.	passage	păs'ĭj	pas-sage	A means of passing; a channel or course.
44.	perhaps	pĕr·hăps'	per-haps	Possibly but not certainly; maybe.
45.	pleasant	plĕz'ănt	pleas-ant	Agreeable.
46.	please	plēz	please	To afford pleasure or satisfaction.
47.	position	pŏ·zĭsh'ŭn	po-si-tion	Place; station; site.
48.	possible	pŏs'ĭ·b'l	pos-si-ble	Within one's power to perform or attain.
49.	prepare	prĕ·pâr'	pre-pare	To make ready; to fit or adapt.
50.	presents	prĕ·zĕnts'	pre-sents	Bestows; introduces.

▶

51.	president	prĕz'ĭ·dĕnt	pres-i-dent	One who presides by election or appointment.
52.	presidents	prĕz'ĭ·dĕnts	pres-i-dents	Plural of *president* (see above).
53.	probably	prŏb'à·blĭ	prob-a-bly	Very likely.
54.	problem	prŏb'lĕm	prob-lem	A question that must be solved.
55.	produce	prŏ·dūs'	pro-duce	To bring forth; to exhibit or show.
56.	producer	prŏ·dūs'ĕr	pro-duc-er	One who produces or brings forth.
57.	producing	prŏ·dūs'ĭng	pro-duc-ing	Yielding; bearing; exhibiting.
58.	promise	prŏm'ĭs	prom-ise	A pledge.
59.	provide	prŏ·vīd'	pro-vide	To obtain beforehand.
60.	providing	prŏ·vīd'ĭng	pro-vid-ing	Supplying for use.
61.	purpose	pûr'păs	pur-pose	Intention; aim; goal.
62.	quarter	kwôr'tĕr	quar-ter	A fourth part or portion.
63.	question	kwĕs'chŭn	ques-tion	Interrogation; inquiry.
64.	really	rē'ăl·ĭ	re-al-ly	Actually.
65.	refuse	rĕ·fūz'	re-fuse	To fail to accept; to reject.
66.	require	rĕ·kwīr'	re-quire	To need; to demand; to compel.
67.	second	sĕk'ŭnd	sec-ond	Immediately following the first.
68.	sense	sĕns	sense	Wisdom; correct judgment.
69.	service	sûr'vĭs	serv-ice	Performance of work for the benefit of another.
70.	servicing	sûr'vĭs·ĭng	serv-ic-ing	Performing services of repair, supply, maintenance, or installation.
71.	society	sŏ·sī'ĕ·tĭ	so-ci-e-ty	Association with one's fellows.
72.	system	sĭs'tĕm	sys-tem	Regular method or order.
73.	systematize	sĭs'tĕm·à·tīz	sys-tem-a-tize	To arrange methodically.
74.	until	ŭn·tĭl'	un-til	Up to the time of.
75.	wait	wāt	wait	To stay for; to be in expectation of.

Lesson 3

1.	allow	ă·lou'	al-low	To approve of; to admit; to concede.
2.	appear	ă·pēr'	ap-pear	To become visible.
3.	belong	bĕ·lŏng'	be-long	To be the property of.
4.	British	brĭt'ĭsh	Brit-ish	Pertaining to Great Britain.
5.	caught	kôt	caught	Past tense and past participle of *catch*.
6.	cause	kôz	cause	Reason; motive.

7. certain	sûr′tĭn	cer-tain	Sure; reliable; settled.
8. corner	kôr′nẽr	cor-ner	Angle formed where two lines or sides join.
9. cotton	kŏt′'n	cot-ton	A soft, white, fibrous substance used in textiles.
10. couldn't	kŏŏd′'nt	could-n't	Contraction of *could not*.
11. daily	dā′lĭ	dai-ly	Happening each day.
12. death	dĕth	death	Loss of life.
13. described	dĕ·skrībd′	de-scribed	Related; recounted.
14. describing	dĕ·skrīb′ĭng	de-scrib-ing	Relating; recounting.
15. destroy	dĕ·stroi′	de-stroy	To demolish; to abolish.
16. discover	dĭs·kŭv′ẽr	dis-cov-er	To reveal; to disclose; to unearth.
17. distance	dĭs′tăns	dis-tance	Space between two objects.
18. division	dĭ·vĭzh′ŭn	di-vi-sion	Separation.
19. doubt	dout	doubt	To question; to be undecided.
20. earliest	ûr′lĭ·ĕst	ear-li-est	The superlative of *early*.
21. early	ûr′lĭ	ear-ly	At a time near the beginning of a period.
22. enough	ē·nŭf′	e-nough	Sufficient; ample.
23. except	ĕk-sĕpt′	ex-cept	To leave out; to exclude.
24. expect	ĕks·pĕkt′	ex-pect	To look forward to; to hope.
25. factual	făk′tū·ăl	fac-tu-al	Containing facts; actual.
26. February	fĕb′rŏŏ·ĕr′ĭ	Feb-ru-ar-y	Second month in the year.
27. further	fûr′thẽr	fur-ther	In addition; furthermore.
28. governors	gŭv′ẽr·nẽrz	gov-er-nors	Those who govern.
29. handling	hăn′dlĭng	han-dling	Touching or controlling with the hands.
30. height	hīt	height	Summit; altitude; elevation.
31. history	hĭs′tô·rĭ	his-to-ry	A narrative of events.
32. hundred	hŭn′drĕd	hun-dred	Cardinal number, following *ninety-nine*.
33. individual	ĭn′dĭ·vĭd′ū·ăl	in-di-vid-u-al	A person; a single being or group of beings.
34. introductory	ĭn′trô·dŭk′tô·rĭ	in-tro-duc-to-ry	Serving to introduce; preliminary.
35. military	mĭl′ĭ·tĕr′ĭ	mil-i-tar-y	Pertaining to soldiers, arms, or war.
36. month	mŭnth	month	The twelfth part of a year.
37. mouth	mouth	mouth	An opening through which food is taken into the body.
38. national	năsh′ŭn·ăl	na-tion-al	Of or pertaining to a nation.
39. naturally	năt′ū·răl·ĭ	nat-u-ral-ly	Normally; innately.
40. numerous	nū′mẽr·ŭs	nu-mer-ous	Plentiful.
41. opinion	ô·pĭn′yŭn	o-pin-ion	Belief; view; judgment.
42. period	pẽr′ĭ·ŭd	pe-ri-od	An extent of time.
43. realize	rē′ăl·īz	re-al-ize	To accomplish; to make real.
44. receivable	rĕ·sēv′à·b'l	re-ceiv-a-ble	Capable of being received.
45. religious	rĕ·lĭj′ŭs	re-li-gious	Devout; displaying devotion to religion.

46.	remain	rĕ·mān′	re-main	To be left; to stay behind.
47.	return	rĕ·tûrn′	re-turn	To come or go back.
48.	settle	sĕt′'l	set-tle	To decide; to fix by agreement.
49.	several	sĕv′ĕr·ăl	sev-er-al	Made up of an indefinite number more than two.
50.	silence	sī′lĕns	si-lence	Absence of sound.

►

51.	simple	sĭm′p'l	sim-ple	Not complicated.
52.	soldier	sōl′jĕr	sol-dier	One engaged in military service.
53.	spirit	spĭr′ĭt	spir-it	State or disposition of mind.
54.	strange	strānj	strange	Alien; unnatural; unfamiliar.
55.	subject	sŭb′jĕkt	sub-ject	Matter; theme; topic.
56.	supplies	sŭ·plīz′	sup-plies	Provisions.
57.	supplying	sŭ·plī′ĭng	sup-ply-ing	Providing for a want.
58.	support	sŭ·pōrt′	sup-port	To sustain; to uphold.
59.	surprise	sẽr·prīz′	sur-prise	To astonish; to amaze; to astound.
60.	surprised	sẽr·prīzd′	sur-prised	Astonished; amazed.
61.	third	thûrd	third	Ordinal number, following *second*.
62.	thirty	thûr′tĭ	thir-ty	Cardinal number, following *twenty-nine*.
63.	tomorrow	tŏŏ·mŏr′ō	to-mor-row	The day after the present.
64.	toward	tō′ẽrd	to-ward	Approaching to; in the direction of.
65.	travel	trăv′ĕl	trav-el	To make a journey.
66.	traveling	trăv′ĕl·ĭng	trav-el-ing	Journeying.
67.	trouble	trŭb′'l	trou-ble	Affliction; misfortune.
68.	usually	ū′zhŏŏ·ăl·ĭ	u-su-al-ly	Ordinarily; customarily.
69.	valleys	văl′ĭz	val-leys	The depression between hills or mountains.
70.	value	văl′ū	val-ue	Assessed or estimated worth.
71.	various	vâr′ĭ·ŭs	var-i-ous	Diversified; several.
72.	voice	vois	voice	Sound uttered by living beings.
73.	women	wĭm′ĕn	wom-en	Plural of *woman*.
74.	women's	wĭm′ĕnz	wom-en's	Possessive of *women*.
75.	yellow	yĕl′ō	yel-low	A color having a hue resembling lemons, butter, or sunflowers.

Lesson 4

1.	accident	ăk′sĭ·dĕnt	ac-ci-dent	An event that takes place without expectation.
2.	accompanied	ă·kŭm′på·nĭd	ac-com-pa-nied	Escorted; attended.
3.	accompany	ă·kŭm′på·nĭ	ac-com-pa-ny	To escort; to attend.
4.	actual	ăk′tŭ·ăl	ac-tu-al	Real.
5.	actually	ăk′tŭ·ăl·ĭ	ac-tu-al-ly	Really; truly.
6.	ancient	ān′shĕnt	an-cient	Old; venerable.
7.	appearance	ă·pẽr′ăns	ap-pear-ance	The act of appearing; look.
8.	average	ăv′ẽr·ĭj	av-er-age	Medium; fair; mediocre.

9. capital	kăp′ĭ·tăl	cap-i-tal	A stock of accumulated wealth; net worth.
10. cease	sēs	cease	To come to an end; to stop.
11. central	sĕn′trăl	cen-tral	Relating to the center.
12. certainly	sûr′tĭn·lĭ	cer-tain-ly	With certainty; surely.
13. circumstances	sûr′kŭm·stăns·ĕz	cir-cum-stanc-es	Conditions affecting a person or agent.
14. citizen	sĭt′ĭ·zĕn	cit-i-zen	An inhabitant of a specified place.
15. colonel	kûr′nĕl	colo-nel	A commissioned officer in charge of a regiment.
16. command	kŏ·mánd′	com-mand	v. To direct; to order. n. Act of commanding; an order.
17. commence	kŏ·mĕns′	com-mence	To begin; to start.
18. commission	kŏ·mĭsh′ŭn	com-mis-sion	v. To appoint and authorize. n. A form of compensation usually based on performance; a body of commissioners.
19. confidence	kŏn′fĭ·dĕns	con-fi-dence	Trust; reliance.
20. contain	kŏn·tān′	con-tain	To hold within fixed limits.
21. couple	kŭp′′l	cou-ple	A pair.
22. department	dĕ·pärt′mĕnt	de-part-ment	A division of a business firm.
23. detail	dĕ·tāl′	de-tail	A small part; an item.
24. detailed	dĕ·tāld′	de-tailed	Full of details.
► 25. determining	dĕ·tûr′mĭn·ĭng	de-ter-min-ing	Deciding; impelling.
26. diamond	dī′á·mŭnd	di-a-mond	A precious stone of crystallized carbon.
27. difficulty	dĭf′ĭ·kŭl·tĭ	dif-fi-cul-ty	Hardship; rigor.
28. earlier	ûr′lĭ·ẽr	ear-li-er	The comparative of early.
29. easier	ēz′ĭ·ẽr	eas-i-er	The comparative of easy.
30. easily	ēz′ĭ·lĭ	eas-i-ly	In an easy manner.
31. eastern	ēs′tẽrn	east-ern	Of or from the east.
32. editor	ĕd′ĭ·tẽr	ed-i-tor	One who revises and prepares copy for publication.
33. evidence	ĕv′ĭ·dĕns	ev-i-dence	That which furnishes proof.
34. factory	făk′tŏ·rĭ	fac-to-ry	A building where goods are made.
35. field	fēld	field	Open country.
36. foreign	fŏr′ĭn	for-eign	Not native or domestic.
37. forest	fŏr′ĕst	for-est	A dense growth of trees on a large tract.
38. friend	frĕnd	friend	One attached to another by esteem, respect, or affection.
39. guessed	gĕst	guessed	Supposed; believed; surmised.
40. guide	gīd	guide	v. To direct; to conduct. n. One who directs or guides.
41. impossible	ĭm·pŏs′ĭ·b′l	im-pos-si-ble	Incapable of being or of occurring.
42. incriminate	ĭn·krĭm′ĭ·nāt	in-crim-i-nate	To charge with a crime.

43.	irate	ī′rāt	i-rate	Angry; enraged.
44.	liberty	lĭb′ẽr·tĭ	lib-er-ty	Privilege; freedom.
45.	locate	lō′kāt	lo-cate	To assign a place to; to settle.
46.	manage	măn′ĭj	man-age	To conduct business or affairs.
47.	market	mär′kĕt	mar-ket	A body of men organized for the buying and selling of goods.
48.	master	mȧs′tẽr	mas-ter	One who controls.
49.	music	mū′zĭk	mu-sic	Sounds that have rhythm and melody.
50. ▶	narrow	năr′ō	nar-row	Limited or restricted in width or scope.
51.	natural	năt′ụ·răl	nat-u-ral	Innate; normal.
52.	nothing	nŭth′ĭng	noth-ing	Not any thing.
53.	official	ŏ·fĭsh′ăl	of-fi-cial	One holding an office.
54.	operation	ŏp′ẽr·ā′shŭn	op-er-a-tion	Method or way of functioning.
55.	organization	ôr′găn·ĭ·zā′shŭn	or-gan-i-za-tion	Act or process of organizing.
56.	particularly	pẽr·tĭk′ụ·lẽr·lĭ	par-tic-u-lar-ly	Especially; expressly.
57.	patient	pā′shĕnt	pa-tient	A person under treatment or care.
58.	political	pŏ·lĭt′ĭ·kăl	po-lit-i-cal	Pertaining to politics.
59.	portion	pōr′shŭn	por-tion	An allotted part; a share.
60.	possession	pō·zĕsh′ŭn	pos-ses-sion	Ownership; control.
61.	practical	prăk′tĭ·kăl	prac-ti-cal	Useful.
62.	practically	prăk′tĭ·kăl·ĭ	prac-ti-cal-ly	In a practical manner.
63.	precious	prĕsh′ŭs	pre-cious	Costly; highly esteemed.
64.	presence	prĕz′ĕns	pres-ence	State of being present.
65.	principal	prĭn′sĭ·păl	prin-ci-pal	Highest in rank or authority; main.
66.	principle	prĭn′sĭ·p'l	prin-ci-ple	A fundamental truth.
67.	record	rê·kôrd′	re-cord	To commit to writing.
68.	regard	rê·gärd′	re-gard	To look at or observe closely.
69.	season	sē′z'n	sea-son	One of the divisions of a year.
70.	square	skwâr	square	A parallelogram having all sides equal.
71.	suddenly	sŭd′'n·lĭ	sud-den-ly	Unexpectedly.
72.	together	tŏŏ·gĕth′ẽr	to-geth-er	In one group.
73.	union	ūn′yŭn	un-ion	A junction; a combination.
74.	written	rĭt′'n	writ-ten	In writing or in print.
75.	zenith	zē′nĭth	ze-nith	The point of the heavens directly above one.

Lesson 5 Check-Up

Unit Test. Your teacher will dictate 50 words chosen from the lessons in Unit 1. These words are selected to test your mastery of the new words in this unit. Listen closely as each word is dictated, spell each word carefully, and write plainly to assure yourself of a fair test.

Proofreading Test. In the following letter, some of the italicized words are misspelled. Copy the entire letter, making any corrections necessary in the spelling of the words.

Dear Mr. Roskin:

As a member of a *famious busness famaly*, you are *certin* to be *intrested* in the *busness histry* that we are compiling. *Evry artical* in this unusual book is *different* from any that you will find *writen* about the historical background of *busness*.

Busness Histry discusses such problems as *capatal controll, factry* needs, general *bookeeping sistems, sentral manajement*, and *numrous* other topics *important* to the *oparation* of a *busness* enterprise. You will find the *answer* to almost any *question* that has arisen in the long *pereod* of *busness histry*.

A *detaled* graph will *acompany* your copy. Send for it today.

Sincerely yours,

Checking Your Tests. Your teacher will give you directions for checking both the unit test and the proofreading test.

Error Analysis. Classify the errors that you made by noting the type of error beside each word that you misspelled.

Review. Use the appropriate attack procedures when you study the words that you misspelled on the unit test and on the proofreading test.

Retest. The retest will tell you if you have mastered the words in Unit 1. If you misspelled words on the retest, continue your attack procedures until you are sure that you can spell all the words correctly.

Unit 2 Meaning Words

Meaning is the key to the correct spelling of the words in this unit. Spend a few moments reviewing "Spotting Meaning Errors," beginning on page 6, and then begin your study of Lessons 1-4 of this unit, applying the following procedures:

Preview. Your teacher will dictate a list of 75 general-vocabulary words. Number a sheet of paper from 1 to 75. Spell as many of the words as you can, but attempt only the words that you are quite sure you know how to spell. If you do not know the spelling of a word, place a question mark (?) beside the number.

Checking Performance. Compare your spellings with the words given in the appropriate lesson. Place an X beside each word that you misspelled. To the right of any misspelled or omitted word, write the correct spelling. If you are not certain of the correct meaning of the word, study the definition and then use the word in a sentence.

Error Analysis. Classify the errors that you made by noting the type of error beside each word that you misspelled. For instance, if an error was caused by confusion of similar words, write "similar words" beside the word.

Attack Procedures. Attack procedures for meaning-type errors were presented in Section One, beginning on page 16. Review the corrective techniques recommended for each type of error.

Learning to Spell New Words. The pretest words that you did not know how to spell now appear on your answer sheet preceded by a question mark. Use a separate sheet of paper to practice those words, following the SEE, SAY, SPELL, and WRITE routine (see pages 39-41). Hand in the drill paper to your instructor.

Lesson 1

1. accept	ăk·sĕpt′	ac-cept	To receive with favor; to approve.
2. except	ĕk·sĕpt′	ex-cept	To take or leave out; to omit.
3. expect	ĕks·pĕkt′	ex-pect	To look for; to look forward to.
4. add	ăd	add	To join or unite so as to increase the quantity.
5. ad	ăd	ad	An advertisement.
6. air	âr	air	The gases that surround the earth.
7. heir	âr	heir	One who inherits or is entitled to inherit.
8. allowed	ă·loud′	al-lowed	Permitted; granted.
9. aloud	á·loud′	a-loud	Loudly; with a speaking voice.
10. ascend	ă·sĕnd′	as-cend	To mount; to rise; to climb.
11. ascent	ă·sĕnt′	as-cent	An upward slope.
12. assent	ă·sĕnt′	as-sent	To agree; to admit a thing is true.
13. bad	băd	bad	Defective; below standard.
14. bade	băd	bade	Past tense of *bid*.
15. bear	bâr	bear	To produce; to yield.
16. bare	bâr	bare	Exposed; uncovered.
17. blue	blōō	blue	Of the color blue.
18. blew	blōō	blew	Past tense of *blow*.
19. board	bōrd	board	A piece of sawed lumber.
20. bored	bōrd	bored	Weary from tedious repetition.
21. born	bôrn	born	Brought into existence by birth.
22. borne	bōrn	borne	Past participle of *bear*.
23. break	brāk	break	To pull apart suddenly and violently.
24. brake	brāk	brake	A device for slowing down or stopping motion.
25. build	bĭld	build	To erect; to construct.

▶

26. billed	bĭld	billed	Past tense and past participle of *bill*.
27. captain	kăp′tĭn	cap-tain	A chief; a leader.
28. caption	kăp′shŭn	cap-tion	The heading for a chapter, section, or page.
29. cent	sĕnt	cent	One 100th of a dollar.
30. sent	sĕnt	sent	Past tense and past participle of *send*.
31. scent	sĕnt	scent	An odor.
32. close	klōz	close	To shut; to confine.
33. clothes	klōthz	clothes	Covering for the body.
34. countries	kŭn′trĭz	coun-tries	Plural of *country*.
35. counties	koun′tĭz	coun-ties	Plural of *county*.
36. course	kōrs	course	Direction of progress.
37. coarse	kōrs	coarse	Unrefined.
38. chorus	kō′rŭs	cho-rus	Simultaneous singing of a number of persons.
39. days	dāz	days	Plural of *day*.
40. daze	dāz	daze	To stun.

41. die	dī	die	To cease to live.
42. dye	dī	dye	To stain; to color.
43. fair	fâr	fair	A festival or carnival.
44. fare	fâr	fare	The price of transportation.
45. flour	flour	flour	Finely ground meal of wheat or of other cereals.
46. flower	flou′ĕr	flow-er	A bloom or blossom.
47. forward	fôr′wĕrd	for-ward	Onward; moving toward a position in front.
48. foreword	fōr′wûrd′	fore-word	A preface.
49. forth	fōrth	forth	Forward; onward.
50. fourth	fōrth	fourth	Ordinal number, following *third*.

▶

51. further	fûr′thĕr	fur-ther	In addition.
52. farther	fär′thĕr	far-ther	At a greater distance.
53. great	grāt	great	Large in size.
54. grate	grāt	grate	To fret; to irritate; to make a rasping noise.
55. later	lāt′ĕr	lat-er	After, afterwards, in the future.
56. latter	lăt′ĕr	lat-ter	Being more recent.
57. loss	lŏs	loss	A decrease in value.
58. lose	lōōz	lose	To miss from one's possession.
59. loose	lōōs	loose	Unattached; disconnected.
60. minute	mĭn′ĭt	min-ute	The sixtieth part of an hour.
61. minute	mī·nūt′	mi-nute	Very small; little.
62. promises	prŏm′ĭs·ĕz	prom-is-es	One's pledges to another.
63. premises	prĕm′ĭs·ĕz	prem-is-es	Propositions that are supposed or proved; a piece of land or real estate.
64. purpose	pûr′pŭs	pur-pose	Intention; determination.
65. propose	prŏ·pōz′	pro-pose	To offer for consideration; to state.
66. quiet	kwī′ĕt	qui-et	Free from noise; still.
67. quite	kwīt	quite	Positively; completely; wholly.
68. their	thâr	their	Possessive of *they*.
69. there	thâr	there	In or at that place.
70. through	thrōō	through	In at one side and out at the opposite side of.
71. thorough	thûr′ŏ	thor-ough	Very careful about details.
72. very	vĕr′ĭ	ver-y	Extremely; exceedingly.
73. vary	vâr′ĭ	var-y	To modify; to diversify.
74. your	yŏŏr	your	Possessive of *you*.
75. you're	yŏŏr	you're	Contraction of *you are*.

Lesson 2

1. abroad	à·brôd′	a-broad	Beyond the limits of a country; widely.
2. aboard	à·bōrd′	a-board	On board.
3. addition	ă·dĭsh′ŭn	ad-di-tion	Process of adding.
4. edition	ĕ·dĭsh′ŭn	e-di-tion	All the copies of a work published at one time.
5. adopted	à·dŏpt′ĕd	a-dopt-ed	Taken as one's own.
6. adapted	à·dăpt′ĕd	a-dapt-ed	Made suitable; adjusted.

7. advice	ăd·vīs′	ad-vice	The recommendations given regarding a decision or course of conduct.
8. advise	ăd·vīz′	ad-vise	To give advice to; to counsel.
9. affect	ă·fĕkt′	af-fect	To produce an effect upon.
10. effect	ĕ·fĕkt′	ef-fect	Result; consequence; outcome.
11. angel	ān′jĕl	an-gel	A spiritual, celestial being.
12. angle	ăng′g'l	an-gle	A figure formed by the merging of two lines.
13. area	ā′rĕ·ȧ	a-re-a	Any flat surface, as of the ground; extent.
✗ 14. aria	ä′rĭ·ȧ	a-ri-a	An air, melody, or tune.
15. attack	ă·tăk′	at-tack	To assault; to storm.
16. attach	ă·tăch′	at-tach	To fasten; to connect; to tie.
17. basis	bā′sĭs	ba-sis	Foundation; fundamental principle.
18. bases	bā′sēz	ba-ses	Plural of *basis* (see above).
19. bath	bȧth	bath	Act of bathing.
20. bathe	bāth	bathe	To wash by emersion.
21. breath	brĕth	breath	The air inhaled and exhaled in breathing.
22. breathe	brēth	breathe	To inhale and exhale air.
23. cease	sēs	cease	To come to an end.
24. seize	sēz	seize	To take possession of by force.
25. cents	sĕnts	cents	Plural of *cent*.
► 26. since	sĭns	since	From a definite past time until now.
✗ 27. scents	sĕnts	scents	Characteristic odors.
28. choose	chōōz	choose	To select; to make a choice of.
29. chose	chōz	chose	Past tense of *choose*.
30. cloth	klŏth	cloth	A piece of fabric.
31. clothe	klōth	clothe	To provide with clothes; to dress.
32. colonel	kûr′nĕl	colo-nel	A commissioned officer in charge of a regiment.
33. colonial	kŏ·lō′nĭ·ăl	co-lo-ni-al	Of or pertaining to a colony or colonies.
34. conscience	kŏn′shĕns	con-science	Sense of obligation to do right.
35. conscious	kŏn′shŭs	con-scious	Aware; mentally awake or active.
36. corporation	kôr′pŏ·rā′shŭn	cor-po-ra-tion	A body of associated persons.
37. co-operation	kŏ·ŏp′ēr·ā′shŭn	co-op-er-a-tion	Collective action for common benefit or profit.
38. debt	dĕt	debt	A thing owed; an obligation.
39. debit	dĕb′ĭt	deb-it	Any of the entries on the left-hand side of an account.
40. desert	dĕz′ĕrt	des-ert	An arid or deserted region.
41. dessert	dĭ·zûrt′	des-sert	A course of fruit, cake, or the like, served at the end of a meal.
42. diseased	dĭ·zēzd′	dis-eased	Sick; ill.
43. deceased	dĕ·sēst′	de-ceased	Dead.
44. gray	grā	gray	Of the color gray.
45. grey	grā	grey	Of the color gray.

46. guessed	gĕst	guessed	Supposed; surmised. Past tense and past participle of *guess*.
47. guest	gĕst	guest	A person entertained at one's house.
48. hear	hẹr	hear	To perceive by the ear.
49. here	hẹr	here	In this place.
50. heard	hûrd	heard	Past tense and past participle of *hear*.
▶			
51. herd	hûrd	herd	A number of large animals gathered in one group.
52. here's	hẹrz	here's	Contraction of *here is*.
53. hears	hẹrz	hears	Perceives by the ear.
54. interrupt	ĭn'tĕ·rŭpt'	in-ter-rupt	To make a break in the continuity of.
55. interpret	ĭn·tûr'prĕt	in-ter-pret	To explain; to translate.
56. moral	mŏr'ăl	mor-al	Ethical; virtuous.
57. morale	mŏ·răl'	mo-rale	Prevailing mood or spirit.
58. personal	pûr'sŭn·ăl	per-son-al	Not public or general; private.
59. personnel	pûr'sŏ·nĕl'	per-son-nel	The group of persons employed in some service.
60. popular	pŏp'ŭ·lẽr	pop-u-lar	Approved by the people; prevelant.
61. poplar	pŏp'lẽr	pop-lar	A North American shade tree.
62. practical	prăk'tĭ·kăl	prac-ti-cal	Useful.
63. practicable	prăk'tĭ·ká·b'l	prac-ti-ca-ble	Usable; feasible.
64. proceed	prŏ·sēd'	pro-ceed	To go forward; to advance.
65. precede	prĕ·sēd'	pre-cede	To go before; to be earlier than.
66. register	rĕj'ĭs·tẽr	reg-is-ter	To enroll; to record.
67. registrar	rĕj'ĭs·trär	reg-is-trar	One who keeps a record, as of names.
68. surely	shoor'lĭ	sure-ly	Securely; assuredly.
69. surety	shoor'tĭ	sure-ty	Security; a sponsor or bondsman.
70. weather	wĕth'ẽr	weath-er	Condition of the air or atmosphere.
71. whether	hwĕth'ẽr	wheth-er	A conjunction used to introduce alternative conditions.
72. won't	wōnt	won't	Will not; colloquial contraction of *woll not*.
73. want	wŏnt	want	To be without; to desire; to wish.
74. worship	wûr'shĭp	wor-ship	*n.* Respect; honor. *v.* To venerate.
75. warship	wôr'shĭp'	war-ship	A government vessel armed for attack.

Lesson 3

1. adapt	á·dăpt'	a-dapt	To make suitable; to fit; to adjust.
2. adept	ăd'ĕpt	ad-ept	*n.* One fully skilled in something. *adj.* Proficient; expert.
3. adopt	á·dŏpt'	a-dopt	To accept; to take by choice.
4. compliment	kŏm'plĭ·mĕnt	com-pli-ment	A flattering speech or attention.
5. complement	kŏm'plĕ·mĕnt	com-ple-ment	That which fills up or completes.
6. corps	kōr	corps	A body of persons under common direction.
7. corpse	kôrps	corpse	A dead body.

8. dairy	dâr′ĭ	dair-y	The business of producing milk, cheese, and butter.
9. diary	dī′á·rĭ	di-a-ry	A daily record.
10. descent	dĕ·sĕnt′	de-scent	Change from higher to lower.
11. decent	dē′sĕnt	de-cent	Proper; respectable.
12. device	dĕ·vīs′	de-vice	A scheme; a mechanical appliance.
13. devise	dĕ·vīz′	de-vise	To contrive; to invent.
14. envelope	ĕn′vĕ·lōp	en-ve-lope	A folded gummed paper used to enclose a letter.
15. envelop	ĕn·vĕl′ŭp	en-vel-op	To wrap up or in.
16. excess	ĕk·sĕs′	ex-cess	State of going beyond limits; that which exceeds what is usual.
17. access	ăk′sĕs	ac-cess	A way of approach; an admittance.
18. formerly	fôr′mĕr·lĭ	for-mer-ly	Once; heretofore; in the time past.
19. formally	fôr′măl·ĭ	for-mal-ly	In a formal manner.
20. genius	jēn′yŭs	gen-ius	Inborn mental gift or endowment.
21. genus	jē′nŭs	ge-nus	A class; order; kind; sort.
22. guarantee	găr′ăn·tē′	guar-an-tee	To give security to; to secure.
23. guaranty	găr′ăn·tĭ	guar-an-ty	Something given or held as security.
24. hour	our	hour	The twenty-fourth part of a day; sixty minutes.
25. our ▶	our	our	Plural possessive of pronoun *I*.
26. immigrant	ĭm′ĭ·grănt	im-mi-grant	One who comes into a country for permanent residence, but of which country one is not a native.
27. emigrant	ĕm′ĭ·grănt	em-i-grant	One who leaves his country to settle elsewhere.
28. kill	kĭl	kill	To slay; to deprive of life.
29. kiln	kĭl	kiln	A large oven for hardening, burning, or drying anything.
30. led	lĕd	led	Past tense and past participle of *lead*.
31. lead	lĕd	lead	A heavy, pliable metal.
32. lease	lēs	lease	*n.* A contract by which one transfers real estate for a specified period. *v.* To hire; to rent; to grant by lease; to let.
33. leash	lēsh	leash	A cord by which a dog is tied or led.
34. lets	lĕts	lets	Permits; allows.
35. let's	lĕts	let's	Contraction of *let us*.
36. lightening	līt′′n·ĭng	light-en-ing	Making lighter.
37. lightning	līt′nĭng	light-ning	A flashing of light caused by a discharge of atmospheric electricity.
38. mean	mēn	mean	Vicious; unmanageable; bad.
39. mien	mēn	mien	Bearing; demeanor.
40. meter	mē′tĕr	me-ter	A measuring instrument.
41. meteor	mē′tĕ·ĕr	me-te-or	Any phenomenon in the atmosphere.
42. mind	mīnd	mind	Power of remembering; opinion.
43. mined	mīnd	mined	Extracted from the earth.

44. morning	môr′nĭng	morn-ing	The early part of the day.
45. mourning	mōrn′ĭng	mourn-ing	Act of sorrowing.
46. pair	pâr	pair	Two of a kind; a couple.
47. pear	pâr	pear	A fruit of the apple family.
48. pare	pâr	pare	To shave off; to cut off.
49. past	pȧst	past	Pertaining to a former time.
▶ 50. passed	pȧst	passed	Gone by; elapsed.
51. pasture	pȧs′tụ̄r	pas-ture	Land used for grazing.
52. pastor	pȧs′tẽr	pas-tor	A minister or a priest in charge of a church or parish.
53. peace	pēs	peace	State of tranquillity or quiet.
54. piece	pēs	piece	A fragment separated from the whole.
55. perish	pĕr′ĭsh	per-ish	To be destroyed or ruined.
56. parish	păr′ĭsh	par-ish	A part of a diocese assigned to the spiritual care of a minister or a priest.
57. permanent	pûr′mȧ·nĕnt	per-ma-nent	Not subject to alteration.
✗ 58. prominent	prŏm′ĭ·nĕnt	prom-i-nent	Standing out or projecting; conspicuous.
59. plain	plān	plain	Void of embellishments; free from obstructions.
60. plane	plān	plane	A flat or level material surface.
61. presence	prĕz′ĕns	pres-ence	State of being present.
62. presents	prĕz′ĕnts	pres-ents	Gifts; things given.
63. purely	pūr′lĭ	pure-ly	Merely; solely; completely.
64. poorly	po͞or′lĭ	poor-ly	Unsatisfactorily; inefficiently.
65. realty	rē′ăl·tĭ	re-al-ty	A piece of real property.
66. reality	rē·ăl′ĭ·tĭ	re-al-i-ty	The character of being true to life.
67. receipt	rē·sēt′	re-ceipt	A written acknowledgment of the taking or receiving of goods or money.
68. recipe	rĕs′ĭ·pē	rec-i-pe	A formula for preparing food.
69. statue	stăt′ū	stat-ue	The likeness of a person sculptured in some solid substance, like stone or wood.
70. statute	stăt′ūt	stat-ute	A law enacted by a legislative branch of government.
71. stature	stăt′ụ̄r	stat-ure	Natural height.
✗ 72. veil	vāl	veil	A piece of fabric that conceals or protects.
73. veal	vēl	veal	The flesh of a calf used as food.
74. vile	vīl	vile	Mean; worthless; odious.
75. vial	vī′ăl	vi-al	A small vessel for liquids.

Lesson 4

✗ 1. biennial	bī·ĕn′ĭ·ăl	bi-en-ni-al	Taking place once in two years.
✗ 2. biannual	bī·ăn′ū·ăl	bi-an-nu-al	Occurring twice a year.
3. cartoon	kär·to͞on′	car-toon	A pictorial caricature.
4. carton	kär′tŏn	car-ton	A light covered box of pasteboard.

X	5. censure	sĕn′shēr	cen-sure	To criticize adversely; to condemn as wrong.
	6. censor	sĕn′sēr	cen-sor	A person who oversees morals and conduct.
	7. cereal	sēr′ē·ăl	ce-re-al	A prepared foodstuff of grain.
	8. serial	sēr′ĭ·ăl	se-ri-al	Appearing in successive parts.
X	9. collision	kŏ·lĭzh′ŭn	col-li-sion	Act of colliding.
	10. collusion	kŏ·lū′zhŭn	col-lu-sion	A secret scheme for a fraudulent purpose.
	11. creditable	krĕd′ĭt·à·b'l	cred-it-a-ble	Deserving of praise.
	12. credible	krĕd′ĭ·b'l	cred-i-ble	Worthy of belief.
	13. eligible	ĕl′ĭ·jĭ·b'l	el-i-gi-ble	Legally suitable; qualified to be chosen.
	14. illegible	ĭl·lĕj′ĭ·b'l	il-leg-i-ble	Not legible.
	15. eminent	ĕm′ĭ·nĕnt	em-i-nent	Notable; standing out clearly.
	16. imminent	ĭm′ĭ·nĕnt	im-mi-nent	Impending; overhanging.
	17. eraser	ē·rās′ēr	e-ras-er	A piece of rubber used to erase marks.
	18. erasure	ē·rā′zhēr	e-ra-sure	Act of erasing.
	19. whole	hōl	whole	Entire; not broken; intact.
	20. hole	hōl	hole	A hollow place; a cavity; a pit.
	21. ingenuous	ĭn·jĕn′û·ŭs	in-gen-u-ous	Honorable; noble; frank; candid.
	22. ingenious	ĭn·jēn′yŭs	in-gen-ious	Inventive; clever; possessed of unusual mental powers.
	23. interstate	ĭn′tēr·stāt′	in-ter-state	Existing between different states.
	24. intestate	ĭn·tĕs′tāt	in-tes-tate	Without having made a valid will.
▶	25. intrastate	ĭn′trà·stāt′	in-tra-state	Within one state.
	26. liable	lī′à·b'l	li-a-ble	Obliged by law; answerable.
	27. libel	lī′bĕl	li-bel	Anything written, printed, or pictured tending to degrade another's character or reputation.
	28. nucleus	nū′klē·ŭs	nu-cle-us	A central point about which matter is gathered.
	29. nuclear	nū′klē·ēr	nu-cle-ar	Pertaining to a nucleus.
	30. persecute	pûr′sĕ·kūt	per-se-cute	To cause to suffer because of belief.
	31. prosecute	prŏs′ĕ·kūt	pros-e-cute	To institute and carry on a legal suit.
	32. petition	pē·tĭsh′ŭn	pe-ti-tion	A formal written request.
	33. partition	pär·tĭsh′ŭn	par-ti-tion	A separation; that which divides one part from another.
	34. president's	prĕz′ĭ·dĕnts	pres-i-dent's	Singular possessive of *president*.
	35. presidents	prĕz′ĭ·dĕnts	pres-i-dents	Those who preside.
	36. prophecy	prŏf′ē·sĭ	proph-e-cy	A prediction.
	37. prophesy	prŏf′ē·sī	proph-e-sy	To predict; to foretell.
	38. prospective	prŏ·spĕk′tĭv	pro-spec-tive	Anticipated; expected.
	39. perspective	pēr·spĕk′tĭv	per-spec-tive	The ability to see objects in respect to their relative position or importance.
	40. quantitative	kwŏn′tĭ·tā′tĭv	quan-ti-ta-tive	That may be estimated by quantity.
	41. qualitative	kwŏl′ĭ·tā′tĭv	qual-i-ta-tive	Relating to quality.
	42. rain	rān	rain	Water falling in drops.

43. reign	rān	reign	To govern as king or emperor.
44. rein	rān	rein	The strap of a bridle.
45. raise	rāz	raise	To elevate; to cause to rise.
46. raze	rāz	raze	To destroy; to demolish.
47. respectively	rĕ·spĕk′tĭv·lĭ	re-spec-tive-ly	Each in the order given.
48. respectfully	rĕ·spĕkt′fŏŏl·ĭ	re-spect-ful-ly	With respect or deference.
49. roll	rōl	roll	To revolve by turning over and over.
▶ 50. role	rōl	role	A part, or character, performed by an actor.
51. sight	sīt	sight	The power of seeing; a view.
52. site	sīt	site	The seat or scene of any thing; a location.
53. cite	sīt	cite	To quote.
54. soul	sōl	soul	The immortal spirit.
55. sole	sōl	sole	One and no more; one and only.
56. straight	strāt	straight	Not curved; direct; uninterrupted; unbroken.
57. strait	strāt	strait	A narrow passageway connecting two bodies of water.
58. tear	tẽr	tear	Moisture in the eye.
59. tier	tẽr	tier	A row, rank, or layer.
60. through	thrōō	through	By means of; because of.
61. threw	thrōō	threw	Past tense of *throw*.
62. too	tōō	too	Likewise; also.
63. two	tōō	two	A pair; a couple.
64. to	tōō	to	In a direction toward.
65. wait	wāt	wait	To stay for; to be in expectation.
66. weight	wāt	weight	Quantity of heaviness.
67. waste	wāst	waste	Useless expenditure.
68. waist	wāst	waist	The middle part of the body.
69. wave	wāv	wave	To swing back and forth; to motion with the hand.
70. waive	wāv	waive	To give up a claim to.
71. week	wēk	week	A period of seven days.
72. weak	wēk	weak	Lacking physical strength; feeble.
73. write	rīt	write	To form letters or words on paper.
74. right	rīt	right	Not mistaken or wrong.
75. rite	rīt	rite	A form of conducting a ceremony.

Lesson 5 Check-Up

Unit Test. Your teacher will dictate 50 words chosen from the lessons in Unit 2. These words are selected to test your mastery of the new words in this unit. Listen closely as each word is dictated, determine the proper meaning, spell the word carefully, and write plainly to assure yourself of a fair test.

Proofreading Test. In the following letter, some of the italicized words are misspelled. Copy the entire letter, making any corrections necessary in the spelling of the words.

Dear Mr. Johnson:

We of the Acme Company regret that we cannot *except* the amount of *breakage* that your company *aloud* us on our recent shipment of dishes. Although we must *complement* you on your fast action—we did not *expect* the settlement *quiet* so soon—*farther* negotiation will be necessary to reach a *prominent* agreement. We feel that there is no other *coarse* open to us.

For *your* own *piece* of mind, as well as for ours, will you please make a more *thorough* investigation and *advice* us of the results. The new findings will, of *course*, *effect* our *latter* decision to reorder.

Respectively yours,

Cumulative Test. Your teacher will now dictate 40 words chosen from Unit 1. These words will test your retention of the correct spelling of the words in Unit 1. Spell carefully and write plainly.

Checking Your Tests. Your teacher will give you directions for checking the unit test, the proofreading test, and the cumulative test.

Error Analysis. Classify the errors that you made by noting the type of error beside each word that you misspelled.

Review. Use the appropriate attack procedures for studying the words that you misspelled on the unit test, on the proofreading test, and on the cumulative test. Remember that Unit 1 contained sound words.

Retest. The retest will tell you if you have mastered the words in Units 1 and 2. If you misspelled words on the retest, continue your attack procedures until you are sure that you can spell all the words correctly.

Unit 3 Sound Words

Sound is the key to the correct spelling of the words in this unit. Spend a few moments reviewing "Spotting Sound Errors," beginning on page 3, and then begin your study of Lessons 1-4 of this unit, applying the following procedures:

Preview. Your teacher will dictate a list of 75 general-vocabulary words. Number a sheet of paper from 1 to 75. Spell as many of the words as you can, but attempt only the words that you are quite sure you know how to spell. If you do not know the spelling of a word, place a question mark (?) beside the number.

Checking Performance. Compare your spellings with the words given in the appropriate lesson. Place an X beside each word that you misspelled. To the right of any misspelled or omitted word, write the correct spelling.

Error Analysis. Classify the errors that you made by noting the type of error beside each word that you misspelled. For instance, if an error was caused by adding unnecessary letters, write "addition" beside the word. Refer to Section One if you need to be reminded of the types of errors.

Attack Procedures. Attack procedures for sound-type errors were presented in Section One, beginning on page 7. Review the corrective techniques recommended there.

Learning to Spell New Words. The pretest words that you did not know how to spell now appear on your answer sheet preceded by a question mark. Use a separate sheet of paper to practice those words, following the SEE, SAY, SPELL, and WRITE routine (see pages 39-41). Hand in the drill paper to your instructor.

Lesson 1

1. admire	ăd·mīr′	ad-mire	To regard highly.
2. apparently	ă·păr′ĕnt·lĭ	ap-par-ent-ly	Evidently; seemingly.
3. carefully	kâr′fŏŏl·ĭ	care-ful-ly	Meticulously; scrupulously.
4. collectible	kŏ·lĕkt′ĭ·b'l	col-lect-i-ble	Capable of being assembled or gathered.
5. comfortable	kŭm′fẽrt·a·b'l	com-fort-a-ble	In a state of content.
6. committee	kŏ·mĭt′ĭ	com-mit-tee	A body of persons appointed or elected to take action upon some matter.
7. concern	kŏn·sûrn′	con-cern	Regard; anxiety.
8. considerable	kŏn·sĭd′ẽr·a·b'l	con-sid-er-a-ble	Worthy of consideration; of large extent.
9. council	koun′sĭl	coun-cil	An assembly summoned for consultation.
10. current	kûr′ĕnt	cur-rent	Prevalent; belonging to the present time.
11. defense	dĕ·fĕns′	de-fense	Protection from attack.
12. defensible	dĕ·fĕn′sĭ·b'l	de-fen-si-ble	Capable of being defended.
13. each	ēch	each	All, considered one by one.
14. entrance	ĕn′trăns	en-trance	Admittance; entry.
15. everywhere	ĕv′ẽr·ĭ·hwâr′	ev-er-y-where	In every place.
16. excellent	ĕk′sĕ·lĕnt	ex-cel-lent	Extremely good; of great worth.
17. excusable	ĕks·kūz′a·b'l	ex-cus-a-ble	Pardonable; forgivable.
18. expense	ĕks·pĕns′	ex-pense	Outlay; expenditure.
19. experiment	ĕks·pĕr′ĭ·mĕnt	ex-per-i-ment	The conducting of tests.
20. expression	ĕks·prĕsh′ŭn	ex-pres-sion	Process of representing by language.
21. final	fī′năl	fi-nal	Conclusive; last.
22. finalize	fī′năl·īz	fi-nal-ize	To carry into the final stage.
23. frequently	frĕ′kwĕnt·lĭ	fre-quent-ly	At short intervals.
24. furniture	fûr′nĭ·tŭr	fur-ni-ture	Necessary equipment.
25. generally	jĕn′ẽr·ăl·ĭ	gen-er-al-ly	In a general manner.
26. gradually	grăd′ů·ăl·ĭ	grad-u-al-ly	By steps or degrees.
27. half	häf	half	One of two equal parts of something.
28. harbor	här′bẽr	har-bor	v. To shelter; to give refuge to. n. A port or haven.
29. heard	hûrd	heard	Past tense and past participle of hear.
30. hospitalization	hŏs′pĭt·′l·ĭ·zā′shŭn	hos-pi-tal-i-za-tion	Placement in a hospital for treatment.
31. hour	our	hour	Sixty minutes.
32. imagine	ĭ·măj′ĭn	im-ag-ine	To suppose; to think to be.

33. improve	ĭm·prōōv′	im-prove	To increase in value.
34. indicate	ĭn′dĭ·kāt	in-di-cate	To point out.
35. individually	ĭn′dĭ·vĭd′û·ăl·ĭ	in-di-vid-u-al-ly	Particularly; inseparably.
36. information	ĭn′fŏr·mā′shŭn	in-for-ma-tion	Knowledge derived from reading, observation, or instruction.
37. interesting	ĭn′tĕr·ĕs·tĭng	in-ter-est-ing	Engaging the attention.
38. introduce	ĭn′trŏ·dūs′	in-tro-duce	To institute; to bring in.
39. island	ī′lănd	is-land	A tract of land surrounded by water.
40. journey	jûr′nĭ	jour-ney	A trip.
41. journeys	jûr′nĭz	jour-neys	Plural of *journey* (see above).
42. knew	nū	knew	Past tense of *know.*
43. knowledge	nŏl′ĕj	knowl-edge	Enlightenment; learning; acquaintance with facts.
44. known	nōn	known	Past participle of *know.*
45. lesson	lĕs′′n	les-son	Something that is learned or taught.
46. library	lī′brĕr′ĭ	li-brar-y	A building devoted to a collection of books.
47. major	mā′jĕr	ma-jor	Greater in dignity, rank, or importance.
48. manageable	măn′ĭj·à·b'l	man-age-a-ble	Submitting to control.
49. manufacturing	măn′û·făk′tûr·ĭng	man-u-fac-tur-ing	The making by hand, machinery, or other agency.
50. marriage ▶	măr′ĭj	mar-riage	State of being married.
51. memory	mĕm′ŏ·rĭ	mem-o-ry	Faculty of remembering.
52. message	mĕs′ĭj	mes-sage	A communication sent from one person to another.
53. misspell	mĭs·spĕl′	mis-spell	To spell incorrectly.
54. model	mŏd′′l	mod-el	A miniature representation of a thing.
55. monograph	mŏn′ŏ·grȧf	mon-o-graph	A written account of a single thing.
56. necessity	nĕ·sĕs′ĭ·tĭ	ne-ces-si-ty	An inevitable need.
57. occasion	ŏ·kā′zhŭn	oc-ca-sion	A favorable opportunity; a happening; an occurrence.
58. occur	ŏ·kûr′	oc-cur	To appear; to happen.
59. occurred	ŏ·kûrd′	oc-curred	Appeared; happened.
60. official	ŏ·fĭsh′ăl	of-fi-cial	Authorized; authoritative.
61. operation	ŏp′ĕr·ā′shŭn	op-er-a-tion	Method of functioning.
62. opportunities	ŏp′ŏr·tū′nĭ·tĭz	op-por-tu-ni-ties	Plural of *opportunity* (see below).
63. opportunity	ŏp′ŏr·tū′nĭ·tĭ	op-por-tu-ni-ty	Fit time; a good chance.
64. original	ŏ·rĭj′ĭ·năl	o-rig-i-nal	Not copied or imitated.
65. passenger	păs′ĕn·jĕr	pas-sen-ger	A traveler by a public conveyance.

66. passion	păsh′ŭn	pas-sion	Feeling; emotion.
67. per cent	pēr sĕnt′	per cent	Amount measured by the number of units in proportion to one hundred.
68. personal	pûr′sŭn·ăl	per-son-al	Private; relating to an individual.
69. proceed	prŏ·sēd′	pro-ceed	To advance; to go forward.
70. recently	rē′sĕnt·lĭ	re-cent-ly	In the immediate past.
71. recover	rĕ·kŭv′ēr	re-cov-er	To win back; to regain.
72. reduce	rĕ·dūs′	re-duce	To diminish; to lower.
73. regular	rĕg′ū·lēr	reg-u-lar	Steady or uniform in practice.
74. secretarial	sĕk′rĕ·târ′ĭ·ăl	sec-re-tar-i-al	Pertaining to a type of position related to attending to organizational records.
75. student	stū′dĕnt	stu-dent	A learner; a scholar; one who studies.

Lesson 2

1. activities	ăk·tĭv′ĭ·tĭz	ac-tiv-i-ties	Physical motions; normal functions.
2. addition	ă·dĭsh′ŭn	ad-di-tion	Process of increasing; a part added to a building.
3. balance	băl′ăns	bal-ance	*n.* An equality between the totals of two sides. *v.* To equal in weight, force, or value; to make proportionate.
4. cattle	kăt′′l	cat-tle	Bovine animals, as cows, bulls, steers.
5. choose	chōōz	choose	To select; to pick.
6. chose	chōz	chose	Past tense of *choose.*
7. civil	sĭv′ĭl	civ-il	Courteous; polite; pertaining to a whole body of citizens.
8. communities	kŏ·mū′nĭ·tĭz	com-mu-ni-ties	Bodies of people having common interests or living in the same place.
9. develop	dĕ·vĕl′ŭp	de-vel-op	To promote the growth of; to mature; to ripen.
10. development	dĕ·vĕl′ŭp·mĕnt	de-vel-op-ment	Process or result of developing.
11. exactly	ĕg·zăkt′lĭ	ex-act-ly	Strictly; rigorously; precisely.
12. exist	ĕg·zĭst′	ex-ist	To live; to have actual being.
13. heed	hēd	heed	To regard with care; to take notice of.
14. importance	ĭm·pôr′tăns	im-por-tance	Consequence; significance.
15. inquire	ĭn·kwīr′	in-quire	To question; to make examination.
16. league	lēg	league	An agreement between two or more nations, parties, or persons.

17.	least	lēst	least	Smallest; shortest; slightest.
18.	leave	lēv	leave	n. A formal parting. v. To go away.
19.	listen	lĭs''n	lis-ten	To give heed; to give ear.
20.	machinery	mȧ·shēn'ēr·ĭ	ma-chin-er-y	The working parts of a machine; machines in general or collectively.
21.	majority	mȧ·jŏr'ĭ·tĭ	ma-jor-i-ty	The number greater than half.
22.	measure	mĕzh'ēr	meas-ure	n. Prescribed limit; the measured dimensions, capacity, or quantity of anything. v. To determine extent or degree.
23.	might	mīt	might	v. Past tense of *may*. n. Power.
24.	mistake	mĭs·tāk'	mis-take	To err in recognizing or estimating.
25. ▶	often	ôf'ĕn	of-ten	Frequently; many times.
26.	opposite	ŏp'ŏ·zĭt	op-po-site	Opposed; contrary; facing.
27.	ordinary	ôr'dĭ·nĕr'ĭ	or-di-nar-y	Commonplace; usual; normal.
28.	paint	pānt	paint	v. To tinge; to adorn with colors. n. A mixture of liquid pigment used to color a surface.
29.	parent	pâr'ĕnt	par-ent	A father or a mother.
30.	parents	pâr'ĕnts	par-ents	Plural of *parent* (see above).
31.	pattern	păt'ērn	pat-tern	Anything designed as a guide or model for making things.
32.	perform	pĕr·fôrm'	per-form	To accomplish; to achieve; to execute.
33.	permit	pĕr·mĭt'	per-mit	To tolerate; to consent to; to allow.
34.	permitted	pĕr·mĭt'ĕd	per-mit-ted	Allowed; tolerated.
35.	policies	pŏl'ĭ·sĭz	pol-i-cies	Plural of *policy* (see below).
36.	policy	pŏl'ĭ·sĭ	pol-i-cy	An insurance certificate; a course adopted and followed by a group.
37.	policyholder	pŏl'ĭ·sĭ·hōl'dĕr	pol-i-cy-hold-er	One to whom an insurance policy has been issued.
38.	possess	pŏ·zĕs'	pos-sess	To hold; to own; to control.
39.	possesses	pŏ·zĕs'ĕz	pos-ses-ses	Owns; controls.
40.	possibly	pŏs'ĭ·blĭ	pos-si-bly	Perhaps.
✗ 41.	potato	pŏ·tā'tō	po-ta-to	An edible starchy tuber.
42.	potatoes	pŏ·tā'tōz	po-ta-toes	Plural of *potato* (see above).
43.	powerful	pou'ēr·fŏol	pow-er-ful	Potent; influential; cogent.
44.	prefer	prĕ·fûr'	pre-fer	To like better; to choose.
45.	preferred	prĕ·fûrd'	pre-ferred	Set above something else in estimation.
46.	preserve	prĕ·zûrv'	pre-serve	To protect; to keep from intact.
47.	principal	prĭn'sĭ·păl	prin-ci-pal	*adj.* Chief; main; head. n. A capital sum invested at interest; a leader, chief, or head.

48. product	prŏd′ŭkt	prod-uct	Anything produced.
49. production	prŏ·dŭk′shŭn	pro-duc-tion	Act of producing.
50. professor	prŏ·fĕs′ĕr	pro-fes-sor	One who publicly teaches.
▶			
51. profit	prŏf′ĭt	prof-it	Excessive income over expenditures.
52. progress	prŏg′rĕs	prog-ress	Movement forward; advancement.
53. protect	prŏ·tĕkt′	pro-tect	To defend; to guard; to shield.
54. protest	prŏ·tĕst′	pro-test	To complain; to object.
55. purchasing	pûr′chĭs·ĭng	pur-chas-ing	Buying; acquiring.
56. recognize	rĕk′ŏg·nīz	rec-og-nize	To know again a person or thing previously known; to take notice of.
57. religion	rĕ·lĭj′ŭn	re-li-gion	The practice of religious beliefs.
58. representative	rĕp′rĕ·zĕn′tȧ·tĭv	rep-re-sent-a-tive	One who acts as the agent for another.
59. sacrifice	săk′rĭ·fīs	sac-ri-fice	To give up for something considered to be better.
60. scarcely	skârs′lĭ	scarce-ly	Barely; hardly.
61. secretaries	sĕk′rĕ·tĕr′ĭz	sec-re-tar-ies	Plural of secretary (see below).
62. secretary	sĕk′rĕ-tĕr′ĭ	sec-re-tar-y	One who attends to correspondence and records of an organization.
63. senator	sĕn′ȧ·tĕr	sen-a-tor	A member of a senate.
64. serious	sēr′ĭ·ŭs	se-ri-ous	Earnest; thoughtful; solemn.
65. shown	shōn	shown	Past participle of show.
66. situation	sĭt′û·ā′shŭn	sit-u-a-tion	The combination of circumstances at any given time.
67. source	sōrs	source	The origin; the first cause.
68. succeed	sŭk·sēd′	suc-ceed	To follow another in order.
69. sufficient	sŭ·fĭsh′ĕnt	suf-fi-cient	Adequate; enough.
70. superior	sū·pēr′ĭ·ĕr	su-pe-ri-or	Higher; far above in comparison.
71. trial	trī′ăl	tri-al	A test; an effort; attempt.
72. urged	ûrjd	urged	Advocated; advanced.
73. variety	vȧ·rī′ĕ·tĭ	va-ri-e-ty	A diversity; a varied assortment.
74. vegetable	vĕj′ĕ·tȧ·b'l	veg-e-ta-ble	A plant cultivated for food.
75. weighed	wād	weighed	Considered carefully; pondered in the mind.

Lesson 3

1. acre	ā′kĕr	a-cre	A measure of land.
2. active	ăk′tĭv	ac-tive	Live; dynamic; brisk.
3. address	ă·drĕs′	ad-dress	A lecture; manner of speaking to another.
4. addresses	ă·drĕs′ĕz	ad-dress-es	Plural of address (see above).

5. adopted	á·dŏpt′ĕd	a-dopt-ed	Taken and applied as one's own.
6. affect	ă·fĕkt′	af-fect	To influence or impress; to sway.
7. afford	ă·fōrd′	af-ford	To incur or stand without serious detriment.
8. announce	ă·nouns′	an-nounce	To give public notice of; to proclaim.
9. announcing	ă·noun′sĭng	an-nounc-ing	Giving public notice of.
10. area	ā′rē·á	a-re-a	Range; scope; tract on the earth.
11. August	ô′gŭst	Au-gust	The eighth month of the year.
12. burden	bûr′d'n	bur-den	Something borne with difficulty.
13. campaign	kăm·pān′	cam-paign	A connected series of operations to bring about a desired result.
14. conclude	kŏn·klōōd′	con-clude	To bring to an end; to close.
15. consent	kŏn·sĕnt′	con-sent	To give approval.
16. courage	kûr′ĭj	cour-age	Valor; bravery.
17. creature	krē′tûr	crea-ture	Anything created.
18. curtain	kûr′tĭn	cur-tain	Drapery of cloth at a window.
19. defeat	dĕ·fēt′	de-feat	To overcome; to conquer.
20. delight	dĕ·līt′	de-light	Extreme satisfaction; pleasure.
21. engage	ĕn·gāj′	en-gage	To involve; to promise; to betroth.
22. exclaim	ĕks·klām′	ex-claim	To cry out; to speak loudly.
23. familiar	fá·mĭl′yĕr	fa-mil-iar	Intimate; well known.
24. favorite	fā′vĕr·ĭt	fa-vor-ite	One unduly trusted or enriched with favors.
25. invite	ĭn·vīt′	in-vite	To solicit; to request graciously the presence of another.
26. justice	jŭs′tĭs	jus-tice	Administration of law; merited reward or punishment.
27. latter	lăt′ĕr	lat-ter	Being more recent.
28. magazine	măg′á·zēn′	mag-a-zine	A periodical containing miscellaneous articles.
29. merchant	mûr′chănt	mer-chant	A shopkeeper; one who carries on a retail business.
30. metal	mĕt′'l	met-al	Any of a class of minerals that may be fused with others to produce substances that conduct electricity and heat.
31. moral	mŏr′ăl	mor-al	Right and proper; ethical; virtuous.
32. noble	nō′b'l	no-ble	Highborn; of high birth; grand.
33. ordinarily	ôr′dĭ·nĕr′ĭ·lĭ	or-di-nar-i-ly	Normally; commonly; usually.
34. palace	păl′ĭs	pal-ace	A large stately house.
35. particular	pĕr·tĭk′ū·lĕr	par-tic-u-lar	Specific; noteworthy.
36. perfect	pûr′fĕkt	per-fect	Flawless; sound.
37. perfectly	pûr′fĕkt·lĭ	per-fect-ly	In a perfect manner.
38. prisoner	prĭz′'n·ĕr	pris-on-er	A person under arrest.
39. process	prŏs′ĕs	proc-ess	A series of actions definitely leading to an end.
40. properties	prŏp′ĕr·tĭz	prop-er-ties	Plural of *property* (see below).
41. property	prŏp′ĕr·tĭ	prop-er-ty	A piece of real estate; an estate; a characteristic quality of a thing.

42. proportion	prŏ·pōr'shŭn	pro-por-tion	The relation of one part to another.
43. proposed	prŏ·pōzd'	pro-posed	Stated; suggested; propounded.
44. protected	prŏ·tĕk'tĕd	pro-tect-ed	Guarded; shielded.
45. purchasable	pûr'chĭs·à·b'l	pur-chas-a-ble	Capable of being purchased.
46. qualities	kwŏl'ĭ·tĭz	qual-i-ties	Plural of *quality* (see below).
47. quality	kwŏl'ĭ·tĭ	qual-i-ty	Grade; characteristic; distinctive trait.
48. quantities	kwŏn'tĭ·tĭz	quan-ti-ties	Plural of *quantity* (see below).
49. quantity	kwŏn'tĭ·tĭ	quan-ti-ty	An amount or portion.
50. quarreled	kwŏr'ĕld	quar-reled	Found fault; wrangled.

▶

51. raise	rāz	raise	To cause to arise; to elevate.
52. ready	rĕd'ĭ	read-y	To arrange for immediate use.
53. reason	rē'z'n	rea-son	A statement offered as an explanation; a cause.
54. represent	rĕp'rĕ·zĕnt'	rep-re-sent	To portray or depict; to act the part of.
55. right	rīt	right	Correct; fit; suitable.
56. royal	roi'ăl	roy-al	Kingly; regal.
57. salable	sāl'à·b'l	sal-a-ble	Marketable.
58. salaries	săl'à·rĭz	sal-a-ries	Plural of *salary* (see below).
59. salary	săl'à·rĭ	sal-a-ry	Fixed compensation paid regularly for services.
60. scene	sēn	scene	A division of a drama; stage setting; a view.
61. science	sī'ĕns	sci-ence	Knowledge obtained by study and practice.
62. senate	sĕn'ĭt	sen-ate	A legislative body.
63. series	sēr'ēz	se-ries	A number of things succeeding in order.
64. shoulders	shōl'dĕrs	shoul-ders	The upper part of the back.
65. sight	sīt	sight	*n.* A view; a vision. *v.* To see.
66. signed	sīnd	signed	Marked; noted.
67. similar	sĭm'ĭ·lĕr	sim-i-lar	Nearly corresponding.
68. smooth	smōōth	smooth	Having an even surface.
69. successful	sŭk·sĕs'fŏŏl	suc-cess-ful	Achieving success.
70. surround	sŭ·round'	sur-round	To enclose on all sides; to encircle.
71. taxable	tăk'sà·b'l	tax-a-ble	Capable of being taxed; tollable.
72. temperature	tĕm'pēr·à·t̥ûr	tem-per-a-ture	Degree of hotness or coldness measured on a definite scale.
73. territory	tĕr'ĭ·tō'rĭ	ter-ri-to-ry	A region; a large tract of land.
74. tracer	trās'ēr	trac-er	Device used in tracing.
75. valuable	văl'û·à·b'l	val-u-a-ble	Having monetary value; worth a good price.

Lesson 4

1. acquaintance	à·kwān'tăns	ac-quaint-ance	A person with whom one is acquainted.
2. administration	ăd·mĭn'ĭs·trā'shŭn	ad-min-is-tra-tion	Process of administering.
3. advise	ăd·vīz'	ad-vise	To recommend; to counsel.

4. anxious	ăngk'shŭs	anx-ious	Eager; disquieted over an impending ill.
5. appeal	ă·pēl'	ap-peal	A plea; a petition.
6. appealing	ă·pēl'ĭng	ap-peal-ing	Petitioning; pleading.
7. apply	ă·plī'	ap-ply	To put to use.
8. applying	ă·plī'ĭng	ap-ply-ing	Devoting to a particular purpose.
9. approach	ă·prōch'	ap-proach	v. To come near. n. Act of approaching.
10. arrange	ă·rānj'	ar-range	To put in proper order; to adjust; to settle.
11. artist	är'tĭst	art-ist	A person skilled in one of the fine arts.
12. association	ă·sō'sĭ·ā'shŭn	as-so-ci-a-tion	A body of persons organized for some common purpose.
13. assumed	ă·sūmd'	as-sumed	Supposed; pretended.
14. assure	ă·shōōr'	as-sure	To state confidently; to confirm.
15. assuring	ă·shōōr'ĭng	as-sur-ing	Confirming; securing.
16. attempting	ă·tĕmpt'ĭng	at-tempt-ing	Endeavoring to do; trying.
17. attend	ă·tĕnd'	at-tend	To be present with; to accompany; to take charge of.
18. attitude	ăt'ĭ·tūd	at-ti-tude	Feeling; mood.
19. autumn	ô'tŭm	au-tumn	The season between summer and winter.
20. avenue	ăv'ĕ·nū	av-e-nue	A street; a broad passageway.
21. benefited	bĕn'ĕ·fĭt·ĕd	ben-e-fit-ed	Profited.
22. careful	kâr'fŏŏl	care-ful	Full of care; anxious; marked by care.
23. chapter	chăp'tĕr	chap-ter	A main division of a book; an organized body of a society.
24. collect	kŏ·lĕkt'	col-lect	To assemble; to gather.
25. collection ▶	kŏ·lĕk'shŭn	col-lec-tion	Process of collecting; things that have been collected.
26. column	kŏl'ŭm	col-umn	A perpendicular line of figures; a supporting post or pillar.
27. commerce	kŏm'ûrs	com-merce	The buying and selling of commodities.
28. companion	kŏm·păn'yŭn	com-pan-ion	An associate; a comrade.
29. conference	kŏn'fĕr·ĕns	con-fer-ence	Formal consultation or discussion.
30. connection	kŏ·nĕk'shŭn	con-nec-tion	Union; alliance; relationship.
31. consist	kŏn·sĭst'	con-sist	To be composed or made up of.
32. constitution	kŏn'stĭ·tū'shŭn	con-sti-tu-tion	The mode of organization of a social group.

33. decision	dē·sĭzh′ŭn	de-ci-sion	A conclusion arrived at after consideration.
34. descend	dē·sĕnd′	de-scend	To pass from a higher to a lower place.
35. element	ĕl′ē·mĕnt	el-e-ment	One of the component parts, principles, or traits of anything.
36. encourage	ĕn·kûr′ĭj	en-cour-age	To inspire with courage.
37. enormous	ē·nôr′mŭs	e-nor-mous	Huge; immense; vast.
38. federal	fĕd′ĕr·ăl	fed-er-al	Pertaining to a political unit formed when several states unite under a central government.
39. handled	hăn′d′ld	han-dled	Directed; managed.
40. hungry	hŭng′grĭ	hun-gry	Feeling hunger; having a desire or craving.
41. institution	ĭn′stĭ·tū′shŭn	in-sti-tu-tion	An establishment; an established corporation.
42. laughter	läf′tēr	laugh-ter	A facial expression together with sounds from the throat indicating amusement.
43. manufacture	măn′û·făk′tûr	man-u-fac-ture	To make by machinery or by hand; to produce mechanically; to fabricate.
44. minister	mĭn′ĭs·tēr	min-is-ter	One duly authorized to conduct worship.
45. murmur	mûr′mēr	mur-mur	A low, indistinct sound.
46. northern	nôr′thērn	north-ern	Being in the north.
47. perceive	pēr·sēv′	per-ceive	To see; to hear; to understand.
48. physical	fĭz′ĭ·kăl	phys-i-cal	Pertaining to physics; pertaining to the laws of nature.
49. proof	pro͞of	proof	Any process designed to establish the truth.
50. proud ▶	proud	proud	Showing too great self-esteem.
51. pursue	pēr·sū′	pur-sue	To chase; to go after.
52. pursuing	pēr·sū′ĭng	pur-su-ing	Chasing; following.
53. region	rē′jŭn	re-gion	A large tract of land.
54. respect	rē·spĕkt′	re-spect	*v.* To consider worthy of esteem. *n.* Regard; consideration.
55. reveal	rē·vēl′	re-veal	To disclose; to divulge.
56. satisfied	săt′ĭs·fīd	sat-is-fied	Made content; requited.
57. secret	sē′krĕt	se-cret	Hidden from others; furtive.
58. secretive	sē·krē′tĭv	se-cre-tive	Not frank; reticent.
59. separate	sĕp′à·rāt	sep-a-rate	To disconnect; to detach; to come apart.
60. separating	sĕp′à·rāt·ĭng	sep-a-rat-ing	Severing; disconnecting.
61. September	sĕp·tĕm′bēr	Sep-tem-ber	Ninth month of the year.

62. settlement	sĕt′′l·mĕnt	set-tle-ment	A disposition of property; state of being settled.
63. telephone	tĕl′ĕ·fōn	tel-e-phone	An instrument for reproducing sounds.
64. theater	thē′à·tĕr	the-a-ter	A place where events are enacted.
65. though	thō	though	Supposing that; although.
66. thought	thôt	thought	Reflection; capacity to think or judge; idea.
67. through	thrōō	through	From one end or side to another.
68. title	tī′t′l	ti-tle	A claim; a right; a descriptive name.
69. uniform	ū′nĭ·fôrm	u-ni-form	Conforming to one rule or mode.
70. university	ū′nĭ·vûr′sĭ·tĭ	u-ni-ver-si-ty	An institution organized for teaching and study.
71. velocity	vĕ·lŏs′ĭ·tĭ	ve-loc-i-ty	Quickness of motion; speed.
72. weather	wĕth′ĕr	weath-er	Condition of the air or atmosphere.
73. whole	hōl	whole	Total; undivided; entire.
74. whose	hōōz	whose	Possessive of *who*.
75. witness	wĭt′nĕs	wit-ness	One who furnishes evidence.

Lesson 5 Check-Up

Unit Test. Your teacher will dictate 50 words chosen from the lessons in Unit 3. These words are selected to test your mastery of the new words in this unit. Listen closely as each word is dictated, spell the word carefully, and write plainly to assure yourself of a fair test.

Proofreading Test. In the following letter, some of the italicized words are misspelled. Copy the entire letter, making any corrections necessary in the spelling of the words.

> Dear Mr. James:
>
> The *Commitee* for *Civel Defence* met *resently* in the *Sience* Room of the City *Libary*. As a result of this meeting, the *autum campaign* for this *region* is being *interduced* on a *triel* basis. The program is something of an *experament*, and all citizens are *urjed* to suggest ways in which *defence* procedures can be *emproved*.
>
> Since you are *familiar* with the *polacies* of the *Commitee*, and since you have previously *handeled* programs in *conection* with *defence*, we *invite* you to participate in our weekly *conferance* next Wednesday. May we count on you to *atend?*
>
> Cordially yours,

Cumulative Test. Your teacher will now dictate 40 words chosen from Units 1 and 2. These words will test your retention of the correct spelling of the words in these units. Spell carefully, determine the correct meanings, and write plainly.

Checking Your Tests. Your teacher will give you directions for checking the unit test, the proofreading test, and the cumulative test.

Error Analysis. Classify the errors that you made by noting the type of error beside each word that you misspelled.

Review. Use the appropriate attack procedures for studying the words that you misspelled on the unit test, on the proofreading test, and on the cumulative test. Remember that the cumulative test contained both sound and meaning words.

Retest. The retest will tell you if you have mastered the words in Units 1 through 3. If you misspelled words on the retest, continue your attack procedures until you are sure that you can spell all the words correctly.

Unit 4 Carelessness, Demons, and Homonyms

The words in this unit are commonly involved in errors that are made through carelessness, misspelling of demons, or the improper use of homonyms. Other types of errors may occur as you are tested on the words in this unit. Identify all the errors that you make and use the appropriate attack procedures, following this usual daily lesson routine.

Preview. Your teacher will dictate a list of 75 general-vocabulary words. Number a sheet of paper from 1 to 75. Spell as many of the words as you can, but attempt only the words that you are quite sure you know how to spell. If you do not know the spelling of a word, place a question mark (?) beside the number.

Checking Performance. Compare your spellings with the words given in the appropriate lesson. Place an X beside each word that you misspelled. To the right of any misspelled or omitted word, write the correct spelling. If you are not certain of the correct meaning of the word, study the definition and then use the word in a sentence.

Error Analysis. Classify the errors that you made by noting the type of error beside each word that you misspelled. For instance, if an error was caused by carelessness, write "carelessness" beside the word. Refer to Section One if you have forgotten the types of errors.

Attack Procedures. Attack procedures for errors due to carelessness, demons, or improper use of homonyms were presented in Section One, on pages 17 and 35. Review the corrective technique recommended for each type of error.

Learning to Spell New Words. The pretest words that you did not know how to spell now appear on your answer sheet preceded by a question mark. Use a separate sheet of paper to practice those words, following the SEE, SAY, SPELL, and WRITE routine (see pages 39-41). Hand in the drill paper to your instructor.

Lesson 1

1. accommodate	ă·kŏm′ō·dāt	ac-com-mo-date	To oblige; to favor.
2. accommodation	ă·kŏm′ō·dā′shŭn	ac-com-mo-da-tion	State of being accommodated; adaptation; adjustment.
3. amateur	ăm′á·tûr′	am-a-teur	One who is not rated as a professional.

4. Arkansas	är′kăn·sô	Ar-kan-sas	A south central state of the United States.
5. beach	bēch	beach	The shore of a sea or of a lake.
6. beech	bēch	beech	A hardwood timber tree.
7. benefited	bĕn′ĕ·fĭt·ĕd	ben-e-fit-ed	Past tense of *benefit;* profited.
8. birth	bûrth	birth	Act of being born.
9. berth	bûrth	berth	The place where a ship lies at anchor.
10. besiege	bĕ·sēj′	be-siege	To surround with armed forces.
11. bow	bou	bow	To bend the head, knee, or body in reverence.
12. bough	bou	bough	A branch of a tree.
13. Britain	brĭt′′n	Brit-ain	Short for *Great Britain.*
14. can't	kănt	can't	Contraction of *cannot.*
15. capital	kăp′ĭ·tăl	cap-i-tal	Chief; principal; main.
16. capitol	kăp′ĭ·tŏl	cap-i-tol	A statehouse.
17. captain	kăp′tĭn	cap-tain	A leader; a person having authority over others.
18. certain	sûr′tĭn	cer-tain	Fixed; settled; sure.
19. certainly	sûr′tĭn·lĭ	cer-tain-ly	Surely; without doubt.
20. council	koun′sĭl	coun-cil	An assembly summoned for consultation.
21. counsel	koun′sĕl	coun-sel	To recommend; to give advice to.
22. corps	kōr	corps	A body of persons under common direction.
23. current	kûr′ĕnt	cur-rent	Circulating; prevailing.
24. currant	kûr′ănt	cur-rant	A small seedless raisin.
25. curtain ▶	kûr′tĭn	cur-tain	Drapery of cloth at a window.
26. depth	dĕpth	depth	Perpendicular measurement from the surface down.
27. determining	dĕ·tûr′mĭn·ĭng	de-ter-min-ing	Deciding; impelling.
28. each	ēch	each	All, considered one by one.
29. ecstasy	ĕk′stȧ·sĭ	ec-sta-sy	A state of joy; rapture.
30. eighth	ātth	eighth	Ordinal number, following *seventh.*
31. embroidery	ĕm·broi′dĕr·ĭ	em-broi-der-y	Art of ornamenting cloths with needlework.
32. enemies	ĕn′ĕ·mĭz	en-e-mies	Hostile forces; military foes.
33. exaggerate	ĕg·zăj′ĕr·āt	ex-ag-ger-ate	To overstate the truth about something.

34. exquisite	ĕks′kwĭ·zĭt	ex-qui-site	Choice; pleasing by reason of excellence.
35. extemporaneous	ĕks·tĕm′pō·rā′nē·ŭs	ex-tem-po-ra-ne-ous	Without prior preparation.
36. extraordinary	ĕks·trôr′dĭ·nĕr′ĭ	ex-traor-di-nar-y	Exceeding the common degree; remarkable.
37. false	fôls	false	Not true; incorrect.
38. familiar	fȧ·mĭl′yēr	fa-mil-iar	Well known; closely acquainted.
39. fulfill	fōōl·fĭl′	ful-fill	To carry into effect.
40. grown	grōn	grown	Mature.
41. groan	grōn	groan	To utter a sound that is expressive of pain, grief, or disapproval.
42. heir	âr	heir	One who inherits.
43. I've	īv	I've	Contraction of *I have*.
44. colonel	kûr′nĕl	colo-nel	A commissioned officer ranking above a lieutenant colonel.
45. kernel	kûr′nĕl	ker-nel	A whole grain or seed of a cereal.
46. lean	lēn	lean	To bend from a vertical position.
47. lien	lē′ĕn	li-en	A charge upon real or personal property to satisfy a debt.
48. length	lĕngth	length	A portion of space or of time.
49. lesson	lĕs′'n	les-son	Instruction.
50. lessen	lĕs′'n	less-en	To decrease; to reduce.
51. ludicrous	lū′dĭ·krŭs	lu-di-crous	Ridiculous.
52. mail	māl	mail	Letters, papers, etc., received through the post office.
53. male	māl	male	Masculine; manly.
54. main	mān	main	The chief part; the essential point.
55. mane	mān	mane	The long, heavy hair on the upper side of the neck of some animals.
56. manufacturing	măn′ṳ·făk′t̬ṳr·ĭng	man-u-fac-tur-ing	Producing mechanically.
57. material	mȧ·tēr′ĭ·ăl	ma-te-ri-al	Physical; pertinent.
58. medieval	mē′dĭ·ē′văl	me-di-e-val	Characteristic of the Middle Ages.
59. meeting	mēt′ĭng	meet-ing	A gathering; assembly.
60. mountain	moun′tĭn	moun-tain	A marked elevation of land; a great mass.
61. necessary	nĕs′ĕ·sĕr′ĭ	nec-es-sar-y	Indispensable.

62.	necessity	nĕ·sĕs′ĭ·tĭ	ne-ces-si-ty	An urgent need.
63.	parallel	păr′ă·lĕl	par-al-lel	Anything resembling or equal to another in all essential details.
64.	particularly	pēr·tĭk′ů·lēr·lĭ	par-tic-u-lar-ly	Especially; unusually; in a particular manner.
65.	proportion	prŏ·pōr′shŭn	pro-por-tion	The relation of one portion to another.
66.	representative	rĕp′rĕ·zĕn′tȧ·tĭv	rep-re-sent-a-tive	One who acts as an agent for another.
67.	return	rĕ·tûrn′	re-turn	To go or come back again to a place, person, or condition.
68.	roof	rŏŏf	roof	The cover of any building.
69.	sheriff	shĕr′ĭf	sher-iff	The chief executive officer of a county, charged with executing the laws and preserving the peace.
70.	similar	sĭm′ĭ·lēr	sim-i-lar	Having a general likeness.
71.	soldier	sōl′jēr	sol-dier	One engaged in military service.
72.	square	skwâr	square	A parallelogram having four equal sides and four right angles.
73.	trial	trī′ăl	tri-al	The action of putting to the proof; a test.
74.	wrote	rōt	wrote	Past tense of *write*.
75.	rote	rōt	rote	Repetition of forms or phrases, often without attention to meaning.

Lesson 2

1.	accelerate	ăk·sĕl′ēr·āt	ac-cel-er-ate	To move or act faster; to quicken.
2.	accompaniment	ȧ·kŭm′pȧ·nĭ·mĕnt	ac-com-pa-ni-ment	That which accompanies as a circumstance or an embellishment; a supporting musical instrument or musical part.
3.	administration	ăd·mĭn′ĭs·trā′shŭn	ad-min-is-tra-tion	Act or process of administering; executive management.
4.	attain	ȧ·tān′	at-tain	To reach; to gain; to accomplish.
5.	auxiliary	ôg·zĭl′yȧ·rĭ	aux-il-ia-ry	Supporting; subsidiary; assistant.
6.	bargain	bär′gĭn	bar-gain	To try to get, buy, or sell something on good terms.

7. breadth	brĕdth	breadth	Distance from side to side of any surface.
8. bruise	brōōz	bruise	v. To crush. n. A surface injury to the flesh.
9. buoyant	bōō′yănt	buoy-ant	Able to float; not easily depressed.
10. Cairo	kī′rō	Cai-ro	Capital city of Egypt.
11. candidate	kăn′dĭ·dāt	can-di-date	One who declares himself a suitable person for an office.
12. ceiling	sēl′ĭng	ceil-ing	The overhead lining of a room.
13. sealing	sēl′ĭng	seal-ing	Securing; enclosing.
14. census	sĕn′sŭs	cen-sus	An official enumeration of the population of an area.
15. colossal	kŏ·lŏs′ăl	co-los-sal	Enormous; huge.
16. connoisseur	kŏn′ĭ·sûr′	con-nois-seur	One competent to act as a critical judge of art, or in matters concerning taste.
17. convenience	kŏn·vēn′yĕns	con-ven-ience	Fitness; personal comfort.
18. convenient	kŏn·vēn′yĕnt	con-ven-ient	Suited to one's easy performance of some act or function.
19. debris	dĕ·brē′	de-bris	Rubbish; ruins.
20. demonstrate	dĕm′ŭn·strāt	dem-on-strate	To show publicly.
21. drudgery	drŭj′ĕr·ĭ	drudg-er-y	Wearisome toil.
22. dying	dī′ĭng	dy-ing	Ceasing to live; perishing; vanishing; fading.
23. dyeing	dī′ĭng	dye-ing	Process of coloring fibers uniformly and permanently.
24. eighteen	ā′tēn′	eight-een	Cardinal number, following *seventeen*.
25. eighty ▶	ā′tĭ	eight-y	Cardinal number, following *seventy-nine*.
26. ensemble	än·sŏm′b'l	en-sem-ble	adv. All at once; together. n. A whole.
27. environment	ĕn·vī′rŭn·mĕnt	en-vi-ron-ment	Surroundings.
28. etiquette	ĕt′ĭ·kĕt	et-i-quette	Actions required by good breeding or social conventions.
29. fountain	foun′tĭn	foun-tain	An artificial jet of water.
30. gaseous	găs′ĕ·ŭs	gas-e-ous	Lacking substance or solidity; in the form of gas.
31. gauge	gāj	gauge	A measure; an instrument for measuring.
32. guardian	gär′dĭ·ăn	guard-i-an	One who keeps safe; one who secures.
33. holy	hō′lĭ	ho-ly	Sacred; worthy of adoration.
34. wholly	hōl′lĭ	whol-ly	Fully; totally; solely.

35. idle	ĭ′d′l	i-dle	Useless; not employed.
36. idol	ī′dŭl	i-dol	A false god; an image or representative of a deity.
37. impious	ĭm′pĭ·ŭs	im-pi-ous	Irreverent; profane.
38. indict	ĭn·dīt′	in-dict	To charge with an of-fense.
39. innumerable	ĭ·nū′mĕr·a̤·b′l	in-nu-mer-a-ble	Numberless; too many to be counted.
40. interpret	ĭn·tûr′prĕt	in-ter-pret	To translate; to explain.
41. Louisiana	lŏo′ĭ·zĭ·ăn′a̤	Lou-i-si-an-a	A southern state in the United States.
42. maneuver	ma̤·nōō′vĕr	ma-neu-ver	*v.* To manipulate; to exe-cute tactical movements. *n.* A military or naval movement of troops or vessels.
43. manufacturer	măn′ṷ·făk′t̤ŭr·ēr	man-u-fac-tur-er	One who manufactures.
44. merry	mĕr′ĭ	mer-ry	Pleasant; delightful.
45. marry	măr′ĭ	mar-ry	To unite in wedlock.
46. museum	mṷ·zē′ŭm	mu-se-um	A building in which are preserved and exhibited objects of permanent in-terest.
47. necessarily	nĕs′ĕ·sĕr′ĭ·lĭ	nec-es-sar-i-ly	By necessity; inevitably.
48. nucleus	nū′klĕ·ŭs	nu-cle-us	The central portion; the core.
49. permanent	pûr′ma̤·nĕnt	per-ma-nent	Lasting; continuing in the same state.
50. pray	prā	pray	To beg for; to entreat.
51. prey	prā	prey	Any animal seized by an-other to be devoured.
52. prerogative	prĕ·rŏg′a̤·tĭv	pre-rog-a-tive	A right to exercise a power to the exclusion of others.
53. principal	prĭn′sĭ·pa̤l	prin-ci-pal	Chief; main; highest in rank.
54. principle	prĭn′sĭ·p′l	prin-ci-ple	A basic law; a rule.
55. profit	prŏf′ĭt	prof-it	The excess of receipts over expenditures.
56. prophet	prŏf′ĕt	proph-et	One who prophesies future events.
57. proof	prōōf	proof	Evidence that convinces the mind of a truth or fact.
58. rendezvous	rän′dĕ·vōō	ren-dez-vous	A place appointed for a meeting.
59. reservation	rĕz′ēr·vā′shŭn	res-er-va-tion	Act of reserving some-thing for oneself or for others; a record of an act of reserving.

60. resolve	rĕ·zŏlv′	re-solve	To determine; to decide; to settle on.
61. reward	rĕ·wôrd′	re-ward	*v.* To make a return; to repay. *n.* Something given as a return for good or evil done or received.
62. route	rōōt	route	The way that is to be traveled.
63. root	rōōt	root	Any part of a plant that is underground.
64. satellite	săt′ĕ·līt	sat-el-lite	A secondary planet (sometimes artificial) revolving around a larger one.
65. seed	sēd	seed	That from which anything springs.
66. cede	sēd	cede	To yield; to grant.
67. steel	stēl	steel	A commercial form of iron.
68. steal	stēl	steal	To take away illegally.
69. superintendent	sū′pĕr·ĭn·tĕn′dĕnt	su-per-in-tend-ent	One who has the charge of a place.
70. supersede	sū′pĕr·sēd′	su-per-sede	To take the place of.
71. thrown	thrōn	thrown	Past participle of *throw.*
72. throne	thrōn	throne	A royal seat on a dais, as for a king, prince, bishop, etc.
73. tragedy	trăj′ĕ·dĭ	trag-e-dy	A literary composition that excites pity and terror by a series of unhappy events.
74. vane	vān	vane	An instrument used to show direction of wind.
75. vain	vān	vain	Manifesting undue pride in one's appearance.

Lesson 3

1. administrative	ăd·mĭn′ĭs·trā′tĭv	ad-min-is-tra-tive	Having to do with management; executive.
2. Albuquerque	ăl′bŭ·kûr′kē	Al-bu-quer-que	A city in central New Mexico.
3. altar	ôl′tĕr	al-tar	A raised structure on which sacrifices are offered.
4. alter	ôl′tĕr	al-ter	To vary; to change.
5. aluminum	à·lū′mĭ·nŭm	a-lu-mi-num	A bluish, silver-white malleable metal.
6. anniversary	ăn′ĭ·vûr′sà·rĭ	an-ni-ver-sa-ry	Annual return of a date on which some special event took place.
7. ascent	ă·sĕnt′	as-cent	An upward slope.
8. assent	ă·sĕnt′	as-sent	To consent; to agree; to acquiesce.

9. assistance	ă·sĭs′tăns	as-sist-ance	Help; aid.
10. assistants	ă·sĭs′tănts	as-sist-ants	Helpers; those who assist.
11. attendance	ă·tĕn′dăns	at-tend-ance	Act of attending.
12. attendants	ă·tĕn′dănts	at-tend-ants	Those who attend or accompany.
13. authoritatively	ô·thŏr′ĭ·tā′tĭv·lĭ	au-thor-i-ta-tive-ly	With authority; dictatorially.
14. bankruptcy	băngk′rŭpt·sĭ	bank-rupt-cy	State of being legally bankrupt.
15. cancellation	kăn′sĕ·lā′shŭn	can-cel-la-tion	Deletion; annulment.
16. canvas	kăn′vȧs	can-vas	A heavy, closely woven cloth made of hemp or flax.
17. canvass	kăn′vȧs	can-vass	To solicit; to seek orders.
18. civilian	sĭ·vĭl′yăn	ci-vil-ian	One not professionally in the armed services.
19. consensus	kŏn·sĕn′sŭs	con-sen-sus	Agreement in matters of opinion.
20. core	kōr	core	The central part of anything.
21. corps	kōr	corps	A group of persons under common direction.
22. corroborate	kŏ·rŏb′ō·rāt	cor-rob-o-rate	To confirm; to establish; to make more certain.
23. debut	dā′bū	de-but	The first public appearance.
24. denomination	dĕ·nŏm′ĭ·nā′shŭn	de-nom-i-na-tion	A general name; a category.
► 25. desiccate	dĕs′ĭ·kāt	des-ic-cate	To dry up; to preserve by drying.
26. disseminate	dĭ·sĕm′ĭ·nāt	dis-sem-i-nate	To spread abroad; to scatter.
27. dominant	dŏm′ĭ·nănt	dom-i-nant	Controlling; ruling.
28. encore	äng′kōr	en-core	The call for a repetition of an appearance or a performance.
29. epitome	ê·pĭt′ō·mê	e-pit-o-me	A brief statement of the contents of a topic or work.
30. exemplary	ĕg·zĕm′plȧ·rĭ	ex-em-pla-ry	Deserving imitation; serving as a pattern.
31. exhilaration	ĕg·zĭl′ȧ·rā′shŭn	ex-hil-a-ra-tion	Stimulation; enlivenment; animation.
32. exorbitant	ĕg·zôr′bĭ·tănt	ex-or-bi-tant	Excessive.
33. facilitate	fȧ·sĭl′ĭ·tāt	fa-cil-i-tate	To make easy.
34. familiarity	fȧ·mĭl′ĭ·ăr′ĭ·tĭ	fa-mil-i-ar-i-ty	Intimacy; state of being familiar.
35. heinous	hā′nŭs	hei-nous	Hateful; atrocious; offending greatly.
36. hereditary	hĕ·rĕd′ĭ·tĕr′ĭ	he-red-i-tar-y	Innate; transmitted or capable of being transmitted from parent to offspring.
37. inconvenience	ĭn′kŏn·vēn′yĕns	in-con-ven-ience	Discomfort; that which causes trouble or uneasiness.

38. indebtedness	ĭn·dĕt'ĕd·nĕs	in-debt-ed-ness	State of being in debt; the sum owed.
39. inexhaustible	ĭn'ĕg·zôs'tĭ·b'l	in-ex-haust-i-ble	Incapable of being exhausted; indefatigable.
40. innocuous	ĭ·nŏk'ū·ŭs	in-noc-u-ous	Harmless.
41. inoculate	ĭn·ŏk'ū·lāt	in-oc-u-late	To infuse; to inject an immunizing serum into.
42. inveigle	ĭn·vē'g'l	in-vei-gle	To lure; to cajole; to lead astray by deceiving.
43. irrelevant	ĭr·rĕl'ĕ·vănt	ir-rel-e-vant	Not pertinent; extraneous.
44. irresistible	ĭr'rē·zĭs'tĭ·b'l	ir-re-sist-i-ble	That cannot be resisted successfully; resistless.
45. aisle	īl	aisle	A passageway between rows of seats.
46. isle	īl	isle	A small island.
47. mahogany	mȧ·hŏg'ȧ·nĭ	ma-hog-a-ny	Valuable wood yielded by the mahogany tree.
48. maintenance	mān't'n·ăns	main-te-nance	Support; upkeep of property.
49. manual	măn'ū·ăl	man-u-al	adj. Done, made, or operated by hand. n. A small book.
50. marshal	mär'shăl	mar-shal	An officer authorized to regulate ceremonies, preserve order, etc.
51. martial	mär'shăl	mar-tial	Pertaining to a military life; warlike.
52. materially	mȧ·tẽr'ĭ·ăl·ĭ	ma-te-ri-al-ly	Substantially; essentially.
53. miner	mīn'ẽr	min-er	A worker in a mine.
54. minor	mī'nẽr	mi-nor	Less; smaller; not of legal age.
55. pageant	păj'ĕnt	pag-eant	A theatrical exhibition.
56. peer	pēr	peer	To gaze; to look curiously.
57. pier	pẽr	pier	A structure built out into the water and used as a landing place for boats.
58. plebeian	plē·bē'yăn	ple-be-ian	Common.
59. preliminary	prē·lĭm'ĭ·nẽr'ĭ	pre-lim-i-nar-y	Introductory; preceding the main event.
60. presentation	prĕz'ĕn·tā'shŭn	pres-en-ta-tion	Formal introduction; the formal offering of a gift.
61. preservation	prĕz'ẽr·vā'shŭn	pres-er-va-tion	Protection; the state of being preserved from injury.
62. probability	prŏb'ȧ·bĭl'ĭ·tĭ	prob-a-bil-i-ty	Likelihood; that which appears probable.
63. reconnoiter	rĕk'ŏ·noi'tẽr	rec-on-noi-ter	To make a preliminary examination.
64. remembrance	rē·mĕm'brăns	re-mem-brance	Recollection; a souvenir.
65. residence	rĕz'ĭ·dĕns	res-i-dence	A place where one has his home.

66. residents	rĕz′ĭ·dĕnts	res-i-dents	Those who reside in a place.
67. slay	slā	slay	To kill; to destroy.
68. sleigh	slā	sleigh	A vehicle on runners, used on snow or ice.
69. souvenir	sōō′vē·nẹr′	sou-ve-nir	A memento.
70. stake	stāk	stake	A pointed piece of wood driven into the ground as a mark or support.
71. steak	stāk	steak	A slice of meat cut from a fleshy part of an animal.
72. synonym	sĭn′ŏ·nĭm	syn-o-nym	A word having the same or nearly the same meaning as another word.
73. thermometer	thẽr·mŏm′ĕ·tẽr	ther-mom-e-ter	An instrument used to determine the temperature of a body or space.
74. unanimous	û·năn′ĭ·mŭs	u-nan-i-mous	Being of one mind; agreeing.
75. vacillate	văs′ĭ·lāt	vac-il-late	To fluctuate; to oscillate; to waver.

Lesson 4

1. absenteeism	ăb′sĕn·tē′ĭz′m	ab-sen-tee-ism	The practice of being absent.
2. acclimate	ă·klī′mĭt	ac-cli-mate	To become accustomed to a climate.
3. accrediting	ă·krĕd′ĭt·ĭng	ac-cred-it-ing	Approving; sanctioning.
4. acoustics	à·kōōs′tĭks	a-cous-tics	The science of sound and its transmission.
5. administrator	ăd·mĭn′ĭs·trā′tẽr	ad-min-is-tra-tor	One who has the legal right of administration of an estate.
6. adviser	ăd·vīz′ẽr	ad-vis-er	One who gives warning or advice.
7. advisor	ăd·vīz′ẽr	ad-vis-or	Same as *adviser*.
8. appellate	ă·pĕl′ăt	ap-pel-late	Vested with the power to review law cases.
9. awkward	ôk′wẽrd	awk-ward	Clumsy; ungraceful.
10. Baton Rouge	băt′′n rōōzh′	Bat-on Rouge	Capital city of Louisiana.
11. bouquet	bōō·kā′	Bou-quet	A bunch of flowers.
12. Buenos Aires, Argentina	bwā′nŭs âr′ĕz är′jĕn·tē′nà	Bue-nos Ai-res, Ar-gen-ti-na	Capital city of Argentina.
13. cardiac	kär′dĭ·ăk	car-di-ac	Pertaining to or near the heart.
14. codicil	kŏd′ĭ·sĭl	cod-i-cil	An added provision to a will.
15. constitution	kŏn′stĭ·tū′shŭn	con-sti-tu-tion	The fundamental laws or principles of government of a nation, state, or society.
16. decipher	dē·sī′fẽr	de-ci-pher	To find out the meaning of.
17. dittoed	dĭt′ōd	dit-toed	Repeated the same as before.
18. duodenal	dū′ŏ·dē′n′l	du-o-de-nal	Pertaining to the first part of the small intestine.
19. eligible	ĕl′ĭ·jĭ·b′l	el-i-gi-ble	Fit to be chosen.

20.	exonerate	ĕg·zŏn'ĕr·āt	ex-on-er-ate	To free from blame.
21.	facsimile	făk·sĭm'ĭ·lē	fac-sim-i-le	An exact copy.
22.	flair	flâr	flair	A natural power of discerning.
23.	flare	flâr	flare	A blaze of fire used to signal or to attract attention.
24.	illegible	ĭl·lĕj'ĭ·b'l	il-leg-i-ble	Not capable of being read.
25.	inconvenient ▶	ĭn'kŏn·vēn'yĕnt	in-con-ven-ient	Giving trouble, delay, or uneasiness.
26.	indelible	ĭn·dĕl'ĭ·b'l	in-del-i-ble	Cannot be blotted out or removed.
27.	inimitable	ĭn·ĭm'ĭ·ta·b'l	in-im-i-ta-ble	Not able to be matched or imitated.
28.	instance	ĭn'stăns	in-stance	Occasion; step in an action.
29.	instants	ĭn'stănts	in-stants	Moments; very brief periods of time.
30.	integral	ĭn'tĕ·grăl	in-te-gral	Composed of parts making a whole.
31.	irresponsible	ĭr'rē·spŏn'sĭ·b'l	ir-re-spon-si-ble	Not reliable.
32.	liaison	lē'ā·zŏn'	li-ai-son	A bond or link.
33.	magnanimous	măg·năn'ĭ·mŭs	mag-nan-i-mous	Great of mind or soul; honorable.
34.	materialize	ma·tēr'ĭ·ăl·īz	ma-te-ri-al-ize	To assume material form.
35.	medal	mĕd''l	med-al	A special piece of metal that serves as a reward.
36.	meddle	mĕd''l	med-dle	To interfere.
37.	misdemeanor	mĭs'dĕ·mēn'ĕr	mis-de-mean-or	A petty crime.
38.	misrepresent	mĭs'rĕp·rē·zĕnt'	mis-rep-re-sent	To represent improperly or falsely.
39.	nuclear	nū'klē·ēr	nu-cle-ar	Pertaining to a nucleus.
40.	ordinance	ôr'dĭ·năns	or-di-nance	A decree; a prescribed practice or usage.
41.	ordnance	ôrd'năns	ord-nance	Military supplies.
42.	pedal	pĕd'ăl	ped-al	n. A lever acted on by the foot. v. To drive oneself onward by use of pedals.
43.	peddle	pĕd''l	ped-dle	To travel from place to place selling goods.
44.	perseverance	pûr'sĕ·vēr'ăns	per-se-ver-ance	Steadfastness.
45.	plagiarism	plā'jĭ·a·rĭz'm	pla-gi-a-rism	The act of stealing the ideas or writings of another.
46.	pole	pōl	pole	A long slender piece of wood or timber.
47.	poll	pōl	poll	The casting or recording of votes of a group of people.
48.	posthumous	pŏs'tῠ·mŭs	post-hu-mous	Following or happening after one's death.
49.	predominant	prē·dŏm'ĭ·nănt	pre-dom-i-nant	Prevailing; superior in position.
50.	proportionate	prŏ·pōr'shŭn·ĭt	pro-por-tion-ate	Being in proportion; adjusted proportionately.

▶

51. pseudonym	sū′dŏ·nĭm	pseu-do-nym	A fictitious name; a pen name.
52. qualitative	kwŏl′ĭ·tā′tĭv	qual-i-ta-tive	Relating to or concerned with quality.
53. quantitative	kwŏn′tĭ·tā′tĭv	quan-ti-ta-tive	That may be estimated by quantity.
54. quire	kwīr	quire	A unit of measure for paper, usually 24 sheets of paper of the same size and quality.
55. choir	kwīr	choir	An organized group of singers.
56. registration	rĕj′ĭs·trā′shŭn	reg-is-tra-tion	An entry in a record book.
57. remuneration	rĕ·mū′nẽr·ā′shŭn	re-mu-ner-a-tion	Pay or compensation.
58. rhythmically	rĭth′mĭ·kăl·ĭ	rhyth-mi-cal-ly	In a manner marked with rhythm or beat.
59. sacrilegious	săk′rĭ·lē′jŭs	sac-ri-le-gious	Involving sacrilege; profane.
60. scene	sēn	scene	A division of a drama.
61. seen	sēn	seen	Past participle of see.
62. seam	sēm	seam	The line formed by sewing two pieces of cloth together.
63. seem	sēm	seem	To appear.
64. stationary	stā′shŭn·ẽr′ĭ	sta-tion-ar-y	Fixed in a certain place.
65. stationery	stā′shŭn·ẽr′ĭ	sta-tion-er-y	Articles used in writing, as paper and envelopes.
66. strategy	străt′ē·jĭ	strat-e-gy	Large-scale planning in combat or in solving problems.
67. subpoena	sŭ·pē′nȧ	sub-poe-na	A writ that commands a person to appear in court.
68. subtle	sŭt′'l	sub-tle	Cunning; crafty; ingenious.
69. tentative	tĕn′tȧ·tĭv	ten-ta-tive	In the nature of an experiment; not permanent.
70. triumph	trī′ŭmf	tri-umph	Victory; conquest.
71. unanimity	ū′nȧ·nĭm′ĭ·tĭ	u-na-nim-i-ty	State of being of one mind; agreement.
72. wade	wād	wade	To move by stepping through water; to go forward with difficulty.
73. weighed	wād	weighed	Past tense of weigh.
74. wrapping	răp′ĭng	wrap-ping	Enfolding; enveloping; enclosing with a cover.
75. rapping	răp′ĭng	rap-ping	Striking with a quick blow.

Lesson 5 Check-Up

Unit Test. Your teacher will dictate 50 words chosen from the lessons in Unit 4. These words are selected to test your mastery of the new words in this unit. Listen closely as each word is dictated, recall the "type" of word it is, spell the word carefully, and write plainly to assure yourself of a fair test.

Proofreading Test. In the following letter, some of the italicized words are misspelled. Copy the entire letter, making whatever corrections are necessary in the spelling of the words.

Dear Mr. Billings:

The *admistration* of an estate is a difficult job, particularly for an *amatuer*. There are always such problems as *tenative* work assignments, *disemination* of information, *capitol* investments, *leans* on property, maintenance of buildings, *irrevelant* arguments among the *principles*, bankruptcy suits, *assistants* to *airs*, and other major decisions.

The Phillips School of Estate *Admistration* offers courses that have *benefited* many persons. Our students have included businessmen, army *colonials* and *captians*, members of the engineering *core*, and many others. The names on our *stationary* give evidence of our important offerings. Why not join our classes during our *eigth* year of operation?

Sincerely yours,

Cumulative Test. Your teacher will now dictate 40 words chosen from Units 1, 2, and 3. These words will test your retention of the correct spelling of words in these units. Spell carefully and write plainly.

Checking Your Tests. Your teacher will give you directions for checking the unit test, the proofreading test, and the cumulative test.

Error Analysis. Classify the errors that you made by noting the type of error beside each word that you misspelled.

Review. Use the appropriate attack procedures for studying the words that you misspelled on the unit test, on the proofreading test, and on the cumulative test. Remember that both sound and meaning words were included.

Retest. The retest will tell you if you have mastered the words in Unit 1 through 4. If you misspelled words on the retest, continue your attack procedures until you are sure that you can spell all the words correctly.

Unit 5 Sound Words

Sound is the key to the correct spelling of the words in this group. Spend a few moments reviewing "Spotting Sound Errors," beginning on page 3, and then begin your study of Lessons 1-4 of this unit, applying the following procedures:

Preview. Your teacher will dictate a list of 75 general-vocabulary words. Number a sheet of paper from 1 to 75. Spell as many of the words as you can, but attempt only the words that you are quite sure you know how to spell. If you do not know the spelling of a word, place a question mark (?) beside the number.

Checking Performance. Compare your spellings with the words given in the appropriate lesson. Place an X beside each word that you misspelled. To the right of any misspelled or omitted word, write the correct spelling.

Attack Procedures. Attack procedures for sound-type errors were presented in Section One, beginning on page 7. Review the corrective techniques recommended for each type of error.

Learning to Spell New Words. The pretest words that you did not know how to spell now appear on your answer sheet preceded by a question mark. Use a separate sheet of paper to practice those words, following the SEE, SAY, SPELL, and WRITE routine (see pages 39-41). Hand in the drill paper to your instructor.

Lesson 1

1. accomplish	ă·kŏm′plĭsh	ac-com-plish	To effect; to fulfill.
2. acquire	ă·kwīr′	ac-quire	To get as one's own.
3. advantage	ăd·văn′tĭj	ad-van-tage	Condition favorable to success.
4. adventure	ăd·věn′tụ̄r	ad-ven-ture	Chance; risk.
5. afterwards	ȧf′tēr·wērdz	aft-er-wards	At a later time.
6. ahead	ȧ·hĕd′	a-head	At the front or head; in advance.
7. appoint	ă·point′	ap-point	To assign.
8. April	ā′prĭl	A-pril	The fourth month of the year.
9. ashamed	ȧ·shāmd′	a-shamed	Affected by shame.
10. Atlantic	ăt·lăn′tĭk	At-lan-tic	The ocean between the Americas and Europe and Africa.
11. author	ô′thēr	au-thor	One who composes; a writer.
12. basket	bȧs′kĕt	bas-ket	A container made of woven material.
13. bottom	bŏt′ŭm	bot-tom	Lowest surface; base.
14. breakfast	brĕk′fȧst	break-fast	The first meal of the day.
15. bureau	bū′rō	bu-reau	A writing table; a chest; a government division or a civil office established to give out information.
16. California	kăl′ĭ·fôrn′yȧ	Cal-i-for-nia	A western state of the United States, bordering on the Pacific Ocean.
17. candidate	kăn′dĭ·dāt	can-di-date	A person who offers himself as an aspirant for an office.
18. candle	kăn′d′l	can-dle	A cylinder of wax burned for light.
19. career	kȧ·rēr′	ca-reer	The course of a person's life.
20. carriage	kăr′ĭj	car-riage	Act of carrying; bearing.
21. colony	kŏl′ō·nĭ	col-o-ny	A number of persons living more or less isolated from other people; a settlement.
22. commercial	kŏ·mûr′shăl	com-mer-cial	Pertaining to commerce or business.
23. community	kŏ·mū′nĭ·tĭ	com-mu-ni-ty	A body of people living in the same place under the same laws.
24. compel	kŏm·pĕl′	com-pel	To drive or urge with force.
25. complain	kŏm·plān′	com-plain	To utter discontent.
▶			
26. congress	kŏng′grĕs	con-gress	A gathering or formal assembly, especially of representatives or envoys.
27. connect	kŏ·nĕkt′	con-nect	To join; to unite.
28. connected	kŏ·nĕkt′ĕd	con-nect-ed	Joined together.
29. consequence	kŏn′sĕ·kwĕns	con-se-quence	Act of following something else as a result.
30. consideration	kŏn·sĭd′ēr·ā′shŭn	con-sid-er-a-tion	Careful thought.

31. continent	kŏn'tĭ·nĕnt	con-ti-nent	A continuous extent of land.
32. correct	kŏ·rĕkt'	cor-rect	To make right; to chastise.
33. cruel	krōō'ĕl	cru-el	Inhuman; merciless.
34. current	kûr'ĕnt	cur-rent	Belonging to the present time or season.
35. delay	dĕ·lā'	de-lay	v. To stop; to detain; to hinder for a while. n. A postponement.
36. delayed	dĕ·lād'	de-layed	Postponed; put off.
37. deliver	dĕ·lĭv'ĕr	de-liv-er	To set free; to give or transfer.
38. disappear	dĭs'ă·pēr'	dis-ap-pear	To vanish; to be lost.
39. diseases	dĭ·zēz'ĕz	dis-eas-es	Maladies; sicknesses.
40. dozen	dŭz''n	doz-en	A group of twelve.
41. drowned	dround	drowned	Suffocated in water or other liquid.
42. effect	ĕ·fĕkt'	ef-fect	n. Immediate result. v. To bring about; to accomplish.
43. emperor	ĕm'pēr·ĕr	em-per-or	The supreme monarch of an empire.
44. equally	ē'kwăl·ĭ	e-qual-ly	In an equal manner or degree.
45. excite	ĕk·sīt'	ex-cite	To rouse; to stimulate.
46. existence	ĕg·zĭs'tĕns	ex-ist-ence	The state of existing; actual occurrence.
47. fierce	fērs	fierce	Raging; ferocious; savage.
48. fortune	fôr'tŭn	for-tune	Chance; luck.
49. glorious	glō'rĭ·ŭs	glo-ri-ous	Praiseworthy; splendid in appearance.
50. holiday	hŏl'ĭ·dā	hol-i-day	A period of recreation or rest.
51. immediately	ĭ·mē'dĭ·ĭt·lĭ	im-me-di-ate-ly	Without delay.
52. impression	ĭm·prĕsh'ŭn	im-pres-sion	Influence on feeling, sense, or intellect.
53. instant	ĭn'stănt	in-stant	A moment.
54. instruction	ĭn·strŭk'shŭn	in-struc-tion	Act of imparting knowledge.
55. intend	ĭn·tĕnd'	in-tend	To have in mind as a plan or purpose.
56. justify	jŭs'tĭ·fī	jus-ti-fy	To free from blame.
57. lawyer	lô'yĕr	law-yer	One skilled in law and its practice.
58. level	lĕv'ĕl	lev-el	adj. Well balanced and steady. v. To make flat or level.
59. manufacture	măn'û·făk'tŭr	man-u-fac-ture	To make wares by hand or by machinery.
60. neighborhood	nā'bēr·hŏŏd	neigh-bor-hood	People living near one another; a district or section.
61. oblige	ŏ·blīj'	o-blige	To do a favor for.
62. plunge	plŭnj	plunge	To cast oneself forward.
63. program	prō'grăm	pro-gram	A plan of procedure.
64. prospect	prŏs'pĕkt	pros-pect	Something that is hoped for.
65. protection	prŏ·tĕk'shŭn	pro-tec-tion	Act of protecting.

66. scheme	skēm	scheme	*n.* A plan or plot. *v.* To plan; to plot.
67. suggestion	sŭg·jĕs′chŭn	sug-ges-tion	That which is suggested; a hint.
68. total	tō′tăl	to-tal	Complete; constituting a whole; entire.
69. vary	vâr′ĭ	var-y	To alter; to change.
70. volume	vŏl′yŭm	vol-ume	A book; space occupied by an object.
71. would	wŏŏd	would	Past tense and past participle of *will.*
72. wouldn't	wŏŏd′n't	would-n't	Contraction for *would not.*
73. write	rīt	write	To form letters or words with a pen or pencil.
74. wrong	rŏng	wrong	*adj.* Incorrect. *v.* To do wrong to; to treat badly; to injure.
75. wrote	rōt	wrote	Past tense of *write.*

Lesson 2

1. accustom	ă·kŭs′tŭm	ac-cus-tom	To make familiar by use.
2. accustomed	ă·kŭs′tŭmd	ac-cus-tomed	Usual.
3. agriculture	ăg′rĭ·kŭl′tŭr	ag-ri-cul-ture	Art of cultivating the ground.
4. ambition	ăm·bĭsh′ŭn	am-bi-tion	An eager desire for honor or attainment.
5. approve	ă·pro͞ov′	ap-prove	To confirm; to sanction.
6. arrangement	ă·rānj′mĕnt	ar-range-ment	Act of placing in proper order.
7. assembly	ă·sĕm′blĭ	as-sem-bly	A gathering of persons.
8. associate	ă·sō′shĭ·āt	as-so-ci-ate	To unite in action; to join.
9. audience	ô′dĭ·ĕns	au-di-ence	An assembly of listeners or spectators.
10. beneath	bĕ·nēth′	be-neath	Underneath.
11. bought	bôt	bought	Past tense of *buy;* purchased.
12. breath	brĕth	breath	Air inhaled and exhaled in respiration.
13. breathe	brēth	breathe	To inhale and exhale air.
14. brilliant	brĭl′yănt	bril-liant	Sparkling; very bright.
15. broad	brôd	broad	Wide.
16. canal	kȧ·năl′	ca-nal	A water-filled channel used for purposes of navigation, irrigation, etc.
17. commencement	kŏ·mĕns′mĕnt	com-mence-ment	Act of beginning.
18. conquer	kŏng′kĕr	con-quer	To vanquish; to defeat.
19. copper	kŏp′ĕr	cop-per	A reddish metal.
20. counsel	koun′sĕl	coun-sel	To advise.
21. currency	kûr′ĕn·sĭ	cur-ren-cy	A medium of exchange within a country.
22. debt	dĕt	debt	Obligation.
23. design	dĕ·zīn′	de-sign	Pattern; plan.

24. director	dĭ·rĕk′tẽr	di-rec-tor	One who guides or orders.
25. disturb	dĭs·tûrb′	dis-turb	To confuse; to interrupt.

▶

26. domestic	dŏ·mĕs′tĭk	do-mes-tic	Pertaining to a household.
27. dreadful	drĕd′fŏŏl	dread-ful	Inspiring fear or awe.
28. echo	ĕk′ō	ech-o	Repetition or reflection of sound.
29. education	ĕd′û·kā′shŭn	ed-u-ca-tion	Discipline of the mind through study.
30. electric	ê·lĕk′trĭk	e-lec-tric	Consisting of or producing electricity.
31. endure	ĕn·dūr′	en-dure	To last.
32. energy	ĕn′ẽr·jĭ	en-er-gy	Power.
33. evidently	ĕv′ĭ·dĕnt·lĭ	ev-i-dent-ly	Apparently.
34. fastener	fás′n·ẽr	fas-ten-er	That which holds objects firmly together.
35. financial	fĭ·năn′shăl	fi-nan-cial	Related to money matters.
36. generous	jĕn′ẽr·ŭs	gen-er-ous	Liberal.
37. illustrate	ĭl′ŭs·trāt	il-lus-trate	To make clear by examples.
38. illustrated	ĭl′ŭs·trāt·ĕd	il-lus-trat-ed	Made clear.
39. incline	ĭn·klīn′	in-cline	To bend toward.
40. instruments	ĭn′strŏŏ·mĕnts	in-stru-ments	Tools; implements.
41. interrupt	ĭn′tĕ·rŭpt′	in-ter-rupt	To break into.
42. invention	ĭn·vĕn′shŭn	in-ven-tion	Act of inventing.
43. jewel	jōō′ĕl	jew-el	A precious stone; a gem.
44. linen	lĭn′ĕn	lin-en	Cloth made of flax.
45. meadow	mĕd′ō	mead-ow	Grassland; a field of grass.
46. medicine	mĕd′ĭ·sĭn	med-i-cine	Any preparation used in the treatment of diseases.
47. mental	mĕn′tăl	men-tal	Pertaining to the mind.
48. mirror	mĭr′ẽr	mir-ror	A looking glass.
49. mystery	mĭs′tẽr·ĭ	mys-ter-y	Something not explained.
50. occasionally	ŏ·kā′zhŭn·ăl·ĭ	oc-ca-sion-al-ly	In an infrequent manner.

▶

51. occupy	ôk′û·pī	oc-cu-py	To fill; to keep engaged.
52. organized	ôr′găn·īzd	or-gan-ized	Arranged in separate and logical parts.
53. patience	pā′shĕns	pa-tience	Forbearance.
54. physician	fĭ·zĭsh′ăn	phy-si-cian	A doctor of medicine.
55. police	pŏ·lēs′	po-lice	The department of government that enforces law and order.
56. population	pŏp′û·lā′shŭn	pop-u-la-tion	The number of people in an area.
57. possibilities	pŏs′ĭ·bĭl′ĭ·tĭz	pos-si-bil-i-ties	Things that may be attained or may occur.
58. possibility	pŏs′ĭ·bĭl′ĭ·tĭ	pos-si-bil-i-ty	That which may be attained or may occur.
59. preparation	prĕp′á·rā′shŭn	prep-a-ra-tion	Act of making ready for use.
60. present	prĕ·zĕnt′	pre-sent	To give; to introduce.
61. province	prŏv′ĭns	prov-ince	Region of a country; a district.

62. radio	rā'dĭ·ō	ra-di-o	An instrument for receiving sounds and signals transmitted by electric waves.
63. register	rĕj'ĭs·tēr	reg-is-ter	v. To record. n. A record.
64. resolve	rĕ·zŏlv'	re-solve	Fixed purpose; intention.
65. revolution	rĕv'ŏ·lū'shŭn	rev-o-lu-tion	Motion of anything around an axis.
66. select	sĕ·lĕkt'	se-lect	To pick out; to choose.
67. sentence	sĕn'tĕns	sen-tence	A group of words expressing a complete thought and containing a subject and a predicate.
68. silent	sī'lĕnt	si-lent	Free from noise; still.
69. substance	sŭb'stăns	sub-stance	Essential elements.
70. suffice	sŭ·fīs'	suf-fice	To meet a need.
71. swallow	swŏl'ō	swal-low	To take through the mouth into the stomach.
72. swept	swĕpt	swept	Past tense of *sweep*.
73. terror	tĕr'ēr	ter-ror	Extreme fear.
74. thoroughly	thûr'ŏ·lĭ	thor-ough-ly	Completely.
75. triumph	trī'ŭmf	tri-umph	Victory.

Lesson 3

1. abandon	a·băn'dŭn	a-ban-don	To desert; to forsake.
2. acid	ăs'ĭd	ac-id	Sour; sharp.
3. agent	ā'jĕnt	a-gent	One who acts for another; a means or instrument.
4. aloud	a·loud'	a-loud	With the speaking voice; loudly.
5. altogether	ôl'tŏŏ·gĕth'ēr	al-to-geth-er	Wholly; thoroughly.
6. annual	ăn'û·ăl	an-nu-al	Occurring yearly.
7. assist	a·sĭst'	as-sist	To lend aid; to help.
8. blossom	blŏs'ŭm	blos-som	n. A flower of a seed plant. v. To bloom; to thrive.
9. Canada	kăn'a·da	Can-a-da	The country north of and adjoining the United States.
10. capable	kā'pa·b'l	ca-pa-ble	Having ability or fitness.
11. capture	kăp'tŭr	cap-ture	To seize.
12. collar	kŏl'ēr	col-lar	Something worn around the neck.
13. comment	kŏm'ĕnt	com-ment	n. A remark. v. To make or write remarks.
14. commit	kŏ·mĭt'	com-mit	To entrust; to perpetrate, as a crime.
15. committed	kŏ·mĭt'ĕd	com-mit-ted	Entrusted; perpetrated.
16. conceal	kŏn·sēl'	con-ceal	To hide; to withhold knowledge of.
17. conscience	kŏn'shĕns	con-science	The power to distinguish right from wrong.
18. construction	kŏn·strŭk'shŭn	con-struc-tion	Act of devising and forming.

19. delicate	dĕl'ĭ·kĭt	del-i-cate	Fragile; finely made.
20. deserve	dĕ·zûrv'	de-serve	To merit.
21. despair	dĕ·spâr'	de-spair	v. To give up hope. n. Loss of hope.
22. desperate	dĕs'pĕr·ĭt	des-per-ate	Reckless; frantic.
23. earn	ûrn	earn	To merit or deserve; to acquire by labor.
24. eleven	ĕ·lĕv'ĕn	e-lev-en	Cardinal number following ten.
25. error ▶	ĕr'ẽr	er-ror	A mistake.
26. estimate	ĕs'tĭ·māt	es-ti-mate	To gauge; to evaluate; to form an opinion of.
27. extreme	ĕks·trēm'	ex-treme	Most remote; last; final.
28. extremely	ĕks·trēm'lĭ	ex-treme-ly	To the utmost point; excessively.
29. faith	fāth	faith	Confidence; trust; belief in God.
30. fault	fôlt	fault	A failing; a flaw; a blemish.
31. features	fē'tûrz	fea-tures	Appearance; form.
32. featuring	fē'tûr·ĭng	fea-tur-ing	Giving prominence to.
33. fourth	fōrth	fourth	Ordinal number, following third.
34. friendly	frĕnd'lĭ	friend-ly	Not hostile.
35. hesitate	hĕz'ĭ·tāt	hes-i-tate	To falter; to pause undecidedly.
36. imagination	ĭ·măj'ĭ·nā'shŭn	im-ag-i-na-tion	A mental image; a conception; a notion.
37. independence	ĭn'dĕ·pĕn'dĕns	in-de-pend-ence	Freedom from control by others.
38. international	ĭn'tẽr·năsh'ŭn·ǎl	in-ter-na-tion-al	Common to two or more nations.
39. interpret	ĭn·tûr'prĕt	in-ter-pret	To explain.
40. invitation	ĭn'vĭ·tā'shŭn	in-vi-ta-tion	Act of inviting; an expression by which one is invited.
41. literature	lĭt'ẽr·á·tûr	lit-er-a-ture	Published materials; the preserved writings of any language or people.
42. madam	măd'ǎm	mad-am	A form of polite address to a lady.
43. magic	măj'ĭk	mag-ic	The art of producing mysterious effects.
44. magnificent	măg·nĭf'ĭ·sĕnt	mag-nif-i-cent	Marked by grandeur or majestic beauty.
45. manager	măn'ĭj·ẽr	man-ag-er	A director; one who manages.
46. marble	mär'b'l	mar-ble	Highly crystallized limestone.
47. mayor	mā'ẽr	may-or	The chief executive officer of a city.
48. merit	mĕr'ĭt	mer-it	n. Worth; excellence. v. To deserve.
49. mineral	mĭn'ẽr·ǎl	min-er-al	Any natural product that is neither animal nor vegetable.
50. nervous ▶	nûr'vŭs	nerv-ous	Spirited; excitable.
51. normal	nôr'mǎl	nor-mal	Regular; natural.
52. novel	nŏv'ĕl	nov-el	adj. Unusual. n. A lengthy, fictitious prose tale.

53. opening	ō′pĕn·ĭng	o-pen-ing	A part that is open; an opportunity.
54. package	păk′ĭj	pack-age	A wrapped parcel.
55. pencil	pĕn′sĭl	pen-cil	An instrument for writing or drawing.
56. performance	pĕr·fôr′măns	per-form-ance	A feat; a deed.
57. persuade	pĕr·swād′	per-suade	To plead with; to urge.
58. poison	poi′z′n	poi-son	*adj.* Venemous. *n.* That which taints or destroys life, purity, or character.
59. possibly	pŏs′ĭ·blĭ	pos-si-bly	Perhaps.
60. prevail	prĕ·vāl′	pre-vail	To triumph; to win mastery.
61. project	prŏj′ĕkt	proj-ect	A plan or design.
62. properly	prŏp′ĕr·lĭ	prop-er-ly	Suitably; rightly.
63. provision	prŏ·vĭzh′ŭn	pro-vi-sion	That which is prepared; preparation.
64. puzzle	pŭz′′l	puz-zle	A difficult problem.
65. radioactive	rā′dĭ·ō·ăk′tĭv	ra-di-o-ac-tive	Characterized by radiant energy resulting from the disintegration of the atom.
66. relative	rĕl′à·tĭv	rel-a-tive	*adj.* Pertinent; comparative. *n.* A kinsman or kinswoman.
67. republic	rĕ·pŭb′lĭk	re-pub-lic	A state in which the governing power is vested in representatives elected by the people.
68. savage	săv′ĭj	sav-age	Untamed; uncivilized.
69. seventy	sĕv′ĕn·tĭ	sev-en-ty	Cardinal number, following sixty-nine.
70. submit	sŭb·mĭt′	sub-mit	To yield to power or authority; to surrender.
71. truly	trōō′lĭ	tru-ly	Honestly; in a true manner; sincerely.
72. universal	ū′nĭ·vûr′săl	u-ni-ver-sal	Unlimited.
73. vanish	văn′ĭsh	van-ish	To disappear utterly.
74. voyage	voi′ĭj	voy-age	A journey.
75. weapon	wĕp′ŭn	weap-on	Something to fight with.

Lesson 4

1. affection	ă·fĕk′shŭn	af-fec-tion	Tender attachment; love.
2. Africa	ăf′rĭ·kà	Af-ri-ca	A continent in the Eastern Hemisphere, adjoining Asia.
3. arise	à·rīz′	a-rise	To get up; to ascend.
4. arrest	ă·rĕst′	ar-rest	To take or keep in custody lawfully; to stop.
5. arrival	ă·rīv′ăl	ar-riv-al	Act of arriving; attainment.
6. arrow	ăr′ō	ar-row	The weapon that is projected with a bow.

7.	Asia	ā′zhá	A-sia	A continent in the Eastern Hemisphere (the largest continent in the world).
8.	attach	ă·tăch′	at-tach	To bind; to connect.
9.	bargain	bär′gĭn	bar-gain	*n.* Something purchased cheaply. *v.* To trade; to barter.
10.	bloom	bloom	bloom	A blossom; a flower of any seed plant.
11.	champion	chăm′pĭ·ŭn	cham-pi-on	A winner in a contest; a defender.
12.	channel	chăn′ĕl	chan-nel	The bed of a natural stream of water.
13.	charity	chăr′ĭ·tĭ	char-i-ty	An act of kindness; benevolence.
14.	civilization	sĭv′ĭ·lĭ·zā′shŭn	civ-i-li-za-tion	Advancement in social culture; state of being civilized.
15.	commissioner	kŏ·mĭsh′ŭn·ẽr	com-mis-sion-er	A person appointed or elected to perform some office.
16.	concerning	kŏn·sûrn′ĭng	con-cern-ing	Pertaining to; regarding.
17.	condemn	kŏn′dĕm	con-demn	To declare the guilt or unfitness of; to doom.
18.	conscious	kŏn′shŭs	con-scious	Aware or sensible; mentally awake.
19.	convenient	kŏn·vēn′yĕnt	con-ven-ient	Near at hand.
20.	corporation	kôr′pō·rā′shŭn	cor-po-ra-tion	A body of associated persons.
21.	cultivate	kŭl′tĭ·vāt	cul-ti-vate	To till; to refine.
22.	dignity	dĭg′nĭ·tĭ	dig-ni-ty	Stateliness.
23.	discussion	dĭs·kŭsh′ŭn	dis-cus-sion	An argument designed to arrive at the truth.
24.	embrace	ĕm·brās′	em-brace	To encircle; to enclose.
25.	endeavor	ĕn·dĕv′ẽr	en-deav-or	*v.* To try. *n.* An attempt to achieve an end.
26.	essential	ĕ·sĕn′shăl	es-sen-tial	Necessary.
27.	finance	fĭ·năns′	fi-nance	The control of monetary affairs.
28.	freight	frāt	freight	Cargo; anything that is transported.
29.	grateful	grāt′fŏŏl	grate-ful	Thankful.
30.	guest	gĕst	guest	A visitor entertained without payment.
31.	handsome	hăn′sŭm	hand-some	Of pleasing appearance; considerable.
32.	insurance	ĭn·shŏŏr′ăns	in-sur-ance	A system of insuring one against loss or injury.
33.	intention	ĭn·tĕn′shŭn	in-ten-tion	Aim; purpose.
34.	introduction	ĭn′trō·dŭk′shŭn	in-tro-duc-tion	A presentation; a bringing to the attention of others.
35.	juice	joos	juice	The liquid that can be squeezed out of vegetables and fruits.
36.	knife	nīf	knife	An instrument having a thin blade with a sharp edge for cutting.

37. knock	nŏk	knock	To rap; to strike sharply.
38. leather	lĕth'ẽr	leath-er	The tanned skin of an animal.
39. lieutenant	lū·tĕn'ănt	lieu-ten-ant	A commissioned military officer having a grade below a captain.
40. lightning	līt'nĭng	light-ning	The flashing of light caused by an electrical discharge in clouds; the discharge of atmospheric electricity.
41. literary	lĭt'ẽr·ĕr'ĭ	lit-er-ar-y	Pertaining to letters or literature.
42. luxury	lŭk'shŏŏ·rĭ	lux-u-ry	An expensive rarity.
43. marvelous	mär'vĕl·ŭs	mar-vel-ous	Astonishing; incredible.
44. match	măch	match	An equal; a sulfur-tipped piece of wood used to ignite material.
45. meant	mĕnt	meant	Past tense and past participle of *mean.*
46. mixture	mĭks'tŭr	mix-ture	A mixing; a substance consisting of two or more ingredients.
47. mortal	môr'tăl	mor-tal	*adj.* Destined to die. *n.* A human being.
48. muscle	mŭs''l	mus-cle	An organ that produces motion.
49. museum	mū·zē'ŭm	mu-se-um	A place for exhibiting objects of interest.
50. nation ▶	nā'shŭn	na-tion	The group of inhabitants of a country under a single independent government.
51. needle	nē'd'l	nee-dle	A small instrument for sewing.
52. occupational	ŏk'û·pā'shŭn·ăl	oc-cu-pa-tion-al	Pertaining to, or resulting from, a specific occupation.
53. partner	pärt'nẽr	part-ner	An associate; a companion.
54. permanent	pûr'ma·nĕnt	per-ma-nent	Lasting; abiding.
55. photograph	fõ'tõ·gräf	pho-to-graph	A picture made with a camera.
56. plead	plēd	plead	To argue for; to beg; to implore.
57. promptly	prŏmpt'lĭ	prompt-ly	Quickly; at once.
58. punish	pŭn'ĭsh	pun-ish	To afflict with pain for a crime.
59. readily	rĕd'ĭ·lĭ	read-i-ly	Promptly; quickly.
60. release	rê·lēs'	re-lease	To set free; to let go.
61. remarkable	rê·mär'ka·b'l	re-mark-a-ble	Uncommon; extraordinary.
62. remedy	rĕm'ê·dĭ	rem-e-dy	A corrective; a cure.
63. renew	rê·nū'	re-new	To revive; to repeat; to replace.
64. responsibility	rê·spŏn'sĭ·bĭl'ĭ·tĭ	re-spon-si-bil-i-ty	Accountability; reliability.
65. responsible	rê·spŏn'sĭ·b'l	re-spon-si-ble	Accountable; answerable.
66. retain	rê·tān'	re-tain	To hold in possession.
67. retreat	rê·trēt'	re-treat	*v.* To withdraw. *n.* Act of withdrawing.
68. sheriff	shĕr'ĭf	sher-iff	Chief executive officer of a county, charged with executing laws and preserving peace.
69. sheriffs	shĕr'ĭfs	sher-iffs	Plural form of *sheriff* (see above).

70. summon	sŭm′ŭn	sum-mon	To bid to come; to send for.
71. tobacco	tŏ·băk′ō	to-bac-co	The substance used in making cigars, cigarettes, etc.
72. tobaccos	tŏ·băk′ōz	to-bac-cos	Plural of *tobacco* (see above).
73. traffic	trăf′ĭk	traf-fic	The flow of pedestrians or vehicles along a road or highway; trade.
74. vacation	vă·kā′shŭn	va-ca-tion	A holiday; a period for rest and recreation.
75. victim	vĭk′tĭm	vic-tim	One who is injured or destroyed.

Lesson 5 Check-Up

Unit Test. Your teacher will dictate 50 words chosen from the lessons in Unit 5. These words are selected to test your mastery of the new words in this unit. Listen closely as each word is dictated, spell the word carefully, and write plainly to assure yourself of a fair test.

Proofreading Test. In the following letter, some of the italicized words are misspelled. Copy the entire letter, making any corrections necessary in the spelling of the words.

> Dear Mrs. Richards:
>
> The knowledge that every responsible citizen wants to help eliminate *traffic* accidents prompts us to make an appeal for your support in a newly *organized endevor* called "The *Neighborhood* Safety Council." Since our city's *annuel charaty* drive has already begun, we find that we must ask for a separate donation for this *project.*
>
> If you will *atach* your check to the enclosed card and return both to us *promtly,* you can be one of the *enstruments* in a *program* that will help prevent accidents. Thus far, citizen *preformance* has been little short of *briliant.* We will be *gratefull* for your help.
>
> Sincerely yours,

Cumulative Test. Your teacher will now dictate 40 words chosen from Units 1 through 4. These words will test your retention of the correct spelling of words in these units. Spell carefully and write plainly.

Checking Your Tests. Your teacher will give you directions for checking the unit test, the proofreading test, and the cumulative test.

Error Analysis. Classify the errors that you made by noting the type of error beside each word that you misspelled.

Review. Use the appropriate attack procedures for studying the words that you misspelled on the unit test, on the proofreading test, and on the cumulative test.

Retest. The retest will tell you if you have mastered the words in Units 1 through 5. If you misspelled words on the retest, continue your attack procedure until you are sure that you can spell all the words correctly.

Unit 6 Rule Words

Spelling rules are the guides to the correct spelling of the words in this unit. Review briefly the spelling rules discussed on pages 20-29, giving particular attention to those rules that are most troublesome for you. This brief review will help you to spell correctly the words in this unit; then begin your study of Lessons 1-4 of this unit, applying the following procedures:

Preview. Your teacher will dictate a list of 75 general-vocabulary words. Number a sheet of paper from 1 to 75. Spell as many of the words as you can, but attempt only the words that you are quite sure you know how to spell. If you do not know the spelling of a word, place a question mark (?) beside the number.

Checking Performance. Compare your spellings with the words given in the appropriate lesson. Place an *X* beside each word that you misspelled. To the right of any misspelled or omitted word, write the correct spelling.

Error Analysis. Classify the errors that you made by noting the type of error beside each word that you misspelled. For instance, if an error was caused by failure to double a final consonant when adding a suffix, write "final consonant" beside the word. Refer to pages 20-29 if you have forgotten the types of rule errors.

Attack Procedures. Attack procedures for rule-type errors were presented in Section One, beginning on page 32. Review the corrective techniques recommended for each type of error.

Learning to Spell New Words. The pretest words that you did not know how to spell now appear on your answer sheet preceded by a question mark. Use a separate sheet of paper to practice those words, following the SEE, SAY, SPELL, and WRITE routine (see pages 39-41). Hand in the drill paper to your instructor.

Lesson 1

1. admitted	ăd·mĭt′ĕd	ad-mit-ted	Allowed; permitted.
2. affairs	ă·fârz′	af-fairs	Concerns; business.
3. afternoon	ăf′tĕr·noon′	af-ter-noon	The time between noon and evening.
4. allowed	ă·loud′	al-lowed	Permitted; granted.
5. arriving	ă·rīv′ĭng	ar-riv-ing	Reaching a place.
6. attempting	ă·tĕmpt′ĭng	at-tempt-ing	Trying; making an attempt.
7. bases	bās′ĕz	bas-es	Bottoms; goals in various games.
8. beautiful	bū′tĭ·fool	beau-ti-ful	Full of beauty; possessing qualities that charm and delight the senses.
9. becoming	bĕ·kŭm′ĭng	be-com-ing	Suitable; appropriate.
10. belief	bĕ·lēf′	be-lief	Faith; confidence; trust.
11. believing	bĕ·lēv′ĭng	be-liev-ing	Having faith or confidence.
12. boss's	bŏs′ĕz	boss's	Possessive of *boss*.
13. business	bĭz′nĕs	busi-ness	Rightful work or concern.
14. careful	kâr′fool	care-ful	Characterized by care; exercising care.
15. carefully	kâr′fool·ĭ	care-ful-ly	With great caution.
16. carried	kăr′ĭd	car-ried	Supported.
17. cents	sĕnts	cents	Plural of *cent*.
18. changing	chānj′ĭng	chang-ing	Altering.

19. chosen	chō′z'n	cho-sen	Past participle of *choose;* selected.
20. circumstances	sûr′kŭm·stăns·ĕz	cir-cum-stanc-es	The conditions affecting a person or an event.
21. cities	sĭt′ĭz	cit-ies	Large or important towns.
22. closing	klōz′ĭng	clos-ing	Enclosing; ending.
23. coming	kŭm′ĭng	com-ing	Arriving; approaching.
24. companies	kŭm′pȧ·nĭz	com-pa-nies	Assemblages of people; organizations operated as businesses.
25. continuing ▶	kŏn·tĭn′ū·ĭng	con-tin-u-ing	Staying; remaining; extending.
26. controllable	kŏn·trōl′ȧ·b'l	con-trol-la-ble	Able to be checked or restrained.
27. controlling	kŏn·trōl′ĭng	con-trol-ling	Guiding; holding in check.
28. countries	kŭn′trĭz	coun-tries	Regions or tracts of land.
29. coverage	kŭv′ĕr·ĭj	cov-er-age	Extent to which something is covered; protection.
30. days	dāz	days	Plural of *day.*
31. development	dē·vĕl′ŭp·mĕnt	de-vel-op-ment	Act of developing; state of being started, revealed, or promoted.
32. difference	dĭf′ĕr·ĕns	dif-fer-ence	Variation.
33. different	dĭf′ĕr·ĕnt	dif-fer-ent	Dissimilar; distinct.
34. direction	dĭ·rĕk′shŭn	di-rec-tion	Guidance; the course upon which anything is moving.
35. employed	ĕm·ploid′	em-ployed	Made use of the services of; exercised.
36. entered	ĕn′tĕrd	en-tered	Past tense of *enter;* went into.
37. evening	ēv′nĭng	eve-ning	The close of day.
38. everything	ĕv′ĕr·ĭ·thĭng′	ev-er-y-thing	Every object or fact.
39. factual	făk′tụ̄·ăl	fac-tu-al	Relating to, or containing, facts.
40. filled	fĭld	filled	Occupied entirely.
41. filling	fĭl′ĭng	fill-ing	Act of occupying completely.
42. finished	fĭn′ĭsht	fin-ished	Completed; perfected.
43. following	fŏl′ō·ĭng	fol-low-ing	Pursuing; copying after.
44. forwarding	fôr′wĕrd·ĭng	for-ward-ing	Advancing; helping onward.
45. gentlemen	jĕn′t'l·mĕn	gen-tle-men	Well-bred men.
46. good-by	gŏŏd′bī′	good-by	Farewell.
47. government	gŭv′ĕrn·mĕnt	gov-ern-ment	An established form of political administration.
48. hoping	hōp′ĭng	hop-ing	Desiring; trusting.
49. issuance	ĭsh′ụ̄·ȧns	is-su-ance	Act of giving out.
50. issuing ▶	ĭsh′ụ̄·ĭng	is-su-ing	Giving out; going out.
51. later	lāt′ĕr	lat-er	Comparative of *late.*
52. losing	lōōz′ĭng	los-ing	Suffering loss; failing to win.
53. lowest	lō′ĕst	low-est	Having least height.

54. mailing	māl′ĭng	mail-ing	Act of dispatching by mail.
55. mentioned	mĕn′shŭnd	men-tioned	Referred to.
56. movement	mŏŏv′mĕnt	move-ment	Motion; incident.
57. national	năsh′ŭn·ăl	na-tion-al	Pertaining to a nation; concerned with one's country's interests.
58. neither	nē′t͟hēr	nei-ther	Not the one or the other.
59. nevertheless	nĕv′ēr·t͟hē·lĕs′	nev-er-the-less	Yet; not the less.
60. obtaining	ŏb·tān′ĭng	ob-tain-ing	Getting; procuring.
61. otherwise	ŭt͟h′ēr·wīz′	oth-er-wise	In other ways; in other respects.
62. overlooked	ō′vēr·lŏŏkt′	o-ver-looked	Neglected; surveyed.
63. pagination	păj′ĭ·nā′shŭn	pag-i-na-tion	Process of paging a book.
64. per cent	pēr·sĕnt′	per cent	Relative parts to every hundred.
65. piece	pēs	piece	A fragment; a part.
66. placement	plās′mĕnt	place-ment	Act of putting into position.
67. pleasant	plĕz′ănt	pleas-ant	Agreeable; pleasing.
68. presents	prĕ·zĕnts′	pre-sents	Introduces.
69. presidents	prĕz′ĭ·dĕnts	pres-i-dents	Presiding officers; plural of *president*.
70. railroad	rāl′rōd′	rail-road	A permanent road having rails for trains.
71. receivable	rĕ·sēv′à·b'l	re-ceiv-a-ble	Capable of being received; acceptable.
72. society	sō·sī′ĕ·tĭ	so-ci-e-ty	Companionship with one's fellows.
73. somebody else's	sŭm′bŏd′ĭ ĕls′ĕz	some-bod-y else's	Belonging to some other person of no certain identity.
74. their	t͟hâr	their	Possessive of *they*.
75. themselves	t͟hĕm·sĕlvz′	them-selves	Plural of *himself*, *herself*, and *itself*.

Lesson 2

1. announcing	ă·nouns′ĭng	an-nounc-ing	Proclaiming; giving notice of.
2. apartment	ă·pärt′mĕnt	a-part-ment	A suite or set of rooms.
3. appealing	ă·pēl′ĭng	ap-peal-ing	Calling for support or symathy; attractive.
4. appearance	ă·pēr′ăns	ap-pear-ance	Manner of appearing; aspect.
5. assuring	ă·shŏŏr′ĭng	as-sur-ing	Making sure; stating confidently.
6. believe	bĕ·lēv′	be-lieve	To have convictions; to accept as true.
7. boxes	bŏks′ĕz	box-es	Cartons.
8. breakfast	brĕk′fàst	break-fast	The first meal of the day.
9. closely	klŏs′lĭ	close-ly	In a close manner.
10. completely	kŏm·plēt′lĭ	com-plete-ly	Entirely; wholly.
11. conversation	kŏn′vēr·sā′shŭn	con-ver-sa-tion	An informal, oral exchange of views.

12. defensible	dĕ·fĕn′sĭ·b'l	de-fen-si-ble	Capable of being protected.
13. describing	dĕ·skrīb′ĭng	de-scrib-ing	Giving an account of.
14. detailed	dĕ·tāld′	de-tailed	Full of minute points.
15. determining	dĕ·tûr′mĭn·ĭng	de-ter-min-ing	Deciding; settling.
16. diseases	dĭ·zēz′ĕz	dis-eas-es	Illnesses; sicknesses.
17. earlier	ûr′lĭ·ēr	ear-li-er	Comparative of *early*.
18. earliest	ûr′lĭ·ĕst	ear-li-est	Superlative of *early*.
19. easier	ēz′ĭ·ēr	eas-i-er	Comparative of *easy*.
20. either	ē′thĕr	ei-ther	One of two; the one or the other.
21. enemies	ĕn′ĕ·mĭz	en-e-mies	Foes; persons who are hostile to others.
22. entirely	ĕn·tīr′lĭ	en-tire-ly	Wholly; completely.
23. failure	fāl′ûr	fail-ure	Lack of success.
24. families	făm′ĭ·lĭz	fam-i-lies	Groups of persons closely related.
25. feature ►	fē′tụ̄r	fea-ture	*n.* Facial aspect. *v.* To give special prominence to.
26. field	fēld	field	Cleared land; an open expanse.
27. forcible	fōr′sĭ·b'l	for-ci-ble	Powerful; having force or energy.
28. forgetting	fŏr·gĕt′tĭng	for-get-ting	Omitting from the mind; neglecting.
29. formulas	fôr′mū·lăz	for-mu-las	Established forms of words or rules.
30. forwarded	fôr′wĕrd·ĕd	for-ward-ed	Sent forward; advanced.
31. guessed	gĕst	guessed	Formed an opinion of; supposed.
32. happened	hăp′ĕnd	hap-pened	Came to pass; occurred.
33. headquarters	hĕd′kwôr′tērz	head-quar-ters	The center of operation and of authority.
34. heaviest	hĕv′ĭ·ĕst	heav-i-est	Having the most weight.
35. household	hous′hōld	house-hold	Those living under one roof as a family.
36. however	hou·ĕv′ĕr	how-ev-er	Nevertheless; yet.
37. immediately	ĭ·mē′dĭ·ĭt′lĭ	im-me-di-ate-ly	At once; without delay.
38. important	ĭm·pôr′tănt	im-por-tant	Significant.
39. including	ĭn·klōōd′ĭng	in-clud-ing	Enclosing; containing; embracing.
40. largely	lärj′lĭ	large-ly	Mostly; greatly; to a great extent
41. lawyers'	lô′yērz	law-yers'	Plural possessive of *lawyer*.
42. learned	lûrnd	learned	Gained knowledge or understanding of.
43. losses	lŏs′ĕz	loss-es	Decreases in value; instances of losing.
44. morning	môr′nĭng	morn-ing	The early part of the day.
45. neighbor	nā′bēr	neigh-bor	A person who lives near another.
46. numbered	nŭm′bērd	num-bered	Counted; enumerated.
47. offered	ŏf′ĕrd	of-fered	Presented; proposed.
48. offering	ŏf′ĕr·ĭng	of-fer-ing	Presenting; proposing.
49. old-fashioned	ōld′făsh′ŭnd	old-fash-ioned	Following old customs; antiquated.
50. ordered ►	ôr′dĕrd	or-dered	Commanded.

51.	parties	pär'tĭz	par-ties	Persons concerned in an action or affair.
52.	passage	păs'ĭj	pas-sage	Transit from one place to another.
53.	planned	plănd	planned	Devised or projected a method.
54.	planning	plăn'ĭng	plan-ning	Devising a method.
55.	pleasure	plĕzh'ēr	pleas-ure	Delight; joy.
56.	prayer	prâr	prayer	Entreaty; supplication to God.
57.	probably	prŏb'á·blĭ	prob-a-bly	Very likely; possibly.
58.	producing	prô·dūs'ĭng	pro-duc-ing	Bringing forward; bearing; yielding.
59.	proved	prōōvd	proved	Ascertained; established.
60.	providing	prô·vīd'ĭng	pro-vid-ing	Furnishing.
61.	receiving	rē·sēv'ĭng	re-ceiv-ing	Accepting; getting.
62.	rising	rīz'ĭng	ris-ing	Ascending; extending upward.
63.	roofs	rōōfs	roofs	Tops; summits; top coverings of houses or other buildings.
64.	servicing	sûr'vĭs·ĭng	ser-vic-ing	Repairing; taking care of; supplying.
65.	signed	sīnd	signed	Wrote one's name.
66.	soldier	sōl'jēr	sol-dier	One engaged in military service.
67.	sometimes	sŭm'tīmz'	some-times	Now and then; occasionally.
68.	systematize	sĭs'tĕm·á·tīz	sys-tem-a-tize	To arrange methodically.
69.	taxable	tăks'á·b'l	tax-a-ble	Subject to being taxed.
70.	taxes	tăks'ĕz	tax-es	Charges levied on income, property, etc., to meet the needs of a government.
71.	theirs	ᵺârz	theirs	Possessive of *their*.
72.	tonight	tōō·nīt'	to-night	On the night following this day.
73.	using	ūz'ĭng	us-ing	Converting to one's service or use.
74.	vice-president	vīs'prĕz'ĭ·dĕnt	vice-pres-i-dent	An officer next in rank below a president.
75.	women	wĭm'ĕn	wom-en	Adult female persons.

Lesson 3

1.	accompanied	ă·kŭm'pá·nĭd	ac-com-pa-nied	Occurred together.
2.	addresses	ă·drĕs'ĕz	ad-dress-es	Formal speeches.
3.	adopted	á·dŏpt'ĕd	a-dopt-ed	Taken to one's self, as a child, a course of action, etc.
4.	allowance	ă·lou'ăns	al-low-ance	A share or portion granted.
5.	arrangement	ă·rānj'mĕnt	ar-range-ment	Adjustment; act of putting in order.
6.	benefited	bĕn'ĕ·fĭt'ĕd	ben-e-fit-ed	Profited; promoted the welfare of.
7.	branches	brȧnch'ĕz	branch-es	Stems growing out of a trunk of a tree.
8.	brothers-in-law	brŭᵺ'ērz·ĭn·lô'	broth-ers-in-law	Brothers of one's husband or wife.

9. comfortable	kŭm′fẽrt·á·b'l	com-fort-a-ble	Affording comfort; easy and undisturbed.
10. communities	kŏ·mū′nĭ·tĭz	com-mu-ni-ties	The people of particular areas or regions, or the regions themselves.
11. compelled	kŏm·pĕld′	com-pelled	Driven or urged with force.
12. concerning	kŏn·sûrn′ĭng	con-cern-ing	Involving; implicating.
13. conducted	kŏn·dŭkt′ĕd	con-duct-ed	Directed; managed; led.
14. connected	kŏ·nĕkt′ĕd	con-nect-ed	Joined or fastened together.
15. considerable	kŏn·sĭd′ẽr·á·b'l	con-sid-er-a-ble	Rather large in extent or amount.
16. credited	krĕd′ĭt·ĕd	cred-it-ed	Believed; gave credit to.
17. dangerous	dān′jẽr·ŭs	dan-ger-ous	Full of peril or risk.
18. developing	dĕ·vĕl′ŭp·ĭng	de-vel-op-ing	Promoting the growth of; revealing.
19. eastern	ēs′tẽrn	east-ern	Situated in or from the east.
20. employer	ĕm·ploi′ẽr	em-ploy-er	One who hires another.
21. equipment	ē·kwĭp′mĕnt	e-quip-ment	The items that make up an outfit.
22. excusable	ĕks·kūz′á·b'l	ex-cus-a-ble	Justifiable; forgivable.
23. experience	ĕks·pẽr′ĭ·ĕns	ex-pe-ri-ence	Knowledge; skill; previous acquaintance with.
24. featuring	fē′tụ̄r·ĭng	fea-tur-ing	Giving special prominence to.
25. folks ▶	fōks	folks	Groups of kindred people; persons.
26. friendly	frĕnd′lĭ	friend-ly	Kindly disposed; favorable.
27. gasoline	găs′ō·lēn	gas-o-line	An inflammable liquid produced from petroleum and used as motor fuel.
28. good will	gŏŏd wĭl	good will	Kindly feeling.
29. governors	gŭv′ẽr·nẽrz	gov-er-nors	Chief executives of states.
30. handling	hăn′dlĭng	han-dling	Managing with the hands; manner of treatment.
31. height	hīt	height	Summit; utmost degree or limit; altitude.
32. highway	hī′wā′	high-way	A main or public road.
33. hostess'	hōs′tĕs	host-ess'	Possessive of *hostess*.
34. improving	ĭm·prōōv′ĭng	im-prov-ing	Growing better.
35. indicating	in′dĭ·kāt·ĭng	in-di-cat-ing	Pointing out; showing indirectly.
36. industries	ĭn′dŭs·trĭz	in-dus-tries	Businesses in certain branches of trade.
37. inquiring	ĭn·kwīr′ĭng	in-quir-ing	Asking questions; seeking information.
38. judgment	jŭj′mĕnt	judg-ment	A decision; an opinion.
39. loosing	lōōs′ĭng	loos-ing	Setting free.
40. machinery	má·shēn′ẽr·ĭ	ma-chin-er-y	Machines, in general or collectively.
41. manageable	măn′ĭj·á·b'l	man-age-a-ble	Capable of being controlled.

42. manufacturing	măn′û·făk′tŭr·ĭng	man-u-fac-tur-ing	The process of making wares by hand or by machinery.
43. merely	mēr′lĭ	mere-ly	Purely; simply; barely; only.
44. naturally	năch′ēr·ăl·ĭ	nat-u-ral-ly	Of course; expectedly; through natural means.
45. ninth	nīnth	ninth	Ordinal number, following *eighth*.
46. occasionally	ŏ·kā′zhŭn·ăl·ĭ	oc-ca-sion-al-ly	In an infrequent manner.
47. occupational	ŏk′û·pā′shŭn·ăl	oc-cu-pa-tion-al	Resulting from a business or an occupation.
48. official	ŏ·fĭsh′ăl	of-fi-cial	*adj.* Authorized. *n.* One holding an office.
49. operation	ŏp′ēr·ā′shŭn	op-er-a-tion	Method of functioning.
► 50. organization	ôr′găn·ĭ·zā′shŭn	or-gan-i-za-tion	A group of persons banded together for a specific purpose; act of organizing; organic structure.
51. patient	pā′shĕnt	pa-tient	Long-suffering.
52. platform	plăt′fôrm′	plat-form	A flat, raised horizontal surface.
53. purchasable	pûr′chĭs·á·b′l	pur-chas-a-ble	Able to be purchased.
54. railway	rāl′wā′	rail-way	Track that provides a runway for wheels.
55. receive	rĕ·sēv′	re-ceive	To take; to acquire.
56. repaired	rĕ·pârd′	re-paired	Restored to good condition; fixed; returned.
57. safety	sāf′tĭ	safe-ty	Freedom from danger.
58. shipped	shĭpt	shipped	Transported; sent from one place to another.
59. studies	stŭd′ĭz	stud-ies	Branches of learning that are studied.
60. suggested	sŭg·jĕst′ĕd	sug-gest-ed	Called to mind; aroused the thought of.
61. supplies	sŭ·plīz′	sup-plies	Provisions or materials to meet needs.
62. tailor	tā′lēr	tai-lor	One who makes men's or women's outer garments.
63. therefore	thâr′fôr	there-fore	For that reason.
64. tobaccos	tŏ·băk′ōz	to-bac-cos	Species of tobacco; plural of *tobacco*.
65. together	tŏŏ·gĕth′ēr	to-geth-er	In contact with each other; at one time.
66. traveling	trăv′ĕl·ĭng	trav-el-ing	Journeying; touring.
67. tried	trīd	tried	Tested; endeavored.
68. useful	ūs′fŏŏl	use-ful	Helpful; advantageous.
69. valleys	văl′ĭz	val-leys	Lowlands between hills or mountains.
70. various	vâr′ĭ·ŭs	var-i-ous	Different; diverse; several.
71. weight	wāt	weight	Pressure; influence; a heavy object for holding or pressing something down.

72. wholesale	hōl'sāl'	whole-sale	*n.* Sale of goods in large quantities. *adj.* Extensive and indiscriminate.
73. written	rĭt''n	writ-ten	Past participle of *write;* inscribed.
74. your	yŏŏr	your	Possessive of *you.*
75. yourself	yŏŏr·sĕlf'	your-self	Emphatic form of the second person pronoun.

Lesson 4

1. absolutely	ăb'sŏ·lūt·lĭ	ab-so-lute-ly	Definitely; positively.
2. activities	ăk·tĭv'ĭ·tĭz	ac-tiv-i-ties	Energetic actions.
3. advising	ăd·vīz'ĭng	ad-vis-ing	Giving counsel or warning; informing.
4. amendment	à·mĕnd'mĕnt	a-mend-ment	The correction of a fault; the change made in a bill or law.
5. argument	är'gù·mĕnt	ar-gu-ment	Discussion designed to convince or to persuade.
6. available	à·vāl'à·b'l	a-vail-a-ble	Handy; attainable.
7. availability	à·vāl'à·bĭl'ĭ·tĭ	a-vail-a-bil-i-ty	State of being available.
8. background	băk'ground'	back-ground	The scenery behind something represented; the sum of one's experience or training.
9. by-product	bī'prŏd'ŭkt	by-prod-uct	A secondary result; that which is produced secondarily to the main product in manufacture.
10. ceiling	sēl'ĭng	ceil-ing	An overhead surface; the maximum price fixed by law.
11. children's	chĭl'drĕnz	chil-dren's	Possessive of *children.*
12. churches	chûrch'ĕz	church-es	Buildings for public worship.
13. commercial	kŏ·mûr'shăl	com-mer-cial	Pertaining to commerce or trade.
14. committee	kŏ·mĭt'ĭ	com-mit-tee	A body of persons chosen to take action on business matters.
15. compelling	kŏm·pĕl'ĭng	com-pel-ling	Urging with force; overpowering.
16. conveyed	kŏn·vād'	con-veyed	Carried; imparted, as by words and ideas.
17. copies	kŏp'ĭz	cop-ies	Imitations or reproductions of original work.
18. counties	koun'tĭz	coun-ties	In states, the largest divisions for local government.
19. difficulty	dĭf'ĭ·kŭl·tĭ	dif-fi-cul-ty	A thing that is not easy.
20. easily	ēz'ĭ·lĭ	eas-i-ly	In an easy manner.
21. editor	ĕd'ĭ·tēr	ed-i-tor	One who directs the policy and content of books, newspapers, magazines, etc.
22. elected	ĕ·lĕk'tĕd	e-lec-ted	Chosen; selected.
23. emptied	ĕmp'tĭd	emp-tied	Made vacant.

24.	engineer	ĕn′jĭ·nēr′	en-gi-neer	v. To lay out or construct as an engineer; to guide a course. n. One who operates an engine; one trained in any field of engineering.
25. ▶	enrolling	ĕn·rōl′ĭng	en·roll-ing	Enlisting; rolling or wrapping up.
26.	established	ĕs·tăb′lĭsht	es-tab-lished	v. Fixed firmly. adj. Appointed; affirmed.
27.	exactly	ĕg·zăkt′lĭ	ex-act-ly	Precisely; quite so.
28.	excellent	ĕk′sĕ·lĕnt	ex-cel-lent	Extremely good; of great worth.
29.	excitement	ĕk·sīt′mĕnt	ex-cite-ment	Act of arousing; that which causes agitation.
30.	existing	ĕg·zĭst′ĭng	ex-ist-ing	Having real or actual being.
31.	ex-president	ĕks·prĕz′ĭ·dĕnt	ex-pres-i-dent	A former chief executive.
32.	expression	ĕks·prĕsh′ŭn	ex-pres-sion	A facial aspect; process of representing by language.
33.	finalize	fī′năl·īz	fi-nal-ize	To bring to an end or to completion.
34.	financial	fĭ·năn′shăl	fi-nan-cial	Pertaining to money matters especially as conducted on a large scale.
35.	foreign	fŏr′ĭn	for-eign	Not native; alien in character
36.	grateful	grāt′fŏŏl	grate-ful	Thankful; welcome.
37.	importance	ĭm·pŏr′tăns	im-por-tance	State of being important; weight; significance.
38.	improvement	ĭm·prōōv′mĕnt	im-prove-ment	Betterment; enhanced value.
39.	instances	ĭn·stăns′ĕz	in-stanc-es	Examples; illustrations; specimens.
40.	institution	ĭn′stĭ·tū′shŭn	in-sti-tu-tion	An established society or corporation; a charitable organization.
41.	languages	lăng′gwĭj·ĕz	lan-guag-es	The body of words used and understood by a considerable group of people.
42.	layoffs	lā′ŏfs	lay-offs	Periods of being laid off work.
43.	majority	må·jŏr′ĭ·tĭ	ma-jor-i-ty	The number greater than half.
44.	mankind	măn′kīnd′	man-kind	The human race.
45.	marriage	măr′ĭj	mar-riage	The mutual relation of husband and wife; wedlock.
46.	Miss's	mĭs′ĕz	Miss-'s	Possessive of Miss.
47.	Negroes	nē′grōz	Ne-groes	A member of, or a descendant of, any of the black races of Africa.
48.	opportunities	ŏp′ŏr·tū′nĭ·tĭz	op-por-tu-ni-ties	Good chances or circumstances.
49.	organized	ŏr′găn·īzd	or-gan-ized	Systematized or constituted into a whole of mutually dependent parts.
50. ▶	original	ŏ·rĭj′ĭ·năl	o-rig-i-nal	First in order; primitive.
51.	outstanding	out·stăn′dĭng	out-stand-ing	Conspicuous; noticeable; unpaid.

52. perceive	pĕr·sēv′	per-ceive	To apprehend with the mind; to see; to hear; to understand.
53. possibly	pŏs′ĭ·blĭ	pos-si-bly	Perhaps.
54. proposed	prō·pōzd′	pro-posed	Offered for consideration; intended.
55. published	pŭb′lĭshd	pub-lished	Made public; proclaimed.
56. purchasing	pûr′chĭs·ĭng	pur-chas-ing	Buying for a price.
57. pursuing	pĕr·sū′ĭng	pur-su-ing	Following; seeking.
58. quarreled	kwŏr′ĕld	quar-reled	Disagreed; disputed angrily.
59. quiet	kwī′ĕt	qui-et	Calm; still; peaceful.
60. relief	rĕ·lēf′	re-lief	Comfort; ease; aid.
61. representative	rĕp′rĕ·zĕn′tȧ·tĭv	rep-re-sent-a-tive	One who acts as a special agent for another or others.
62. salable	sāl′ȧ·b'l	sal-a-ble	Marketable.
63. senator	sĕn′ȧ·tēr	sen-a-tor	A member of the upper branch of a legislature.
64. separating	sep′ȧ·rāt·ĭng	sep-a-rat-ing	Intervening or dividing.
65. series	sẽr′ēz	se-ries	A number of related things or events standing or following in order.
66. sheriffs	shĕr′ĭfs	sher-iffs	Chief executive officers of counties, charged with executing laws and preserving peace.
67. situation	sĭt′û·ā′shŭn	sit-u-a-tion	Location; state of affairs; position.
68. statesman	stāts′măn	states-man	A person experienced or engaged in the affairs of government.
69. suitable	sūt′ȧ·b'l	suit-a-ble	Appropriate; fitting.
70. taxation	tăks·ā′shŭn	tax-a-tion	Act of imposing taxes; revenue from taxes.
71. truly	trōō′lĭ	tru-ly	Honestly; genuinely; in a true manner.
72. valuable	văl′û·ȧ·b'l	val-u-a-ble	Having great monetary worth; precious; highly serviceable.
73. weighed	wād	weighed	Measured with scales; pondered; considered carefully.
74. whatsoever	hwŏt′sō·ĕv′ẽr	what-so-ev-er	Intensive form of *whatever*.
75. without	wĭth·out′	with-out	*adv.* On the outside. *prep.* Lacking; free from.

Lesson **5** Check-Up

Unit Test. Your teacher will dictate 50 words chosen from the lessons in Unit 6. These words are selected to test the mastery of the new words in this unit. Listen closely as each word is dictated, recall the rule that determines the correct spelling, spell the word carefully, and write plainly to assure yourself of a fair test.

Proofreading Test. In the following letter, some of the italicized words are misspelled. Copy the entire letter, making whatever corrections are necessary in the spelling of the words.

Dear Mr. Pierson:

Some *companys* sell *goodwill*, some sell *activities*, and others sell merchandise. All are *offerring* something worthwhile. The *Rail Way* Salvage Company, too, offers something worthwhile. Practically *every thing* our company sells will bring improvement to your business.

A quick inspection of our shelves reveals accounts *receiveable* ledgers, *soldier's* uniforms, *feild* glasses, *beautyful* lamps, *lawyers'* code books, special forms for reporting *taxs*, picture-*developping* materials, books on *marriage*, businessmen's *travelling* cases, *childrens'* toys, and numerous other items.

Use the enclosed order blank to send in an order.

Sincerely yours,

Cumulative Test. Your teacher will now dictate 40 words chosen from Units 1 through 5. These words will test your retention of the correct spelling of words in these units. Spell carefully and write plainly.

Checking Your Tests. Your teacher will give you directions for checking the unit test, the proofreading test, and the cumulative test.

Error Analysis. Classify the errors that you made by noting the type of error beside each word that you misspelled.

Review. Use the appropriate attack procedures for studying the words that you misspelled on the unit test, on the proofreading test, and on the cumulative test.

Retest. The retest will tell you if you have mastered the words in Units 1 through 6. If you misspelled words on the retest, continue your attack procedures until you are sure that you can spell all the words correctly.

Unit 7 Sound Words

Sound is the key to the correct spelling of the words in this unit. Spend a few moments reviewing "Spotting Sound Errors," beginning on page 3, and then begin your study of Lessons 1-4 of this unit, applying the following procedures:

Preview. Your teacher will dictate a list of 75 general-vocabulary words. Number a sheet of paper from 1 to 75. Spell as many of the words as you can, but attempt only the words that you are quite sure you know how to spell. If you do not know the spelling of a word, place a question mark (?) beside the number.

Checking Performance. Compare your spellings with the words given in the appropriate lesson. Place an *X* beside each word that you misspelled. To the right of any misspelled or omitted word, write the correct spelling.

Error Analysis. Classify the errors that you made by noting the type of error beside each word that you misspelled. For instance, if an error was caused by faulty syllabication, write "faulty syllabication" beside the word. Refer to Section One if you have forgotten the types of errors.

Attack Procedures. Attack procedures for sound-type errors were presented in Section One, beginning on page 7. Review the corrective technique recommended for each type of error.

Learning to Spell New Words. The pretest words that you did not know how to spell now appear on your answer sheet preceded by a question mark. Use a separate sheet of paper to practice those words, following the SEE, SAY, SPELL, and WRITE routine (see pages 39-41). Hand in the drill paper to your instructor.

Lesson 1

1. aboard	á·bōrd′	a-board	Into or within a boat or railway car.
2. absence	ăb′sĕns	ab-sence	Failure to be present; a want; a lack.
3. absent	ăb′sĕnt	ab-sent	Not present; not existing.
4. acquaint	ă·kwānt′	ac-quaint	To give information; to make one familiar with something or someone.
5. agencies	ā′jĕn·sĭz	a-gen-cies	Establishments that transact business for others.
6. agency	ā′jĕn·sĭ	a-gen-cy	An establishment for transacting business for others; the office or the function of an agent.
7. agreement	á·grē′mĕnt	a-gree-ment	Harmony of opinion.
8. application	ăp′lĭ·kā′shŭn	ap-pli-ca-tion	Close attention; act of applying.
9. assert	ă·sûrt′	as-sert	To state positively.
10. attaches	ă·tăch′ĕz	at-tach-es	Adheres; fastens; takes by legal authority.
11. attain	ă·tān′	at-tain	To achieve; to accomplish.
12. attractive	ă·trăk′tĭv	at-trac-tive	Charming.
13. barrel	băr′ĕl	bar-rel	A round bulging vessel having flat ends of equal diameter.
14. bushels	bŏŏsh′ĕlz	bush-els	Dry measures; four-peck quantities.
15. cellar	sĕl′ẽr	cel-lar	An underground room for storage of provisions.
16. cheerful	chẽr′fŏŏl	cheer-ful	Joyful; hearty.
17. chimney	chĭm′nĭ	chim-ney	A smokestack; an upright flue made of brick, stone, etc.
18. clever	klĕv′ẽr	clev-er	Skillful; talented.
19. correspondent	kŏr′ĕ·spŏn′dĕnt	cor-re-spond-ent	One who writes to another.
20. correspondents	kŏr′ĕ·spŏn′dĕnts	cor-re-spond-ents	Plural of *correspondent* (see above).
21. customers	kŭs′tŭm·ẽrz	cus-tom-ers	Patrons.
22. damaged	dăm′ĭjd	dam-aged	Caused loss, harm, or injury to.
23. description	dĕ·skrĭp′shŭn	de-scrip-tion	The words used to give a mental picture of something.
24. doctrine	dŏk′trĭn	doc-trine	Principles that are observed or adhered to.
25. emotion ►	ĕ·mō′shŭn	e-mo-tion	A strong feeling.
26. enterprise	ĕn′tẽr·prīz	en-ter-prise	An undertaking; a venture.
27. extraordinary	ĕks·trôr′dĭ·nẽr′ĭ	ex-traor-di-nar-y	Exceeding the usual.

28.	failure	fāl′ûr	fail-ure	A deficiency; a want of success.
29.	film	fĭlm	film	A very thin covering; a haze; a motion picture.
30.	front	frŭnt	front	The fore part of an object or surface.
31.	genius	jēn′yŭs	gen-ius	A person of extraordinary talent.
32.	handkerchief	hăng′kĕr·chĭf	hand-ker-chief	A small cloth used for wiping the face.
33.	honorable	ŏn′ĕr·à·b'l	hon-or-a-ble	Worthy of honor; noble.
34.	ideal	ī·dē′ăl	i-de-al	Existing in fancy or imagination as a perfect model.
35.	image	ĭm′ĭj	im-age	A likeness.
36.	immense	ĭ·mĕns′	im-mense	Very large; huge.
37.	inhabitant	ĭn·hăb′ĭ·tănt	in-hab-it-ant	A permanent resident in a place.
38.	instinct	ĭn′stĭngkt	in-stinct	A natural tendency to some form of action; innate perception.
39.	intelligence	ĭn·tĕl′ĭ·jĕns	in-tel-li-gence	Mental power; the mind in operation.
40.	lamb	lăm	lamb	A young sheep.
41.	medical	mĕd′ĭ·kăl	med-i-cal	Dealing with the science of medicine or with healing.
42.	messenger	mĕs′ĕn·jĕr	mes-sen-ger	A courier; one who bears a message.
43.	mighty	mīt′ĭ	might-y	Potent; forceful; extraordinary.
44.	monument	mŏn′û·mĕnt	mon-u-ment	Something that serves as a memorial.
45.	pardon	pär′d'n	par-don	Act of forgiving; freedom from blame.
46.	payment	pā′mĕnt	pay-ment	The amount paid; act of paying.
47.	perish	pĕr′ĭsh	per-ish	To be destroyed or ruined.
48.	personality	pûr′sŭ·năl′ĭ·tĭ	per-son-al-i-ty	Distinctive personal and social traits.
49.	phrase	frāz	phrase	A short, pithy expression; a group of two or more words, not having a subject and a predicate, used as a part of a sentence.
50.	planet	plăn′ĕt	plan-et	A celestial body, except a comet or meteor, that revolves about the sun.
51.	prayer	prâr	prayer	Entreaty; words used in addressing God.
52.	pretend	prē·tĕnd′	pre-tend	To make believe.
53.	previous	prē′vĭ·ŭs	pre-vi-ous	Prior; preceding.
54.	privilege	prĭv′ĭ·lĭj	priv-i-lege	A right or immunity granted.
55.	professional	prŏ·fĕsh′ŭn·ăl	pro-fes-sion-al	Conforming to standards of a profession.

56.	punishment	pŭn′ĭsh·mĕnt	pun-ish-ment	A penalty inflicted on an offender.
57.	reputation	rĕp′û·tā′shŭn	rep-u-ta-tion	Public esteem.
58.	rescue	rĕs′kū	res-cue	*v.* To free from danger; to regain by force. *n.* Act of saving from danger.
59.	rifle	rī′f′l	ri-fle	A firearm with a rifled barrel fired from the shoulder.
60.	scientific	sī′ĕn·tĭf′ĭk	sci-en-tif-ic	Agreeing with the principles of science.
61.	scratch	skrăch	scratch	*v.* To scrape with claws or nails. *n.* The mark or injury made by clawing.
62.	search	sûrch	search	*v.* To explore; to seek. *n.* Act of exploring or seeking.
63.	securities	sĕ·kū′rĭ·tĭz	se-cu-ri-ties	Means of protection or defense; stocks and bonds.
64.	security	sĕ·kū′rĭ·tĭ	se-cu-ri-ty	Safety; means of protection or defense; something given as pledge of payment.
65.	signal	sĭg′năl	sig-nal	*v.* To notify by signs. *n.* A sign made to give notice.
66.	solution	sŏ·lū′shŭn	so-lu-tion	Act of solving a problem; a mixture of different substances.
67.	stomach	stŭm′ăk	stom-ach	The organ in man or animals in which the early stages of digestion take place.
68.	stretch	strĕch	stretch	*v.* To reach out; to draw out. *n.* A length or distance.
69.	survey	sĕr·vā′	sur-vey	To determine the extent of.
70.	sword	sōrd	sword	A weapon with a pointed blade and a sharp cutting edge.
71.	tailor	tā′lĕr	tai-lor	One who makes outer garments for men or women.
72.	theory	thē′ŏ·rĭ	the-o-ry	General or abstract principles drawn from any body of facts.
73.	throughout	thrōō·out′	through-out	In every part.
74.	treasure	trĕzh′ĕr	treas-ure	*n.* A thing of great value. *v.* To cherish; to prize.
75.	yield	yēld	yield	To produce; to give up a right to; to surrender.

Lesson 2

1.	accuse	ă·kūz′	ac-cuse	To blame; to censure.
2.	ache	āk	ache	*v.* To suffer pain. *n.* A continuing pain.
3.	actor	ăk′tĕr	ac-tor	One who acts; a performer in a play or motion picture.
4.	additional	ă·dĭsh′ŭn·ăl	ad-di-tion-al	Added; extra.
5.	amuse	à·mūz′	a-muse	To entertain pleasantly.

6.	appreciate	ȧ·prē′shĭ·āt	ap-pre-ci-ate	To be thankful for; to be fully aware of; to recognize.
7.	ascend	ȧ·sĕnd′	as-cend	To go or move upward.
8.	aspect	ăs′pĕkt	as-pect	Look; appearance; view.
9.	backward	băk′wĕrd	back-ward	Toward the back or rear; in reverse order or direction.
10.	beggar	bĕg′ēr	beg-gar	One who lives by asking alms or gifts.
11.	Berlin	bûr·lĭn′	Ber-lin	A city in Germany.
12.	chemicals	kĕm′ĭ·kȧlz	chem-i-cals	Substances obtained by processes involving the use of chemistry.
13.	condense	kŏn′dĕns	con-dense	To make or become more compact.
14.	consult	kŏn·sŭlt′	con-sult	To ask advice of; to consider.
15.	despite	dė·spīt′	de-spite	In spite of; notwithstanding.
16.	diet	dī′ĕt	di-et	Food and drink that are regularly provided.
17.	disappoint	dĭs′ȧ·point′	dis-ap-point	To fail to come up to expectations.
18.	dissolve	dĭ·zŏlv′	dis-solve	To separate into its parts; to destroy.
19.	drown	droun	drown	To perish by suffocation in water or other liquid.
20.	effective	ĕ·fĕk′tĭv	ef-fec-tive	Impressive; operative.
21.	eighteen	ā′tēn′	eight-een	Cardinal number, following *seventeen*.
22.	enthusiasm	ĕn·thū′zĭ·ăz′m	en-thu-si-asm	Ardent zeal; fervor.
23.	examination	ĕg·zăm′ĭ·nā′shŭn	ex-am-i-na-tion	An investigation; a test; a search.
24.	excite	ĕk·sīt′	ex-cite	To arouse to feeling.
25.	expensive	ĕks′pĕn′sĭv	ex-pen-sive	Costly.
► 26.	explanation	ĕks′plȧ·nā′shŭn	ex-pla-na-tion	That which makes a meaning clear.
27.	forehead	fŏr′ĕd	fore-head	The part of the face above the eyes.
28.	frighten	frīt′′n	fright-en	To alarm; to scare.
29.	gesture	jĕs′tŭr	ges-ture	*v.* To make signs as a mode of expression. *n.* The signs that express ideas or feelings.
30.	graduate	grăd′ů·ȧt	grad-u-ate	One who has completed a course or a complete unit of study.
31.	graduating	grăd′ů·āt·ĭng	grad-u-at-ing	Finishing a prescribed course.
32.	hasten	hās′′n	has-ten	To hurry; to urge forward.
33.	incident	ĭn′sĭ·dĕnt	in-ci-dent	An event; an occurrence.
34.	legal	lē′găl	le-gal	Lawful; established by law.
35.	liquid	lĭk′wĭd	liq-uid	A fluid; a substance that will flow.
36.	management	măn′ĭj·mĕnt	man-age-ment	Skillful direction of affairs.
37.	medieval	mē′dĭ·ē′văl	me-di-e-val	Belonging to the Middle Ages.
38.	miner	mīn′ēr	min-er	A worker in a mine.
39.	moderate	mŏd′ēr·ĭt	mod-er-ate	Kept within bounds; reasonable.
40.	multitude	mŭl′tĭ·tūd	mul-ti-tude	A crowd; a throng.

41.	mysterious	mĭs·tēr′ĭ·ŭs	mys-te-ri-ous	Puzzling; implying mystery.
42.	origin	ŏr′ĭ·jĭn	or-i-gin	Source; beginning; cause.
43.	ornament	ôr′nà·mĕnt	or-na-ment	A decoration; an adornment.
44.	parliament	pär′lĭ·mĕnt	par-lia-ment	A lawmaking body in certain countries.
45.	parlor	pär′lēr	par-lor	A room for the reception of guests, for conversation, etc.
46.	patent	păt′ĕnt	pat-ent	The right given to an inventor to have a monopoly on his product.
47.	philosophy	fĭ·lŏs′ŏ·fĭ	phi-los-o-phy	The body of general principles at the basis of an art, science, etc.
48.	pioneer	pī′ŏ·nēr′	pi-o-neer	One who opens and prepares the way for others.
49.	preservation	prĕz′ēr·vā′shŭn	pres-er-va-tion	Act of keeping intact or keeping from decaying.
50. ▶	prey	prā	prey	v. To plunder; to seek; to seize. n. The person or animal seized as a victim.
51.	procession	prŏ·sĕsh′ŭn	pro-ces-sion	A parade; a group moving onward in an orderly way.
52.	pronounce	prŏ·nouns′	pro-nounce	To speak aloud; to assert.
53.	prosperity	prŏs·pĕr′ĭ·tĭ	pros-per-i-ty	Success; successful progress.
54.	reality	rē·ăl′ĭ·tĭ	re-al-i-ty	Fact of being real or being alive; an actual person, event, etc.
55.	reasonable	rē′z′n·à·b′l	rea-son-a-ble	Just; fair-minded.
56.	rebel	rĕb′ĕl	reb-el	One who rebels.
57.	recommend	rĕk′ŏ·mĕnd′	rec-om-mend	To praise; to commend.
58.	resemble	rē·zĕm′b′l	re-sem-ble	To be like or similar to.
59.	resolution	rĕz′ŏ·lū′shŭn	res-o-lu-tion	A formal expression of opinion adopted by vote.
60.	revenge	rē·vĕnj′	re-venge	The desire to seek vengeance.
61.	sentiment	sĕn′tĭ·mĕnt	sen-ti-ment	Deep mental attitude; feeling.
62.	sparkle	spär′k′l	spar-kle	A little spark; liveliness; a gleam.
63.	sparkling	spär′klĭng	spar-kling	Lively; flashing.
64.	steadily	stĕd′ĭ·lĭ	stead-i-ly	Constantly; firmly; calmly.
65.	substitute	sŭb′stĭ·tūt	sub-sti-tute	A person or thing put in place of another.
66.	surrender	sŭ·rĕn′dĕr	sur-ren-der	To yield to the power of another; to give up.
67.	tendency	tĕn′dĕn·sĭ	tend-en-cy	Inclination.
68.	terribly	tĕr′ĭ·blĭ	ter-ri-bly	In a dreadful manner; appallingly.
69.	thoroughly	thûr′ŏ·lĭ	thor-ough-ly	Completely; carefully; exactly.
70.	transferable	trăns·fûr′à·b′l	trans-fer-a-ble	Capable of being conveyed from one person or place to another.
71.	tremendous	trē·mĕn′dŭs	tre-men-dous	Very large.
72.	upward	ŭp′wērd	up-ward	From lower to higher.
73.	violence	vī′ŏ·lĕns	vi-o-lence	Great force; outrageous assault.
74.	wholly	hōl′lĭ	whol-ly	Entirely; totally; solely.
75.	wrap	răp	wrap	To enclose.

Lesson 3

1. **abundance**	á·bŭn′dăns	a-bun-dance	An excessive fullness; great quantity.
2. **abundant**	á′bŭn·dănt	a-bun-dant	Bountiful; plentiful.
3. **accord**	ă·kôrd′	ac-cord	To agree; to be in harmony; to grant.
4. **accordingly**	ă·kôr′dĭng·lĭ	ac-cord-ing-ly	Consequently; in natural order; suitably.
5. **agony**	ăg′ŏ·nĭ	ag-o-ny	Extreme pain; anguish; torture.
6. **amendment**	á·mĕnd′mĕnt	a-mend-ment	An alteration; a change or correction made in a fault.
7. **anchor**	ăng′kēr	an-chor	v. To fix or fasten; to come to rest. n. An instrument that holds anything fast.
8. **apparent**	ă·păr′ĕnt	ap-par-ent	Evident; visible.
9. **appointment**	ă·point′mĕnt	ap-point-ment	Designation of a person for a certain trust; an arrangement for a meeting.
10. **assistance**	ă·sĭs′tăns	as-sist-ance	Help; aid; support.
11. **assistant**	ă·sĭs′tănt	as-sist-ant	One who aids or helps.
12. **attendant**	ă·tĕn′dănt	at-tend-ant	One who accompanies another.
13. **attendants**	ă·tĕn′dănts	at-tend-ants	Plural of *attendant* (see above).
14. **audible**	ô′dĭ·b'l	au-di-ble	Capable of being heard.
15. **availability**	á·vāl′á·bĭl′ĭ·tĭ	a-vail-a-bil-i-ty	The state of being available.
16. **available**	á·vāl′á·b'l	a-vail-a-ble	Attainable; usable; handy.
17. **basin**	bā′s'n	ba-sin	A wide, hollow utensil for holding water; any hollow or depressed place containing water, as a pond, an ocean basin.
18. **bewilder**	bĕ·wĭl′dēr	be-wil-der	To perplex; to confuse.
19. **boundary**	boun′dá·rĭ	bound-a-ry	Something that marks the limits or bounds.
20. **cabinet**	kăb′ĭ·nĕt	cab-i-net	A set of drawers; a cupboard; a case; an advisory council of an executive.
21. **cable**	kā′b'l	ca-ble	v. To telegraph by a cable. n. A strong rope or chain; an insulated wire for carrying electric current.
22. **ceremony**	sĕr′ĕ·mō′nĭ	cer-e-mo-ny	A ritual; an act prescribed by law or custom for matters of religion, of state, etc.
23. **challenge**	chăl′ĕnj	chal-lenge	v. To assert a right; to object to. n. The summons to a contest.

24. communication	kŏ·mū′nĭ·kā′shŭn	com-mu-ni-ca-tion	A written message; exchange of thoughts or opinions.
25. conquest ▶	kŏng′kwĕst	con-quest	Act of conquering or effecting a victory.
26. countenance	koun′tē·nǎns	coun-te-nance	The expression of the face.
27. despise	dĕ·spīz′	de-spise	To look down upon with contempt.
28. digest	dĭ·jĕst′	di-gest	To think over and arrange methodically in the mind; to change food into a form that can be absorbed.
29. digestible	dĭ·jĕs′tĭ·b'l	di-gest-i-ble	That can be digested or absorbed.
30 distribution	dĭs′trĭ·bū′shŭn	dis-tri-bu-tion	A classification; a dividing into parts for dispensing.
31. entitled	ĕn·tī′t'ld	en-ti-tled	Gave a title to; qualified.
32. everyone	ĕv′ēr·ĭ·wŭn′	ev-er-y-one	This one and all others; everybody.
33. exceed	ĕk·sēd′	ex-ceed	To go or be beyond the limit or measure of; to surpass.
34. exhaust	ĕg·zôst′	ex-haust	To use to the end of the supply; to tire; to fatigue.
35. exhausted	ĕg·zôst′ĕd	ex-haust-ed	Depleted; worn out.
36. favorable	fā′vĕr·à·b'l	fa-vor-a-ble	Advantageous; approving.
37. flourish	flûr′ĭsh	flour-ish	To grow; to thrive.
38. formal	fôr′mǎl	for-mal	Having the form of established custom.
39. gracious	grā′shŭs	gra-cious	Attractive; charming.
40. guilty	gĭl′tĭ	guilt-y	Having one's guilt established.
41. ignorant	ĭg′nō·rǎnt	ig-no-rant	Uninformed; unlearned.
42. immortal	ĭ·môr′tǎl	im-mor-tal	Imperishable; everlasting.
43. impulse	ĭm′pŭls	im-pulse	A motive not governed by reason.
44. innocence	ĭn′ō·sĕns	in-no-cence	Purity of heart; freedom from sin.
45. intimate	ĭn′tĭ·māt	in-ti-mate	To suggest indirectly; to hint.
46. items	ī′tĕmz	i-tems	Separate things; bits of news.
47. jealous	jĕl′ŭs	jeal-ous	Exacting exclusive devotion.
48. knitted	nĭt′ĕd	knit-ted	Past tense and past participle of *knit*.
49. liberal	lĭb′ēr·ǎl	lib-er-al	Generous; not restricted; abundant.
50. limb ▶	lĭm	limb	A leg or arm of a human being or of an animal; a large branch of a tree.

51. marvel	mär'vĕl	mar-vel	v. To be struck with surprise. n. That which causes wonder.
52. mingle	mĭng'g'l	min-gle	To mix; to join in company.
53. miracle	mĭr'à·k'l	mir-a-cle	An extraordinary event that cannot be explained by any known natural law; a wonder; a marvel.
54. miserable	mĭz'ēr·à·b'l	mis-er-a-ble	Wretched; uncomfortable.
55. motive	mō'tĭv	mo-tive	An idea or emotion that prompts one to an action.
56. oxygen	ŏk'sĭ·jĕn	ox-y-gen	A gaseous element in the atmosphere, essential to life.
57. peaceful	pēs'fŏŏl	peace-ful	Tranquil; quiet; undisturbed.
58. peril	pĕr'ĭl	per-il	Danger.
59. pilot	pī'lŭt	pi-lot	One who steers a vessel; a guide.
60. pledge	plĕj	pledge	v. To give as a security; to bind by promise. n. Something given as security.
61. politician	pŏl'ĭ·tĭsh'ăn	pol-i-ti-cian	One versed or experienced in the science of government.
62. prominent	prŏm'ĭ·nĕnt	prom-i-nent	Conspicuous; standing out.
63. prophet	prŏf'ĕt	proph-et	One who foretells future events.
64. reckless	rĕk'lĕs	reck-less	Indifferent; rash; neglectful.
65. reference	rĕf'ēr·ĕns	ref-er-ence	A statement or remark referring to something; an allusion.
66. residence	rĕz'ĭ·dĕns	res-i-dence	A house or a place where one lives.
67. resign	rē·zīn'	re-sign	To give up; to relinquish; to yield.
68. resistance	rē·zĭs'tăns	re-sist-ance	Opposition; any opposing or retarding force.
69. restaurant	rĕs'tō·rănt	res-tau-rant	A public eating place.
70. sandwich	sănd'wĭch	sand-wich	Two slices of bread with an edible mixture spread between them.
71. satisfactorily	săt'ĭs·făk'tō·rĭ·lĭ	sat-is-fac-to-ri-ly	In a satisfying way; in a way that meets requirements or expectations.
72. suitable	sūt'à·b'l	suit-a-ble	Fitting; appropriate.
73. tragedy	trăj'ĕ·dĭ	trag-e-dy	A catastrophe; a calamity; a disastrous event.
74. transportation	trăns'pôr·tā'shŭn	trans-por-ta-tion	Act or system of conveying people or material from one place to another.

75. waist	wāst	waist	The small part of the body between the hips and the thorax.

Lesson 4

1. abide	à·bīd′	a-bide	To remain; to stay; to reside.
2. abuse	à·būz′	a-buse	To mistreat; to use badly.
3. acknowledge	ăk·nŏl′ĕj	ac-knowl-edge	To confess; to recognize as a fact; to admit the claims of.
4. acknowledging	ăk·nŏl′ĕj·ĭng	ac-knowl-edg-ing	Confessing; admitting as true or pertinent.
5. ally	ă·lī′	al-ly	To form a connection between.
6. ample	ăm′p′l	am-ple	More than adequate; of large size.
7. ancestor	ăn′sĕs′tēr	an-ces-tor	A forefather.
8. appetite	ăp′ē·tīt	ap-pe-tite	Desire or craving, as for food.
9. assault	ă·sôlt′	as-sault	*n.* A violent attack. *v.* To make an attack upon.
10. assigned	ă·sīnd′	as-signed	Appointed; designated.
11. attorney	ă·tûr′nĭ	at-tor-ney	A legal agent qualified to represent persons in legal proceedings; a lawyer.
12. attorneys	ă·tûr′nĭz	at-tor-neys	Plural of *attorney* (see above).
13. attribute	ă·trĭb′ût	at-trib-ute	To give as a reason or cause.
14. carbon	kär′bŏn	car-bon	An elementary substance present in all organic compounds.
15. cathedral	kà·thē′drăl	ca-the-dral	The church that contains the bishop's chair.
16. ceiling	sēl′ĭng	ceil-ing	An overhead lining or finish; the maximum price or wage set by law.
17. certificate	sēr·tĭf′ĭ·kĭt	cer-tif-i-cate	A written statement testifying to the truth of a fact.
18. circuit	sûr′kĭt	cir-cuit	The complete path of an electric current.
19. circular	sûr′kû·lēr	cir-cu-lar	Moving in or around a circle; addressed to a number of persons.
20. circularize	sûr′kû·lēr·īz	cir-cu-lar-ize	To make circular; to distribute circulars to.
21. coarse	kōrs	coarse	Common; of inferior quality or appearance; unrefined.
22. comparison	kŏm·păr′ĭ·sŭn	com-par-i-son	Act of estimating relative likenesses.
23. culture	kŭl′t̯ûr	cul-ture	Refinement; social customs; act of developing by training or discipline.
24. decrease	dē·krēs′	de-crease	To diminish gradually in size, number, etc.
25. definitely	dĕf′ĭ·nĭt·lĭ	def-i-nite-ly	Precisely; clearly; assuredly.

▶

26.	delicious	dĕ·lĭsh′ŭs	de-li-cious	Delightful; very tasty.
27.	diminish	dĭ·mĭn′ĭsh	di-min-ish	To make less or smaller.
28.	disciplinary	dĭs′ĭ·plĭ·nĕr′ĭ	dis-ci-pli-nar-y	Of or pertaining to measures that restrain or control.
29.	disguise	dĭs·gīz′	dis-guise	To hide or conceal the identify or true nature of.
30.	employee	ĕm·ploi′ē	em-ploy-ee	One who works for wages in the service of another.
31.	employer	ĕm·ploi′ēr	em-ploy-er	One who hires another for work.
32.	envelope	ĕn′vĕ·lōp	en-ve-lope	A wrapper; a folded gummed paper used to enclose a letter.
33.	excess	ĕk′sĕs	ex-cess	That which exceeds what is usual; surplus.
34.	exhibit	ĕg·zĭb′ĭt	ex-hib-it	To present to view; to show; to display.
35.	facilities	fȧ·sĭl′ĭ·tĭz	fa-cil-i-ties	Things that promote easy action or use.
36.	facility	fȧ·sĭl′ĭ·tĭ	fa-cil-i-ty	Something that promotes ease of operation.
37.	fulfill	fo͝ol·fĭl′	ful-fill	To carry into effect; to bring to pass.
38.	healthy	hĕl′thĭ	health-y	Being in a state of good health; well.
39.	heir	âr	heir	One who is legally entitled to in-herit.
40.	ignorance	ĭg′nŏ·rȧns	ig-no-rance	Lack of knowledge.
41.	inquiries	ĭn·kwīr′ĭz	in-quir-ies	Plural of *inquiry* (see below).
42.	inquiry	ĭn·kwīr′ĭ	in-quir-y	A search for truth or information; an investigation; research.
43.	institute	ĭn′stĭ·tūt	in-sti-tute	*v.* To establish; to found; to or-ganize. *n.* An institution, as a school or college.
44.	invisible	ĭn·vĭz′ĭ·b'l	in-vis-i-ble	Not in sight; not obvious.
45.	isle	īl	isle	A small island.
46.	leaves	lēvz	leaves	Plural of *leaf;* the green, flat parts that grow from the stem of a plant.
47.	legend	lĕj′ĕnd	leg-end	Any story handed down from the past.
48.	legislation	lĕj′ĭs·lā′shŭn	leg-is-la-tion	Act of making laws; laws that are so enacted.
49.	license	lī′sĕns	li-cense	*v.* To permit or authorize. *n.* Formal permission from authori-ties to do something.
50. ▶	luncheon	lŭn′chŭn	lunch-eon	A light meal usually eaten in the middle of the day.
51.	medium	mē′dĭ·ŭm	me-di-um	Intermediate in amount, position, quality, or degree.
52.	mission	mĭsh′ŭn	mis-sion	A definite task or errand.
53.	mourn	mōrn	mourn	To grieve.

54.	multiply	mŭl′tĭ·plī	mul-ti-ply	To increase in number.
55.	obligation	ŏb′lĭ·gā′shŭn	ob-li-ga-tion	A duty; an indebtedness.
56.	obvious	ŏb′vĭ·ŭs	ob-vi-ous	Plainly seen; evident.
57.	paradise	păr′ȧ·dīs	par-a-dise	A place of perfect bliss and happiness; heaven.
58.	parallel	păr′ă·lĕl	par-al-lel	Line, surface, or curve extending in the same direction but never meeting; a counterpart; a similarity.
59.	parcel	pär′sĕl	par-cel	A bundle; a package.
60.	perfume	pûr′fūm	per-fume	A sweet-smelling substance used for scenting.
61.	permission	pĕr·mĭsh′ŭn	per-mis-sion	Formal consent; authorization.
62.	prairie	prâr′ĭ	prai-rie	An extensive tract of flat or rolling land covered by coarse grass but with no trees.
63.	primary	prī′mĕr·ĭ	pri-ma-ry	First in order.
64.	procure	prŏ·kūr′	pro-cure	To obtain; to acquire.
65.	prosperous	prŏs′pĕr·ŭs	pros-per-ous	Thriving; flourishing; successful.
66.	realm	rĕlm	realm	Province; domain.
67.	rejoice	rê·jois′	re-joice	To gladden; to feel great gladness.
68.	remote	rê·mōt′	re-mote	Distant; separate; not obvious.
69.	restless	rĕst′lĕs	rest-less	Unceasing; discontented.
70.	satisfactory	săt′ĭs·făk′tŏ·rĭ	sat-is-fac-to-ry	Meeting expectations or requirements.
71.	sensible	sĕn′sĭ·b′l	sen-si-ble	Reasonable; intelligent.
72.	sketch	skĕch	sketch	v. To make a rough draft or plan of. n. An outline or plan of a design.
73.	sovereign	sŏv′ĕr·ĭn	sov-er-eign	n. A person with highest power or authority in a state. adj. Chief or highest.
74.	spectacle	spĕk′tȧ·k′l	spec-ta-cle	A public display; a noteworthy sight.
75.	succession	sŭk·sĕsh′ŭn	suc-ces-sion	A number of persons or things following each other in a definite sequence.

Lesson 5 Check-Up

Unit Test. Your teacher will dictate 50 words chosen from the lessons in Unit 7. These words are selected to test your mastery of the new words in this unit. Listen closely as each word is dictated, spell the word carefully, and write plainly to assure yourself of a fair test.

Proofreading Test. In the following letter, some of the italicized words are misspelled. Copy the entire letter, making whatever corrections are necessary in the spelling of the words.

Dear Mrs. Cox:

Do you sometimes long for the *priviledge* of exploring the *intamate* operations of the *securaties* market? Do you *exaust* your ideas for meal planning before the week is gone? Would you like to be able to discuss economic *docktrine* and *thery?* Do you sometimes *abbuse* your credit rights? Do *medacal* fees, *lisence* fees, and other *agensy* fees surprise you? Do you *dispise* keeping a budget, and do your expenses *excede* your estimates often?

Consumer News is a monthly magazine *talored* to meet the needs of the housewife. This *asistent* shopper is an *extrordinary* magazine with a wide *destribution.* Send for an *examanation* copy.

Sincerely yours,

Cumulative Test. Your teacher will now dictate 40 words chosen from Units 1 through 6. These words will test your retention of the correct spelling of words in these units. Spell carefully and write plainly.

Checking Your Tests. Your teacher will give you directions for checking the unit test, the proofreading test, and the cumulative test.

Error Analysis. Classify the errors that you made by noting the type of error beside each word that you misspelled.

Review. Use the appropriate attack procedures for studying the words that you misspelled on the unit test, on the proofreading test, and on the cumulative test.

Retest. The retest will tell you if you have mastered the words in Units 1 through 7. If you misspelled words on the retest, continue your attack procedures until you are sure that you can spell all the words correctly.

Unit 8 Rule Words

Spelling rules are the guides to the correct spelling of the words in this unit. Review briefly the spelling rules discussed on pages 20-29, giving particular attention to those rules that are most troublesome for you; then begin your study of Lessons 1-4 of this unit, applying the following procedures:

Preview. Your teacher will dictate a list of 75 general-vocabulary words. Number a sheet of paper from 1 to 75. Spell as many of the words as you can, but attempt only the words that you are quite sure you know how to spell. If you do not know the spelling of a word, place a question mark (?) beside the number.

Checking Performance. Compare your spellings with the words given in the appropriate lesson. Place an *X* beside each word that you misspelled. To the right of any misspelled or omitted word, write the correct spelling.

Error Analysis. Classify the errors that you made by noting the type of error beside each word that you misspelled. For instance, if an error was caused by failure to double a final consonant when adding a suffix, write "final consonant" beside the word. Refer to pages 20-29 if you have forgotten the types of rule errors.

Attack Procedures. Attack procedures for rule-type errors were presented in Section One, beginning on page 32. Review the corrective technique recommended for each type of error.

Learning to Spell New Words. The pretest words that you did not know how to spell now appear on your answer sheet preceded by a question mark. Use a separate sheet of paper to practice those words, following the SEE, SAY, SPELL, and WRITE routine (see pages 39-41). Hand in the drill paper to your instructor.

Lesson 1

1. accustomed	ă·kŭs′tŭmd	ac-cus-tomed	Usual; customary.
2. achievement	à·chēv′měnt	a-chieve-ment	An accomplishment; a feat.
3. adjoining	ă·join′ĭng	ad-join-ing	Situated so as to touch.
4. anything	ĕn′ĭ·thĭng	an-y-thing	Any object, event, or fact.
5. arrival	ă·rīv′ăl	ar-riv-al	Act of reaching a destination; appearance upon a scene.
6. cashier's	kăsh·ērz′	cash-ier's	Possessive of *cashier*.
7. celebrities	sĕ·lĕb′rĭ·tĭz	ce-leb-ri-ties	Celebrated persons; public characters.
8. combination	kŏm′bĭ·nā′shŭn	com-bi-na-tion	Process of combining; the series of letters or numbers used in setting a lock.
9. conference	kŏn′fēr·ĕns	con-fer-ence	A meeting to discuss business of some type.
10. confusion	kŏn·fū′zhŭn	con-fu-sion	A deranged condition.
11. conscience	kŏn′shĕns	con-science	Sense of righteousness or wrongfulness of one's actions.
12. consideration	kŏn·sĭd′ĕr·ā′shŭn	con-sid-er-a-tion	Deliberation; careful thought.
13. constantly	kŏn′stănt·lĭ	con-stant-ly	Faithfully; steadfastly; unchangingly.
14. contributing	kŏn·trĭb′ût·ĭng	con-trib-ut-ing	Helping; assisting.
15. deceive	dĕ·sēv′	de-ceive	To cheat; to mislead.
16. definitely	dĕf′ĭ·nĭt·lĭ	def-i-nite-ly	Precisely; exactly.
17. employees	ĕm·ploi′ēz	em-ploy-ees	Those who work for wages.
18. engagement	ĕn·gāj′měnt	en-gage-ment	An appointment; a betrothal.
19. entertain	ĕn′tēr·tān′	en-ter-tain	To amuse; to receive guests.
20. establishment	ĕs·tăb′lĭsh·měnt	es-tab-lish-ment	Permanent place of residence or business.
21. extremely	ĕks·trēm′lĭ	ex-treme-ly	Radically; excessively; immoderately.
22. financing	fĭ·năn′sĭng	fi-nanc-ing	Providing capital for a business transaction.
23. forever	fŏr·ĕv′ēr	for-ev-er	At all times; perpetually.
24. forgivable	fŏr·gĭv′à·b'l	for-giv-a-ble	Excusable; pardonable.
25. fox's ▶	fŏks′ĭz	fox's	Possessive of *fox*.
26. gaseous	găs′ĕ·ŭs	gas-e-ous	Having the form of gas.
27. good night	good′ nīt′	good night	An expression bidding farewell at the end of a day.
28. halves	hävz	halves	Plural of *half*.
29. imagination	ĭ·măj′ĭ·nā′shŭn	im-ag-i-na-tion	The picture-forming ability of the mind.
30. information	ĭn′fŏr·mā′shŭn	in-for-ma-tion	Knowledge given or acquired.
31. informative	ĭn·fôr′mà·tĭv	in-form-a-tive	Enlightening.

32.	instruments	ĭn′strŏŏ·mĕnts	in-stru-ments	Tools; means; laws.
33.	invitation	ĭn′vĭ·tā′shŭn	in-vi-ta-tion	Act of inviting; an expression by which one is invited.
34.	its	ĭts	its	Possessive of *it*.
35.	journeys	jûr′nĭz	jour-neys	Trips; voyages.
36.	management	măn′ĭj·mĕnt	man-age-ment	The group of those in charge of a business.
37.	millionaire	mĭl′yŭn·âr′	mil-lion-aire	One who has a million or more dollars.
38.	neighborhood	nā′bĕr·hŏŏd	neigh-bor-hood	A region nearby; vicinity.
39.	observation	ŏb′zĕr·vā′shŭn	ob-ser-va-tion	Conclusion based on something noticed.
40.	occurred	ŏ·kûrd′	oc-curred	Existed; happened.
41.	occurring	ŏ·kûr′ĭng	oc-cur-ring	Happening; taking place.
42.	ours	ourz	ours	Possessive of *we* used where no noun follows.
43.	outline	out′līne′	out-line	A profile; a silhouette; a summary or general sketch; significant points of a subject.
44.	parents	pâr′ĕnts	par-ents	Father and mother.
45.	passers-by	păs′ĕrz·bī′	pass-ers-by	Those who pass by.
46.	permitted	pĕr·mĭt′ĕd	per-mit-ted	Tolerated; allowed.
47.	policies	pŏl′ĭ·sĭz	pol-i-cies	Courses followed by a body of people.
48.	possesses	pŏ·zĕs′ĕz	pos-sess-es	Owns; controls.
49.	possession	pŏ·zĕsh′ŭn	pos-ses-sion	Ownership; thing possessed; control; occupancy.
▶ 50.	preparation	prĕp′à·rā′shŭn	prep-a-ra-tion	Act of making ready for use.
51.	production	prŏ·dŭk′shŭn	pro-duc-tion	Act of making goods available for people's wants and needs.
52.	properties	prŏp′ĕr·tĭz	prop-er-ties	Things owned; qualities.
53.	protected	prŏ·tĕk′tĕd	pro-tect-ed	Defended; covered; shielded.
54.	qualities	kwŏl′ĭ·tĭz	qual-i-ties	Characteristics; attributes; distinctive traits.
55.	quantities	kwŏn′tĭ·tĭz	quan-ti-ties	Amounts.
56.	quoted	kwōt′ĕd	quot-ed	Referred to as an authority; repeated the word of another.
57.	rendered	rĕn′dĕrd	ren-dered	Paid back; yielded; furnished.
58.	renewal	rĕ·nū′ăl	re-new-al	State or process of being renewed.
59.	responsibility	rĕ·spŏn′sĭ·bĭl′ĭ·tĭ	re-spon-si-bil-i-ty	A charge for which one is accountable.
60.	responsible	rĕ·spŏn′sĭ·b'l	re-spon-si-ble	Answerable; liable; accountable.
61.	salaries	săl′à·rĭz	sal-a-ries	Compensations paid for services; wages.
62.	satisfied	săt′ĭs·fīd	sat-is-fied	Paid off; convinced; contented.
63.	security	sĕ·kū′rĭ·tĭ	se-cu-ri-ty	Feeling of certainty; surety.

64.	statistics	stá·tĭs′tĭks	sta-tis-tics	Numerical facts; data.
65.	tariffs	tăr′ĭfs	tar-iffs	Taxes or duties imposed by a government on goods imported or exported.
66.	tourist	tŏŏr′ĭst	tour-ist	One who travels for pleasure.
67.	traitor	trā′tẽr	trai-tor	A person who betrays a confidence, a trust, or his country.
68.	twenty-five	twĕn′tĭ·fīv′	twen-ty-five	Cardinal number, following *twenty-four*.
69.	universal	ū′nĭ·vûr′săl	u-ni-ver-sal	Including the whole; prevailing everywhere.
70.	variety	vá·rī′ĕ·tĭ	va-ri-e-ty	Change; diversity.
71.	withdrew	wĭth·drōō′	with-drew	Past tense of *withdraw*.
72.	women's	wĭm′ĕnz	wom-en's	Plural possessive of *woman*.
73.	writing	rīt′ĭng	writ-ing	Handwriting; the act of one who writes.
74.	yield	yēld	yield	To surrender; to permit; to concede.
75.	yielded	yēld′ĕd	yield-ed	Complied; produced; conceded.

Lesson 2

1.	admiration	ăd′mĭ·rā′shŭn	ad-mi-ra-tion	Holding esteem for a person or thing.
2.	affectionate	á·fĕk′shŭn·ĭt	af-fec-tion-ate	Devoted; fond; loving; tender.
3.	amusement	á·mūz′mĕnt	a-muse-ment	That which entertains.
4.	ancient	ān′shĕnt	an-cient	Old; old-fashioned; belonging to the past.
5.	appointment	á·point′mĕnt	ap-point-ment	The designation of power or authority; an engagement.
6.	arguing	är′gū·ĭng	ar-gu-ing	Disputing; reasoning.
7.	broadcast	brôd′kåst′	broad-cast	Scattered in all directions; transmitted by broadcasting.
8.	buyer	bī′ẽr	buy-er	A person who buys.
9.	bylaws	bī′lôz′	by-laws	Rules and regulations for a group or society of persons.
10.	carriage	kăr′ĭj	car-riage	A wheeled vehicle used for transporting persons.
11.	chairman	châr′măn	chair-man	The presiding officer of a meeting or of a group of persons.
12.	clothes	klōthz	clothes	Dress; apparel.
13.	collectible	kŏ·lĕkt′ĭ·b′l	col-lect-i-ble	Capable of being collected.
14.	collection	kŏ·lĕk′shŭn	col-lec-tion	An accumulation; process of collecting.
15.	comparison	kŏm·păr′ĭ·sŭn	com-par-i-son	A relative estimate; act of comparing one to another.
16.	competition	kŏm′pē·tĭsh′ŭn	com-pe-ti-tion	Rivalry; a match; a contest.
17.	conceive	kŏn·sēv′	con-ceive	To form an image; to think; to suppose.

18.	correspondent	kŏr'ĕ·spŏn'dĕnt	cor-re-spond-ent	A person with whom one communicates by letter; a newspaper person who contributes news from a specific location.
19.	correspondents	kŏr'ĕ·spŏn'dĕnts	cor-re-spond-ents	Plural of *correspondent* (see above).
20.	crystallize	krĭs'tăl·īz	crys-tal-lize	To cause to form crystals; to assume a definite form.
21.	customer	kŭs'tŭm·ẽr	cus-tom-er	A patron; one who gives his business to a particular store or firm.
22.	customers	kŭs'tŭm·ẽrz	cus-tom-ers	Plural of *customer* (see above).
23.	deliberately	dĕ·lĭb'ẽr·ĭt·lĭ	de-lib-er-ate-ly	Unhurriedly; voluntarily.
24.	dyeing	dī'ĭng	dye-ing	Process of fixing coloring matters permanently into materials.
25.	earnings	ûr'nĭngs	earn-ings	Wages.
26.	enforceable	ĕn·fōrs'á·b'l	en-force-a-ble	Possible of being put into force.
27.	equality	ĕ·kwŏl'ĭ·tĭ	e-qual-i-ty	A condition of being equal.
28.	examination	ĕg·zăm'ĭ·nā'shŭn	ex-am-i-na-tion	A search; a testing of knowledge or information.
29.	expediency	ĕks·pē'dĭ·ĕn·sĭ	ex-pe-di-en-cy	Fitness; condition of being expedient.
30.	expensive	ĕks·pĕn'sĭv	ex-pen-sive	Costly.
31.	fashionable	făsh'ŭn·á·b'l	fash-ion-a-ble	Conforming to fashion; stylish.
32.	glorious	glō'rĭ·ŭs	glo-ri-ous	Splendid in appearance; magnificent.
33.	graduating	grăd'ū·āt·ĭng	grad-u-at-ing	Passing from one level of education to another; changing gradually.
34.	himself	hĭm·sĕlf'	him-self	A pronoun to place emphasis on the third person singular masculine.
35.	honorable	ŏn'ẽr·á·b'l	hon-or-a-ble	Commendable; respectable; upright.
36.	industrial	ĭn·dŭs'trĭ·ăl	in-dus-tri-al	Having to do with industry.
37.	insurance	ĭn·shoōr'ăns	in-sur-ance	A contract in which one party guarantees another against loss caused by a contingent event.
38.	leisure	lē'zhẽr	lei-sure	Free time; time free from work.
39.	loud-speaker	loud'spēk'ẽr	loud-speak-er	A device to produce sounds loud enough to be heard at a distance.
40.	manufacturer	măn'ū·făk't̬ûr·ẽr	man-u-fac-tur-er	One who manufactures or makes articles.
41.	marvelous	mär'vĕl·ŭs	mar-vel-ous	Astonishing; incredible.
42.	miner	mīn'ẽr	min-er	A worker in a mine; one who digs in a mine.

43. neglected	nĕg·lĕkt′ĕd	neg-lect-ed	Ignored; disregarded; slighted.
44. Negroes'	nē′grōz	Ne-groes'	Plural possessive of *Negro*.
45. ninety	nīn′tĭ	nine-ty	Cardinal number, following *eighty-nine*.
46. opening	ō′pĕn·ĭng	o-pen-ing	A gap; an opportunity.
47. over-all	ō′vēr·ôl′	o-ver-all	Comprising everything.
48. parcel post	pär′sĕl pōst	par-cel post	That branch of the post office charged with collecting, transmitting, and delivering parcels.
49. permitting	pēr·mĭt′ĭng	per-mit-ting	Consenting to; granting; letting.
50. personality	pûr′sŭ·năl′ĭ·tĭ	per-son-al-i-ty	Distinctive personal characteristics.
▶
51. plaintiffs	plăn′tĭfs	plain-tiffs	The complaining parties in lawsuits.
52. possibilities	pŏs′ĭ·bĭl′ĭ·tĭz	pos-si-bil-i-ties	Those things that are attainable or feasible.
53. potatoes	pô·tā′tōz	po-ta-toes	The edible tuber of a plant of the nightshade family.
54. preferred	prē·fûrd′	pre-ferred	Favored; advanced.
55. reign	rān	reign	*v.* To have power or authority as a sovereign. *n.* Royal authority.
56. relating	rē·lāt′ĭng	re-lat-ing	Narrating; recounting.
57. reputation	rĕp′û·tā′shŭn	rep-u-ta-tion	The character commonly identified with a person.
58. requested	rē·kwĕst′ĕd	re-quest-ed	Asked; solicited.
59. scruples	skrōō′p'lz	scru-ples	Qualms.
60. secretarial	sĕk′rē·târ′ĭ·ăl	sec-re-tar-i-al	Pertaining to a secretary.
61. secretaries	sĕk′rē·tĕr′ĭz	sec-re-tar-ies	Business workers who attend to correspondence and records of a confidential nature.
62. shield	shēld	shield	*n.* A cover for protective purposes. *v.* To defend; to protect.
63. smoother	smōōth′ĕr	smooth-er	Comparative of *smooth*.
64. soared	sōrd	soared	Mounted; ascended; rose.
65. somewhat	sŭm′hwŏt′	some-what	Something; an unspecified amount.
66. sparkling	spär′klĭng	spar-kling	Putting forth sparks; flashing.
67. terribly	tĕr′ĭ·blĭ	ter-ri-bly	Dreadfully.
68. trial	trī′ăl	tri-al	An attempt; a test.
69. understanding	ŭn′dĕr·stănd′ĭng	un-der-stand-ing	Capability of comprehending and judging.
70. vacation	vă·kā′shŭn	va-ca-tion	A rest; a period of time away from regular work.
71. Western	wĕs′tĕrn	West-ern	Characteristic of a region specifically called *the West*.
72. wholly	hōl′lĭ	whol-ly	Fully; totally; completely.
73. withdrawal	wĭth·drô′ăl	with-draw-al	A retreat; a recalling.

| 74. wrapping | răp′ĭng | wrap-ping | Enclosing; enfolding something in a wrapper. |
| 75. yours | yŏŏrz | yours | The form of the possessive *your* used when no noun follows. |

Lesson 3

1. acknowledging	ăk·nŏl′ĕj·ĭng	ac-knowl-edg-ing	Recognizing; admitting; confessing.
2. acquaintance	ă·kwān′tăns	ac-quaint-ance	A person whom one knows but may not know well enough to consider a friend.
3. advertising	ăd′vĕr·tīz′ĭng	ad-ver-tis-ing	A form of public announcement for selling a commodity, gaining employment, etc.
4. agencies	ā′jĕn·sĭz	a-gen-cies	Establishments for transacting business in behalf of others.
5. agreeable	à·grē′à·b′l	a-gree-a-ble	Pleasant; conformable; ready to consent.
6. annoyance	ă·noi′ăns	an-noy-ance	A nuisance; a vexation.
7. approximately	ă·prŏk′sĭ·mĭt·lĭ	ap-prox-i-mate-ly	Nearly.
8. astonishment	ăs·tŏn′ĭsh·mĕnt	as-ton-ish-ment	State of amazement.
9. bankers	băngk′ĕrz	bank-ers	Persons who conduct the business of a bank.
10. beginning	bĕ·gĭn′ĭng	be-gin-ning	The origin; the start.
11. bushels	bŏŏsh′ĕlz	bush-els	Dry measures; four-peck quantities.
12. capitalism	kăp′ĭ·tăl·ĭz′m	cap-i-tal-ism	An economic system in which capital and capitalists constitute the principal part.
13. committed	kŏ·mĭt′ĕd	com-mit-ted	Pledged; entrusted; consigned.
14. communication	kŏ·mū′nĭ·kā′shŭn	com-mu-ni-ca-tion	An interchange of thoughts or opinions.
15. congratulations	kŏn·grăt′ŭ·lā′shŭnz	con-grat-u-la-tions	Expressions of happiness for another's joy or success.
16. construction	kŏn·strŭk′shŭn	con-struc-tion	Act of forming or devising.
17. continuous	kŏn·tĭn′û·ŭs	con-tin-u-ous	Continual; without interruption.
18. director	dĭ·rĕk′tĕr	di-rec-tor	One who guides or orders.
19. disciplinary	dĭs′ĭ·plĭ·nĕr′ĭ	dis-ci-pli-nar-y	Corrective; relating to discipline.
20. disposition	dĭs′pŏ·zĭsh′ŭn	dis-po-si-tion	Temperament; character.
21. distribution	dĭs′trĭ·bū′shŭn	dis-tri-bu-tion	Apportionment; arrangement into parts.

22. efficiency	ĕ·fĭsh'ĕn·sĭ	ef-fi-cien-cy	Efficient operation; the competency with which the desired result is produced.
23. eighteen	ā'tēn'	eight-een	Cardinal number, following *seventeen*.
24. enterprise	ĕn'tēr·prīz	en-ter-prise	A venture; an undertaking.
25. existence ▶	ĕg·zĭs'tĕns	ex-ist-ence	State of existing; continuance in life.
26. favorable	fā'vēr·à·b'l	fa-vor-a-ble	Approving; advantageous.
27. fierce	fērs	fierce	Furious; raging; ferocious; inhuman.
28. gracious	grā'shŭs	gra-cious	Cordial; genial; sociable.
29. homeward	hōm'wērd	home-ward	Being in the direction of home.
30. ignorance	ĭg'nô·rǎns	ig-no-rance	Want of information or knowledge.
31. ignorant	ĭg'nô·rǎnt	ig-no-rant	Uninstructed; uninformed; illiterate.
32. inches	ĭnch'ĕz	inch-es	Plural of *inch*, a measure of length.
33. injuries	ĭn'jēr·ĭz	in-ju-ries	Damages to feelings, rights, property, body.
34. instruction	ĭn·strŭk'shŭn	in-struc-tion	A direction; an order.
35. interrupt	ĭn'tĕ·rŭpt'	in-ter-rupt	To break into.
36. leadership	lēd'ēr·shĭp	lead-er-ship	Quality of being a leader.
37. legislation	lĕj'ĭs·lā'shŭn	leg-is-la-tion	Preparation and enactment of laws.
38. lifetime	līf'tīm'	life-time	The length of time that a life continues.
39. meanness	mēn'nĕs	mean-ness	Quality of being mean.
40. meanwhile	mēn'hwīl'	mean-while	At the same time.
41. mysterious	mĭs·tēr'ĭ·ŭs	mys-te-ri-ous	Pertaining to mystery; beyond one's power to explain.
42. obligation	ŏb'lĭ·gā'shŭn	ɔb-li-ga-tion	A duty; a promise by which one is bound.
43. offset	ŏf'sĕt'	off-set	To balance; to counterbalance.
44. our	our	our	Possessive plural of the personal pronoun *I*.
45. package	păk'ĭj	pack-age	A bundle prepared for storage or transportation.
46. postpone	pōst·pōn'	post-pone	To put off; to delay; to defer.
47. priest	prēst	priest	One of the clergy as distinguished from the laity.
48. promotional	prô·mō'shŭn·ǎl	pro-mo-tion-al	Pertaining to advancement or promotion.

49. **proposal**	prô·pōz′ăl	pro-pos-al	A proposition; a plan; an offer
50. **protection** ▶	prô·těk′shŭn	pro-tec-tion	Act of shielding, covering, or guarding.
51. **questionnaire**	kwěs′chŭn·âr′	ques-tion-naire	A set of questions submitted to several persons to get data for a study.
52. **rationing**	răsh′ŭn·ĭng	ra-tion-ing	Allotting in fixed amounts.
53. **readily**	rĕd′ĭ·lĭ	read-i-ly	Quickly; promptly.
54. **reasonable**	rē′z′n·à·b′l	rea-son-a-ble	Just; fair-minded; moderately priced.
55. **receipt**	rĕ·sēt′	re-ceipt	A written acknowledgment of the taking or receiving of goods or money.
56. **reference**	rĕf′ĕr·ĕns	ref-er-ence	Relation; respect.
57. **relieve**	rĕ·lēv′	re-lieve	To lighten; to alleviate.
58. **requirements**	rĕ·kwīr′mĕnts	re-quire-ments	Necessities; needs.
59. **reversible**	rĕ·vûr′sĭ·b′l	re-vers-i-ble	Finished on both sides so that either side may be used.
60. **salesmen**	sālz′mĕn	sales-men	Those whose occupation is selling.
61. **securities**	sĕ·kū′rĭ·tĭz	se-cu-ri-ties	An evidence of property, as bonds, stocks, etc.
62. **self-confidence**	sĕlf′kŏn′fĭ·dĕn s	self-con-fi-dence	Self-reliance; state of being confident of oneself.
63. **sensation**	sĕn·sā′shŭn	scn-sa-tion	A rather indefinite bodily feeling; a condition of excitement.
64. **sensible**	sĕn′sĭ·b′l	sen-si-ble	Intelligent; reasonable.
65. **severely**	sĕ·vĕr′lĭ	se-vere-ly	Gravely; sternly.
66. **someone**	sŭm′wŭn′	some-one	Some person; somebody.
67. **somewhere**	sŭm′hwâr′	some-where	In one place or another.
68. **stationary**	stā′shŭn·ĕr′ĭ	sta-tion-ar-y	Stable; fixed; not moving.
69. **steadily**	stĕd′ĭ·lĭ	stead-i-ly	Evenly; uniformly; unfalteringly; constantly.
70. **submitted**	sŭb·mĭt′ĕd	sub-mit-ted	Yielded; surrendered; offered.
71. **tie-ins**	tī′ĭnz′	tie-ins	Items that may be related to other items as units.
72. **traditional**	trà·dĭsh′ŭn·ăl	tra-di-tion-al	Conforming to tradition.
73. **transferable**	trăns·fûr′à·b′l	trans-fer-a-ble	Capable of being moved from one place to another.
74. **whose**	hōōz	whose	Possessive of *who*.
75. **year's**	yĕrz	year's	Possessive of *year*.

Lesson 4

1. accomplishment	ă·kŏm′plĭsh·mĕnt	ac-com-plish-ment	An acquirement; a completion.
2. advertisement	ăd·vûr′tĭz·mĕnt	ad-ver-tise-ment	A public notice intended to sell a commodity.
3. agricultural	ăg′rĭ·kŭl′tự̂r·ăl	ag-ri-cul-tur-al	Pertaining to the science of cultivating the ground.
4. anybody	ĕn′ĭ·bŏd′ĭ	an-y-bod-y	Any person.
5. anyway	ĕn′ĭ·wā	an-y-way	Anyhow; in any case.
6. assurance	ă·shŏŏr′ăns	as-sur-ance	State of being sure; security; certainty.
7. atomic	ă·tŏm′ĭk	a-tom-ic	Pertaining to atoms; very tiny.
8. attached	ă·tăcht′	at-tached	Adhered; fastened; tied; connected.
9. attorneys	ă·tûr′nĭz	at-tor-neys	Lawyers; legal agents.
10. attractive	ă·trăk′tĭv	at-trac-tive	Charming; having the power to attract.
11. audience	ô′dĭ·ĕns	au-di-ence	An assembly of listeners or spectators; a formal interview.
12. budgeting	bŭj′ĕt·ĭng	budg-et-ing	Estimating the income and expenses of a government, business, or household for a given future period.
13. cargoes	kär′gōz	car-goes	Loads; freight to be transported.
14. chemicals	kĕm′ĭ·kăls	chem-i-cals	Substances obtained by chemical processes.
15. circularize	sûr′kự̂·lēr·ĭz	cir-cu-lar-ize	To make circular; to distribute circulars to.
16. commodities	kŏ·mŏd′ĭ·tĭz	com-mod-i-ties	Things that are bought and sold.
17. company's	kŭm′pȧ·nĭz	com-pa-ny's	Possessive of *company*.
18. contribution	kŏn′trĭ·bū′shŭn	con-tri-bu-tion	The sum contributed or given for a cause.
19. co-operation	kŏ·ŏp′ēr·ā′shŭn	co-op-er-a-tion	Group action for mutual benefit.
20. declaration	dĕk′lȧ·rā′shŭn	dec-la-ra-tion	An announcement; an assertion.
21. decoration	dĕk′ô·rā′shŭn	dec-o-ra-tion	An ornament; a badge of honor.
22. demonstration	dĕm′ŭn·strā′shŭn	dem-on-stra-tion	An outward expression or display; a public display of the merits of a product.
23. desirable	dĕ·zīr′ȧ·b'l	de-sir-a-ble	Agreeable; pleasing.
24. determination	dĕ·tûr′mĭ·nā′shŭn	de-ter-mi-na-tion	Conclusion; impulsion; firmness.

25.	distinction ►	dĭs·tĭngk′shŭn	dis-tinc-tion	Eminence; state of being distinguishable; discrimination.
26.	doubtful	dout′fŏŏl	doubt-ful	Not clear or certain.
27.	edition	ė·dĭsh′ŭn	e-di-tion	The complete number of copies of a work published at one time.
28.	effective	ė·fĕk′tĭv	ef-fec-tive	Impressive; striking; efficient.
29.	efficient	ė·fĭsh′ĕnt	ef-fi-cient	Highly capable or productive.
30.	encouragement	ĕn·kûr′ĭj·mĕnt	en-cour-age-ment	Act of inspiring with courage, spirit, or hope.
31.	everywhere	ĕv′ẽr·ĭ·hwâr′	ev-er-y-where	In every place.
32.	exhausted	ĕg·zôst′ĕd	ex-haust-ed	Depleted; tired.
33.	exports	ĕks′pōrts	ex-ports	Merchandise or commodities sent abroad to foreign countries.
34.	facilities	fȧ·sĭl′ĭ·tĭz	fa-cil-i-ties	Those things that make an operation or task easier.
35.	faculties	făk′ŭl·tĭz	fac-ul-ties	Powers of the mind; natural aptitudes; abilities to act.
36.	falsehood	fôls′hŏŏd	false-hood	A statement that lacks truth or accuracy.
37.	freight	frāt	freight	The amount paid for transporting goods; cargo.
38.	frighten	frīt′′n	fright-en	To alarm; to scare.
39.	handkerchief	hăng′kẽr·chĭf	hand-ker-chief	A small piece of cloth used for wiping the nose, eyes, or face.
40.	healthy	hĕl′thĭ	health-y	Well; sound; wholesome.
41.	horrified	hŏr′ĭ·fīd	hor-ri-fied	Dismayed; stricken with horror.
42.	illustration	ĭl′ŭs·trā′shŭn	il-lus-tra-tion	An instance; an example; a picture, drawing, chart, etc., used to explain or decorate a book, article, etc.
43.	inquiries	ĭn·kwīr′ĭz	in-quir-ies	Questions; investigations.
44.	inspiration	ĭn′spĭ·rā′shŭn	in-spi-ra-tion	Enthusiasm; state of being intellectually or emotionally moved.
45.	interference	ĭn′tẽr·fẽr′ĕns	in-ter-fer-ence	A clashing; a hampering; an obstructing.
46.	investigating	ĭn·vĕs′tĭ·gāt·ĭng	in-ves-ti-gat-ing	Searching into by examination and observation of facts.
47.	knitted	nĭt′ĕd	knit-ted	United closely; grown together; interlocked.

48. lightning	lĭt′nĭng	light-ning	The flashing of light caused by a discharge of electricity in the air; a discharge of atmospheric electricity.
49. meantime	mēn′tīm′	mean-time	At the same time.
▶ 50. measurement	mĕzh′ẽr·mĕnt	meas-ure-ment	Act of determining extent or amount.
51. mechanical	mē·kăn′ĭ·kăl	me-chan-i-cal	Proceeding automatically; pertaining to work done by machine.
52. men's	mĕnz	men's	Possessive of *men*.
53. moreover	mōr·ō′vẽr	more-o-ver	Further.
54. necessarily	nĕs′ĕ·sĕr′ĭ·lĭ	nec-es-sar-i-ly	Inevitably.
55. ourselves	our·sĕlvz′	our-selves	An emphasized form of the pronoun *we*.
56. patience	pā′shĕns	pa-tience	Forbearance; quality of being patient.
57. performance	pẽr·fôr′măns	per-form-ance	A deed; a public presentation.
58. pianos	pĭ·ăn′ōz	pi-an-os	Plural of *piano*.
59. proposition	prŏp′ō·zĭsh′ŭn	prop-o-si-tion	A proposal; a plan.
60. prosperous	prŏs′pẽr·ŭs	pros-per-ous	Favorable; thriving.
61. reaches	rēch′ĕz	reach-es	Influences; impresses; gains; achieves.
62. referred	rē·fûrd′	re-ferred	Directed; related.
63. referring	rē·fûr′ĭng	re-fer-ring	Making reference; directing.
64. regulation	rĕg′ û·lā′shŭn	reg-u-la-tion	A law; a regulating principle; a rule.
65. remarkable	rē·mär′ká·b'l	re-mark-a-ble	Conspicuous; extraordinary; noteworthy.
66. resistance	rē·zĭs′tăns	re-sist-ance	An opposing force.
67. shortly	shôrt′lĭ	short-ly	Soon; briefly; abruptly.
68. simplicity	sĭm·plĭs′ĭ·tĭ	sim-plic-i-ty	Clearness; plainness.
69. situated	sĭt′û·āt′ĕd	sit-u-at-ed	Located; having a site.
70. throughout	thrōō·out′	through-out	Everywhere; in each part.
71. veil	vāl	veil	A piece of fabric that conceals or protects.
72. vein	vān	vein	A tubular vessel that carries blood back to the heart; a strain.
73. vigorous	vĭg′ẽr·ŭs	vig-or-ous	Robust; energetic; strong.
74. whenever	hwĕn·ĕv′ẽr	when-ev-er	At whatever time.
75. wives	wīvz	wives	Plural of *wife*.

Lesson 5 Check-Up

Unit Test. Your teacher will dictate 50 words chosen from the lessons in Unit 8. These words are selected to test your mastery of the new words in this unit. Listen closely as each word is dictated, recall the rule that applies to the word, spell the word carefully, and write plainly in order to assure yourself of a fair test.

Proofreading Test. In the following letter, some of the italicized words are misspelled. Copy the entire letter, making whatever corrections are necessary in the spelling of the words.

Dear Mr. Stone:

Some one with *twenty-five years'* experience in the *freight* business would be a *desireable employee* in your organization. If this experience included almost everything from moving *pianoes* to *wraping* packages, you would be doubly glad to place such a man on your *companies* payroll.

Begining next week, I shall be available. I am *satisfied* that my experience can be *valuable* to you. May I call for an appointment?

Sincerely yours,

Cumulative Test. Your teacher will now dictate 40 words chosen from Units 1 through 7. These words will test your retention of the correct spelling of words in these units. Spell carefully and write plainly.

Checking Your Tests. Your teacher will give you directions for checking the unit test, the proofreading test, and the cumulative test.

Error Analysis. Classify the errors that you made by noting the type of error beside each word that you misspelled.

Review. Use the appropriate attack procedures for studying the words that you misspelled on the unit test, on the proofreading test, and on the cumulative test.

Retest. The retest will tell you if you have mastered the words in Units 1 through 8. If you misspelled words on the retest, continue your attack procedures until you are sure that you can spell all the words correctly.

PART  3

NEW
WORDS
FOR
YOUR
GENERAL
BUSINESS
VOCABULARY

Unit 1 Sound Words

Sound is the key to the correct spelling of the words in this unit. Spend a few moments reviewing "Spotting Sound Errors," beginning on page 3, and then begin your study of Lessons 1-4 of this unit, applying the following procedures:

Preview. Your teacher will dictate a list of 75 general-business-vocabulary words. Number a sheet of paper from 1 to 75. Spell as many of the words as you can, but attempt only the words that you are quite sure you know how to spell. If you do not know the spelling of a word, place a question mark (?) beside the number.

Checking Performance. Compare your spellings with the words in the appropriate lesson. Place an *X* beside each word that you misspelled. To the right of any misspelled or omitted word, write the correct spelling.

Error Analysis. Classify the errors that you made by noting the type of error beside each word that you misspelled. For instance, if an error was caused by adding unnecessary letters, write "addition" beside the word. Refer to Section One if you need to be reminded of the types of errors.

Attack Procedures. Attack procedures for sound-type errors were presented in Section One, beginning on page 7. Review the corrective technique recommended for each type of error.

Learning to Spell New Words. The pretest words that you did not know how to spell now appear on your answer sheet preceded by a question mark. Use a separate sheet of paper to practice those words, following the SEE, SAY, SPELL, and WRITE routine (see pages 39-41). Hand in the drill paper to your instructor.

Lesson 1

1. accuracy	ăk′ů·ra·sĭ	ac-cu-ra-cy	Freedom from error or mistake.
2. agitation	ăj′ĭ·tā′shŭn	ag-i-ta-tion	A disturbance or an excitement caused by agreeable or disagreeable circumstances.
3. alert	a·lûrt′	a-lert	Attentive; watchful; ready to act.
4. alleged	a·lĕjd′	al-leged	Declared as if under oath.
5. analysis	a·năl′ĭ·sĭs	a-nal-y-sis	An examination of an object or statement to study its parts.
6. apparel	a·păr′ĕl	ap-par-el	A person's clothing or garments.
7. applause	a·plôz′	ap-plause	A public demonstration of approval.
8. assets	ăs′ĕts	as-sets	Items of value owned by a person, firm, or estate; cash and/or property.
9. assumption	a·sŭmp′shŭn	as-sump-tion	The act of taking for granted.
10. ballot	băl′ŭt	bal-lot	A method of voting in which a written or printed list is used; the entire number of votes cast at an election.
11. banquet	băng′kwĕt	ban-quet	A ceremonious feast or public dinner often followed by speeches.
12. bottle	bŏt′′l	bot-tle	A glass container for liquids.
13. busy	bĭz′ĭ	bus-y	Actively engaged in some work, play, study, etc.
14. caliber	kăl′ĭ·bĕr	cal-i-ber	The diameter of something that is circular, as a bullet; mental capacity of a person; personal character.
15. cemetery	sĕm′ĕ·tĕr′ĭ	cem-e-ter-y	A graveyard; a burial ground.
16. characteristic	kăr′ăk·tĕr·ĭs′tĭk	char-ac-ter-is-tic	Serving to indicate that which is typical, different, or distinctive.
17. commencement	kŏ·mĕns′mĕnt	com-mence-ment	Act of beginning; the day on which colleges and universities grant degrees.
18. controversy	kŏn′trŏ·vûr′sĭ	con-tro-ver-sy	A dispute; a debate.

19. corrupt	kŏ·rŭpt′	cor-rupt	Depraved; of evil character; dishonest.
20. courteous	kûr′tē·ŭs	cour-te-ous	Having good manners; polite.
21. criticize	krĭt′ĭ·sīz	crit-i-cize	To find fault with; to pass judgment on.
22. currency	kûr′ĕn·sĭ	cur-ren-cy	Coin, government notes, and bank notes in circulation as a medium of exchange.
23. cylinder	sĭl′ĭn·dĕr	cyl-in-der	A curved surface, either solid or hollow; the chamber in an engine.
24. decade	dĕk′ād	dec-ade	A set or series of ten, as ten years.
▶ 25. deface	dĕ·fās′	de-face	To disfigure; to harm the appearance of.
26. delinquent	dĕ·lĭng′kwĕnt	de-lin-quent	Failing in a duty or obligation.
27. delivery	dĕ·lĭv′ēr·ĭ	de-liv-er-y	Transfer of goods from the seller to the buyer; a surrender.
28. deputy	dĕp′û·tĭ	dep-u-ty	A person appointed to act for or represent another.
29. disagreeable	dĭs′à·grē′à·b'l	dis-a-gree-a-ble	Unpleasant; offensive.
30. discover	dĭs·kŭv′ēr	dis-cov-er	To learn of for the first time; to find out; to gain some knowledge of.
31. experience	ĕks·pēr′ĭ·ĕns	ex-pe-ri-ence	Knowledge gained from learning, working, or observing.
32. explain	ĕks·plān′	ex-plain	To make plain; to interpret.
33. foliage	fō′lĭ·ĭj	fo-li-age	A collection of leaves, flowers, and branches.
34. garage	gà·räzh′	ga-rage	A building for automobiles; a repair shop for automobiles.
35. governor	gŭv′ēr·nēr	gov-er-nor	A person appointed as chief executive of a state in the United States; a small attachment for regulating the speed of an engine.
36. grammar	grăm′ēr	gram-mar	The characteristics of a language, including sounds, words, and their arrangement for speaking, reading, or writing.
37. incidentally	ĭn′sĭ·dĕn′tăl·ĭ	in-ci-den-tal-ly	In a casual manner; by the way.

38. incredible	ĭn·krĕd'ĭ·b'l	in-cred-i-ble	Too fantastic to be possible; too improbable to be believed.
39. innocence	ĭn'ô·sĕns	in-no-cence	The state of being free from guilt or wrong-doing.
40. jealousy	jĕl'ŭs·ĭ	jeal-ous-y	State or quality of being envious or resentful.
41. kindergarten	kĭn'dĕr·gär't'n	kin-der-gar-ten	A school for young children.
42. latitude	lăt'ĭ·tūd	lat-i-tude	Freedom from restrictions; freedom of action, thought, and speech; distance measured in degrees north and south from the equator.
43. mathematics	măth'ê·măt'ĭks	math-e-mat-ics	The science that treats of the relationship between measurement and quantities, including arithmetic, geometry, and algebra.
44. meeting	mēt'ĭng	meet-ing	An assembly of people for a purpose; a coming together; a junction.
45. menu	mĕn'ū	men-u	A list of food to be served at a meal.
46. minimum	mĭn'ĭ·mŭm	min-i-mum	The least amount possible, admissible, etc.; the lowest point recorded.
47. modify	mŏd'ĭ·fī	mod-i-fy	To change the form or qualities of; to alter somewhat, as a contract.
48. monograph	mŏn'ô·gráf	mon-o-graph	A treatise or a written account of a single thing or particular subject.
49. municipal	mû·nĭs'ĭ·păl	mu-nic-i-pal	Pertaining to the government of a town or city; pertaining to the internal affairs of a state or nation.
50. omission ►	ô·mĭsh'ŭn	o-mis-sion	Something that has been left out or omitted.
51. omit	ô·mĭt'	o-mit	To leave out; to fail to do something.
52. optician	ŏp·tĭsh'ăn	op-ti-cian	One who makes, or deals in, eyeglasses and optical instruments.
53. organized	ôr'găn·ĭzd	or-gan-ized	Formed into a whole for united action; systematized.

54. paid	pād	paid	Past tense and past participle of *pay;* discharged a debt or obligation; satisfied claims by giving money due.
55. panel	păn′ĕl	pan-el	A group of persons designated to lead a public discussion; a portion of a ceiling, door, or shutter.
56. paragraph	păr′à·gráf	par-a-graph	A subdivision of a letter, chapter, or newspaper article.
57. partial	pär′shăl	par-tial	Incomplete; only a part of the whole.
58. practically	prăk′tĭ·kăl·ĭ	prac-ti-cal-ly	In a practical manner; virtually.
59. presents	prĕ·zĕnts′	pre-sents	Introduces one person to another; bestows a gift formally.
60. propaganda	prŏp′à·găn′dà	prop-a-gan-da	An organized or concerted effort to spread certain doctrines or information.
61. qualify	kwŏl′ĭ·fī	qual-i-fy	To be competent; to modify; to name descriptively.
62. realize	rē′ăl·īz	re-al-ize	To understand clearly; to convert property or goods into money.
63. recommendation	rĕk′ŏ·mĕn·dā′shŭn	rec-om-men-da-tion	A letter or statement calling attention to a person's abilities, character, special qualities, and expressing commendation.
64. reconcile	rĕk′ŏn·sīl	rec-on-cile	To restore to a friendly relationship again; to bring into agreement or balance.
65. recreation	rĕk′rĕ·ā′shŭn	rec-re-a-tion	Agreeable exercise affording relaxation and enjoyment.
66. relatively	rĕl′à·tĭv·lĭ	rel-a-tive-ly	In proportion to other things; in a relative manner; comparatively.
67. repetition	rĕp′ĕ·tĭsh′ŭn	rep-e-ti-tion	The act of repeating an action or a performance.
68. schedule	skĕd′ūl	sched-ule	A detailed statement of plans to be followed or of events to come.
69. seized	sēzd	seized	Taken by force; confiscated.

70. spendthrift	spĕnd′thrĭft′	spend-thrift	A person who spends money unwisely.
71. surprised	sĕr·prīzd′	sur-prised	Astonished; amazed; taken unawares.
72. tyranny	tĭr′ă·nĭ	tyr-an-ny	Abuse of authority; undue harshness.
73. umbrella	ŭm·brĕl′ȧ	um-brel-la	A covering carried in the hand and used to shelter or protect one from rain or sunshine.
74. utilize	ū′tĭ·līz	u-ti-lize	To use profitably; to put to use.
75. voucher	vouch′ĕr	vouch-er	A receipt showing payment of a debt; a statement supporting the correctness of a bill or list of expenditures.

Lesson 2

1. action	ăk′shŭn	ac-tion	Motion or activity; the process of doing something; legal proceedings in which one demands his rights in a court of justice.
2. adjure	ȧ·jŏŏr′	ad-jure	To charge or command solemnly; to entreat or request.
3. airport	âr′pōrt′	air-port	A place where airplanes may land to make repairs, to refuel, or to discharge or take on passengers or cargo.
4. antique	ăn·tēk′	an-tique	Old; old-fashioned.
5. appease	ȧ·pēz′	ap-pease	To bring peace and quiet to a situation; to satisfy; to be willing to be just and fair so as to win over an opponent.
6. auditor	ô′dĭ·tĕr	au-di-tor	A person who examines and checks accounting records; a listener.
7. authentic	ô·thĕn′tĭk	au-then-tic	Reliable; genuine; true.
8. billion	bĭl′yŭn	bil-lion	A thousand millions (1,000,000,-000).
9. bus	bŭs	bus	A motor coach used for transportation.
10. capacity	kȧ·păs′ĭ·tĭ	ca-pac-i-ty	Cubic contents of a room or of space; the ability of receiving and holding knowledge, liquid, etc.; measure of output.
11. charter	chär′tĕr	char-ter	A written document granting a corporation rights or privileges.
12. code	kōd	code	A collection of rules and regulations; a list of letters or words used for secrecy to represent words; a digest of the laws of a country.

13. company	kŭm'pá·nĭ	com-pa-ny	A number of persons associated for a joint purpose, especially for operating a business.
14. condition	kŏn·dĭsh'ŭn	con-di-tion	Something that is established or agreed upon as a prerequisite of something else; an essential part of an agreement.
15. conflict	kŏn·flĭkt'	con-flict	To clash; to oppose; to disagree.
16. consumer	kŏn·sūm'ĕr	con-sum-er	One who uses goods or services.
17. court	kōrt	court	An open space, as a short street; a place where justice is served.
18. data	dā'tá	da-ta	Plural of *datum;* available facts, figures, or information.
19. decline	dě·klīn'	de-cline	To fail to accept; to refuse; to incline downward.
20. default	dě·fôlt'	de-fault	Failure to pay a financial obligation; failure to participate in a scheduled match.
21. definition	děf'ĭ·nish'ŭn	def-i-ni-tion	The explanation of the meaning of a word or of a phrase.
22. delegation	děl'ė·gā'shŭn	del-e-ga-tion	A group of persons chosen to represent others, as at a convention or an assembly.
23. deplete	dě·plēt'	de-plete	To empty or reduce, as the amount of stock on hand.
24. depot	dē'pō	de-pot	A railroad station; a place where supplies are stored.
25. discuss ►	dĭs·kŭs'	dis-cuss	To debate; to talk over.
26. duplicate	dū'plĭ·kåt	du-pli-cate	An exact copy of the original; anything exactly like something else.
27. eloquence	ĕl'ō·kwĕns	el-o-quence	Language characterized by fluency, power, and persuasiveness.
28. eminent	ĕm'ĭ·nĕnt	em-i-nent	Distinguished; high in rank or reputation.
29. energetic	ĕn'ĕr·jět'ĭk	en-er-get-ic	Having vigorous activity.
30. equivalent	ė·kwĭv'á·lĕnt	e-quiv-a-lent	*adj.* Equal in value. *n.* A thing of the same value, weight, power.
31. extravagant	ĕks·trăv'á·gănt	ex-trav-a-gant	Costing more than one can afford; exorbitant; excessively high.
32. fragrant	frā'grănt	fra·grant	Having a sweet-smelling and pleasing odor.
33. horizontal	hŏr'ĭ·zŏn'tăl	hor-i-zon-tal	Pertaining to a position that is parallel to the horizon.
34. hospitality	hŏs'pĭ·tăl'ĭ·tĭ	hos-pi-tal-i-ty	Kind and gracious treatment of guests.
35. humorous	hū'mĕr·ŭs	hu-mor-ous	Amusing; funny; full of humor.
36. implement	ĭm'plě·mĕnt	im-ple-ment	An instrument or a tool necessary for the performance of something.
37. insignificant	ĭn'sĭg·nĭf'ĭ·kănt	in-sig-nif-i-cant	Unimportant; of no consequence.
38. invalidate	ĭn·văl'ĭ·dāt	in-val-i-date	To deprive of legal force.

39.	jurisdiction	jŏŏr′ĭs·dĭk′shŭn	ju-ris-dic-tion	The legal authority of a court to render a binding decision.
40.	maximum	măk′sĭ·mŭm	max-i-mum	The greatest quantity or value possible; the highest value allowed.
41.	miniature	mĭn′ĭ·á·tụ̄r	min-i-a-ture	A representation of something on a very small scale; a very small painting.
42.	monotonous	mŏ·nŏt′ŏ·nŭs	mo-not-o-nous	Lacking in variety; sounded with very little inflection.
43.	mortality	môr·tăl′ĭ·tĭ	mor-tal-i-ty	Frequency of deaths; death rate; the proportion of deaths in a specified number of people.
44.	muscular	mŭs′kû·lĕr	mus-cu-lar	Having well-developed muscles; husky; strong.
45.	mutilate	mū′tĭ·lāt	mu-ti-late	To maim; to disable; to render imperfect by removing or destroying an important part of.
46.	negative	nĕg′á·tĭv	neg-a-tive	Expressing denial; indicating a quantity to be subtracted; lacking positive action.
47.	negligence	nĕg′lĭ·jĕns	neg-li-gence	State of being negligent; failure to exercise that degree of care required of a prudent person under the circumstances.
48.	nominal	nŏm′ĭ·năl	nom-i-nal	Existing in name only; not real or actual.
49.	nominee	nŏm′ĭ·nē′	nom-i-nee	One who is nominated to fill an office or to run for election.
50.	notify	nō′tĭ·fī	no-ti-fy	To give notice of something; to inform.
51.	orbit	ôr′bĭt	or-bit	A curved path followed by a planet around another planet or body; region of activity, influence, etc.
52.	paralyze	păr′á·līz	par-a-lyze	To make helpless or ineffective.
53.	perennial	pĕr·ĕn′ĭ·ăl	per-en-ni-al	Lasting for an indefinite period; continuing without interruption.
54.	postal	pōs′tăl	post-al	Pertaining to the post office or mail service.
55.	predominant	prē·dŏm′ĭ·nănt	pre-dom-i-nant	Having controlling power; surpassing others in position, influence, etc.
56.	prevalent	prĕv′á·lĕnt	prev-a-lent	In general use or acceptance; widespread.
57.	radiator	rā′dĭ·ā′tĕr	ra-di-a-tor	A heating device through which steam or hot water passes.
58.	repetitious	rĕp′ĕ·tĭsh′ŭs	rep-e-ti-tious	That which is characterized by tedious repetition.
59.	resignation	rĕz′ĭg·nā′shŭn	res-ig-na-tion	The act of resigning, as from an office or a position; state of being submissive.
60.	ridiculous	rĭ·dĭk′û·lŭs	ri-dic-u-lous	Too absurd to be considered; laughable.

61. shortage	shôr′tĭj	short-age	A deficiency in the amount required or stated.
62. stimulus	stĭm′ũ·lŭs	stim-u-lus	An incentive that leads to action; something that excites the activity of a muscle, organ, or nerve.
63. subordinate	sŭ·bôr′dĭ·nĭt	sub-or-di-nate	One who is under the authority of a superior; one who is lower in rank; a secondary.
64. suburb	sŭb′ûrb	sub-urb	A district or a residential section outside the limits of a city or town.
65. supplement	sŭp′lĕ·mĕnt	sup-ple-ment	Something that is added to complete a thing; an addition in a book to supply deficiencies or correct errors.
66. symptom	sĭmp′tŭm	symp-tom	A sign or feeling that serves as an indication of a disease or disorder; a circumstance that may accompany something and serve as evidence.
67. technical	tĕk′nĭ·kăl	tech-ni-cal	Pertaining to the useful or mechanic arts; peculiar to a particular trade, art, profession, etc.
68. temperament	tĕm′pĕr·à·mĕnt	tem-per-a-ment	The frame of mind or type of mental outlook of a person.
69. temperance	tĕm′pĕr·ăns	tem-per-ance	Moderation in the use of intoxicants; moderation in eating, drinking, showing emotion, etc.
70. terminate	tûr′mĭ·nāt	ter-mi-nate	To put an end to; to finish; to complete.
71. tournament	tŏŏr′nà·mĕnt	tour-na-ment	An athletic meeting, consisting of contests in numerous sports; a series of contests.
72. treacherous	trĕch′ẽr·ŭs	treach-er-ous	Traitorous; unreliable; betraying a trust.
73. ultimately	ŭl′tĭ·mĭt·lĭ	ul-ti-mate-ly	Finally.
74. verify	vĕr′ĭ·fī	ver-i-fy	To prove to be true; to check the correctness of a statement or of figures.
75. voluntary	vŏl′ŭn·tĕr′ĭ	vol-un-tar-y	Acting on one's own free will or choice; done by intention.

Lesson 3

1. abdomen	ăb·dō′mĕn	ab-do-men	That part of the body that contains most of the digestive organs.
2. accidental	ăk′sĭ·dĕn′tăl	ac-ci-den-tal	Happening unexpectedly or by chance or accident; incidental.
3. adjacent	à·jā′sĕnt	ad-ja-cent	Neighboring; adjoining.
4. aerial	à·ẹr′ĭ·ăl	a-e-ri-al	Existing in the air; produced by the air; lofty.

5. aggregate	ăg′rĕ·gāt	ag-gre-gate	The collection of small parts into a whole.
6. amiable	ā′mĭ·à·b'l	a-mi-a-ble	Having agreeable personal qualities; kindhearted.
7. ammunition	ăm′û·nĭsh′ŭn	am-mu-ni-tion	The materials used as firearms, such as bullets, cartridges, bombs, grenades; material used for attack or defense purposes.
8. anonymous	à·nŏn′ĭ·mŭs	a-non-y-mous	Giving no name; of unknown authorship or donorship.
9. apology	à·pŏl′ŏ·jĭ	a-pol-o-gy	Something said or written that expresses regret for some fault or insult.
10. apprentice	à·prĕn′tĭs	ap-pren-tice	One learning a trade.
11. audible	ô′dĭ·b'l	au-di-ble	Capable of being heard.
12. automatically	ô′tŏ·măt′ĭ·kăl·ĭ	au-to-mat-i-cal-ly	In an automatic manner; in a spontaneous way.
13. aviator	ā′vĭ·ā′tēr	a-vi-a-tor	The pilot of an airplane.
14. capitalist	kăp′ĭ·tăl·ĭst	cap-i-tal-ist	One who has or controls a large amount of money.
15. chauffeur	shŏ·fûr′	chauf-feur	The paid operator of a motor car.
16. circumference	sēr·kŭm′fēr·ĕns	cir-cum-fer-ence	The whole outside boundary of a circular area.
17. collector	kŏ·lĕk′tēr	col-lec-tor	A person who collects money, taxes, objects of art, etc.
18. concession	kŏn·sĕsh′ŭn	con-ces-sion	A grant by a government of land or property or of a right to use land or property for some specified purpose.
19. consolidate	kŏn·sŏl′ĭ·dāt	con-sol-i-date	To unite; to combine; to merge.
20. defend	dĕ·fĕnd′	de-fend	To guard against an attack or an assault; to contest, as a legal claim.
21. delegate	dĕl′ĕ·gāt	del-e-gate	One who is designated to act for or to represent another person or group.
22. determined	dĕ·tûr′mĭnd	de-ter-mined	Decided; resolute; unflinching.
23. diligence	dĭl′ĭ·jĕns	dil-i-gence	A persistent effort to accomplish what is undertaken.
24. disable	dĭs·ā′b'l	dis-a-ble	To weaken; to deprive of the power of action; to make legally incapable.
25. dividend	dĭv′ĭ·dĕnd	div-i-dend	The stockholders' share of corporation earnings.
26. durable	dū′rà·b'l	du-ra-ble	Lasting; enduring; not easily worn out.
27. economic	ē′kŏ·nŏm′ĭk	e-co-nom-ic	Pertaining to the management of production and wealth; pertaining to the management of one's private business.

28. ecstasy	ĕk′stȧ·sĭ	ec-sta-sy	State caused by an overpowering emotion; having a feeling of joy or rapture.
29. elementary	ĕl′ē·mĕn′tȧ·rĭ	el-e-men-ta-ry	Pertaining to the elements or first principles of a thing.
30. emblem	ĕm′blĕm	em-blem	A symbol or the figure of an object suggesting another object or idea.
31. enumerate	ē·nū′mĕr·āte	e-nu-mer-ate	To name one by one; to mention separately.
32. err	ûr	err	To be mistaken or incorrect.
33. evaporate	ē·văp′ō·rāt	e-vap-o-rate	To turn into vapor.
34. extravagance	ĕks·trăv′ȧ·găns	ex-trav-a-gance	Excessive expenditure of money; lavishness.
35. familiarity	fȧ·mĭl′ĭ·ăr′ĭ·tĭ	fa-mil-i-ar-i-ty	Close acquaintance with, or thorough knowledge of, anything.
36. fidelity	fĭ·dĕl′ĭ·tĭ	fi-del-i-ty	Loyalty; faithfulness to promises or duties.
37. grievous	grēv′ŭs	griev-ous	Causing physical pain or suffering; serious.
38. harass	hăr′ȧs	har-ass	To disturb repeatedly; to fatigue.
39. homage	hŏm′ĭj	hom-age	The respect or reverence paid to another; deference.
40. humiliate	hū·mĭl′ĭ·āt	hu-mil-i-ate	To humble; to cause the loss of self-respect.
41. hurricane	hûr′ĭ·kān	hur-ri-cane	A violent tropical storm of intense severity.
42. incentive	ĭn·sĕn′tĭv	in-cen-tive	That which stimulates and leads to action; a motive.
43. incessant	ĭn·sĕs′ănt	in-ces-sant	Unceasing; continuing without interruption.
44. indefinite	ĭn·dĕf′ĭ·nĭt	in-def-i-nite	Not clearly defined; vague.
45. inquisitive	ĭn·kwĭz′ĭ·tĭv	in-quis-i-tive	Improperly curious; inclined to ask questions.
46. intolerable	ĭn·tŏl′ĕr·ȧ·b′l	in-tol-er-a-ble	Unendurable; insufferable.
47. invalid	ĭn′vȧ·lĭd	in-va-lid	A person who is sickly or weak and infirm.
48. juvenile	jōō′vē·nĭl	ju-ve-nile	A young person.
49. kerosene	kĕr′ō·sēn′	ker-o-sene	An oil used for burning in oil stoves and in lamps.
50. laborsaving ▶	lā′bēr·săv′ĭng	la-bor-sav-ing	Made to replace or diminish the labor of men.
51. lemonade	lĕm′ŭn·ād′	lem-on-ade	A beverage made with lemon juice and water.
52. liability	lī′ȧ·bĭl′ĭ·tĭ	li-a-bil-i-ty	A debt; an amount owed.
53. logical	lŏj′ĭ·kăl	log-i-cal	Reasonable; according to the rules of logic.
54. mariner	măr′ĭ·nēr	mar-i-ner	One whose work is the navigation of ships; a seaman.

55. mattress	măt′rĕs	mat-tress	A case stuffed with hair, cotton, or other suitable material, and tufted or fastened together, for use on a bed.
56. maturity	má·tū′rĭ·tĭ	ma-tu-ri-ty	The time fixed for the payment of a note or bond; the date on which a debt is legally collectible.
57. modesty	mŏd′ĕs·tĭ	mod-es-ty	Freedom from vanity; simplicity.
58. motorist	mō′tĕr·ĭst	mo-tor-ist	One who rides in or drives a motor-propelled vehicle, as an automobile.
59. notorious	nŏ·tō′rĭ·ŭs	no-to-ri-ous	Widely known; unfavorably known.
60. paramount	păr′á·mount	par-a-mount	Highest in rank or authority; chief in importance.
61. parasite	păr′á·sīt	par-a-site	One who lives on the hospitality or patronage of others.
62. participate	pär·tĭs′ĭ·pāt	par-tic-i-pate	To take a part in; to share in.
63. patriotic	pā′trĭ·ŏt′ĭk	pa-tri-ot-ic	Inspired by patriotism.
64. premium	prē′mĭ·ŭm	pre-mi-um	A bonus or a gift; the amount due and payable periodically on insurance.
65. qualification	kwŏl′ĭ·fĭ·kā′shŭn	qual-i-fi-ca-tion	A quality or an accomplishment that fits a person for a position.
66. recollect	rĕc′ŏ·lĕkt′	rec-ol-lect	To remember.
67. reliable	rē·lī′á·b'l	re-li-a-ble	Dependable; trustworthy.
68. reluctance	rē·lŭk′tăns	re-luc-tance	Unwillingness.
69. requisite	rĕk′wĭ·zĭt	req-ui-site	That which is necessary or indispensable.
70. solicit	sŏ·lĭs′ĭt	so-lic-it	To beg or request contributions.
71. stapler	stā′plĕr	sta-pler	A machine that fastens papers with wire staples.
72. summary	sŭm′á·rĭ	sum-ma-ry	An abstract, generally of a previous discourse.
73. superficial	sū′pĕr·fĭsh′ăl	su-per-fi-cial	Shallow; lying on the surface.
74. terminal	tûr′mĭ·năl	ter-mi-nal	The end or extremity of something; the end of a transportation line.
75. vigilance	vĭj′ĭ·lăns	vig-i-lance	The quality of being watchful.

Lesson 4

| 1. acceptance | ăk·sĕp′tăns | ac-cept-ance | Act of receiving something offered; favorable reception. |
| 2. accumulation | á·kū′mū·lā′shŭn | ac-cu-mu-la-tion | Act of collecting things in one place; continuous additions, as adding principal to interest. |

3. admission	ăd·mĭsh′ŭn	ad-mis-sion	Entrance; concession; fee paid on entering.
4. alien	āl′yĕn	al-ien	A foreigner; a resident not possessing citizenship.
5. anarchy	ăn′är·kĭ	an-arch-y	A state of society without law or government.
6. anoint	à·noint′	a-noint	To apply oil to.
7. applied	ă·plīd	ap-plied	Put to use in a practical manner.
8. appreciable	ă·prē′shĭ·à·b'l	ap-pre-ci-a-ble	Sufficient in number to be recognized or estimated.
9. apprehend	ăp′rĕ·hĕnd′	ap-pre-hend	To take into custody; to understand the meaning of.
10. ascertain	ăs′ēr·tān′	as-cer-tain	To find out by trial or examination; to discover.
11. benevolent	bĕ·nĕv′ô·lĕnt	be-nev-o-lent	Disposed to do good for others.
12. casualty	kăzh′ů·ăl·tĭ	cas-u-al-ty	An unfortunate accident; a mishap.
13. certification	sûr′tĭ·fĭ·kā′shŭn	cer-ti-fi-ca-tion	Act of certifying or verifying.
14. civic	sĭv′ĭk	civ-ic	Pertaining to a citizen or a city or to citizenship.
15. combine	kŏm·bīn′	com-bine	To unite; to bring together.
16. commendation	kŏm′ĕn·dā′shŭn	com-men-da-tion	Act of commending or praising.
17. complexion	kŏm·plĕk′shŭn	com-plex-ion	The appearance, the aspect, or the character of body or mind; the appearance of the skin.
18. comprise	kŏm·prīz′	com-prise	To comprehend or include.
19. consummate	kŏn′sŭ·māt	con-sum-mate	To complete; to achieve.
20. co-ordinate	kŏ·ôr′dĭ·nāt	co-or-di-nate	To place in the same order or degree; to combine in harmonious relation.
21. culminate	kŭl′mĭ·nāt	cul-mi-nate	To reach the highest point or the summit.
22. debtor	dĕt′ēr	debt-or	One who is in a state of debt.
23. deficit	dĕf′ĭ·sĭt	def-i-cit	The amount of money that falls short of the required amount; a shortage.
24. descendant	dĕ·sĕn′dănt	de-scend-ant	An offspring.
25. excessive	ĕk·sĕs′ĭv	ex-ces-sive	Exceeding the usual limit.
►			
26. fraternal	frà·tûr′năl	fra-ter-nal	Brotherly.
27. gigantic	jī·găn′tĭk	gi-gan-tic	Huge; enormous.
28. headache	hĕd′āk′	head-ache	A pain located in the head; a perplexing problem.
29. hypocrite	hĭp′ô·krĭt	hyp-o-crite	One who pretends to be better than he is.
30. imaginative	ĭ·măj′ĭ·nā′tĭv	im-ag-i-na-tive	Characterized by exceptional powers of imagination.
31. immovable	ĭm·mōōv′à·b'l	im-mov-a-ble	Fixed; stationary; motionless.
32. impediment	ĭm·pĕd′ĭ·mĕnt	im-ped-i-ment	A speech disorder; an obstacle.

33. impressive	ĭm·prĕs′ĭv	im-pres-sive	Making an impression.
34. inflammable	ĭn·flăm′à·b'l	in-flam-ma-ble	Can be set on fire easily.
35. ingenuity	ĭn′jĕ·nū′ĭ·tĭ	in-ge-nu-i-ty	Cleverness; resourcefulness.
36. initial	ĭ·nĭsh′ăl	in-i-tial	*adj.* Relating to the beginning. *n.* The first letter of a name.
37. initiative	ĭ·nĭsh′ĭ·ā′tĭv	in-i-ti-a-tive	An introductory act; a self-reliant enterprise.
38. inspector	ĭn·spĕk′tẽr	in-spec-tor	A person appointed to inspect.
39. interruption	ĭn′tĕ·rŭp′shŭn	in-ter-rup-tion	Act of interrupting; a serious break caused by an obstruction.
40. intervene	ĭn′tẽr·vēn′	in-ter-vene	To intercede in a dispute; to occur between events or series.
41. irritable	ĭr′ĭ·tà·b'l	ir-ri-ta-ble	Can be irritated easily; susceptible of anger.
42. jeweler	jōō′ĕl·ẽr	jew-el-er	One who makes or sells jewelry.
43. latent	lā′tĕnt	la-tent	Hidden; concealed; dormant.
44. legacy	lĕg′à·sĭ	leg-a-cy	A bequest; a gift of property willed to someone.
45. ludicrous	lū′dĭ·krŭs	lu-di-crous	Ridiculous; amusingly absurd.
46. magnitude	măg′nĭ·tūd	mag-ni-tude	Greatness of influence, size, etc.
47. martyr	mär′tẽr	mar-tyr	One who willingly suffers rather than renounce his principles or beliefs.
48. nickel	nĭk′ĕl	nick-el	A hard, silver-white metal.
49. organist	ôr′găn·ĭst	or-gan-ist	One who plays an organ.
▶ 50. pageant	păj′ĕnt	pag-eant	A public display or program illustrating an educational, historical, or other subject.
51. phenomena	fĕ·nŏm′ĕ·nà	phe-nom-e-na	Things that impress the observer as extraordinary.
52. phonograph	fō′nŏ·gráf	pho-no-graph	A machine that reproduces sound from records.
53. presumptuous	prĕ·zŭmp′tů·ŭs	pre-sump-tu-ous	Bold; forward.
54. pretense	prĕ·tĕns′	pre-tense	Make-believe; an excuse.
55. prevention	prĕ·vĕn′shŭn	pre-ven-tion	The act of preventing.
56. promoter	prŏ·mōt′ẽr	pro-mot-er	An organizer; one who promotes.
57. remnant	rĕm′nănt	rem-nant	A small part or scrap remaining, usually cloth.
58. requisition	rĕk′wĭ·zĭsh′ŭn	req-ui-si-tion	A formal application made by one department to another for things needed in business.
59. restriction	rĕ·strĭk′shŭn	re-stric-tion	A regulation that restricts a condition; a limitation.
60. sanction	săngk′shŭn	sanc-tion	Approval given; authoritative confirmation.
61. scholarship	skŏl′ẽr·shĭp	schol-ar-ship	Learning acquired by study.
62. scissors	sĭz′ẽrz	scis-sors	A cutting instrument consisting of two blades that work against each other.

63.	shrewd	shrōōd	shrewd	Astute; piercing.
64.	sincerely	sĭn·sēr′lĭ	sin-cere-ly	Honestly; often used as a complimentary closing of a letter.
65.	slogan	slō′găn	slo-gan	A catchword or phrase used to call attention to a party, class, or group of people, or to advertise a product, business firm, etc.
66.	specified	spĕs′ĭ·fīd	spec-i-fied	Stated in detail; mentioned specifically.
67.	stenographer	stĕ·nŏg′rȧ·fẽr	ste-nog-ra-pher	One who is employed to take dictation and record it.
68.	striker	strīk′ẽr	strik-er	A workman who is on strike.
69.	superfluous	sū·pûr′flŏŏ·ŭs	su-per-flu-ous	More than is necessary; excessive.
70.	tackle	tăk′′l	tack-le	*n.* Equipment for fishing; ropes for hoisting or lowering objects. *v.* To deal with.
71.	teller	tĕl′ẽr	tell-er	One who tells or communicates; a person employed in a bank to receive or to pay out money.
72.	transaction	trăns·ăk′shŭn	trans-ac-tion	The performing of any business; a business deal.
73.	trivial	trĭv′ĭ·ăl	triv-i-al	Not very important; petty.
74.	valuation	văl′û·ā′shŭn	val-u-a-tion	A value estimated and fixed; estimated worth.
75.	zenith	zē′nĭth	ze-nith	The highest point or state; the point in the celestial sphere vertically above an observer.

Lesson 5 Check-Up

Unit Test. Your teacher will dictate 50 words chosen from the lessons in Unit 1 of Part 3. These words are selected to test your mastery of the new words in this unit. Listen closely as each word is dictated, determine the proper meaning, spell the word carefully, and write plainly to assure yourself of a fair test.

Proofreading Test. In the following letter, some of the italicized words are misspelled. Copy the entire letter, making any corrections necessary in the spelling of the words.

Dear Mr. Goldsmith:

We are sending you an *authantic* copy of the *chartre* of *certifikation*, which your *agent* requested. There should be no *controversi* over this. You will be able to *verfi* the *premum* payments before the *maturity* date.

It is *characteristis* of our office to *reconsile otomatically* any difference between the *debtor* and our company. We shall *enumarate* for you the *consessions* that were made by the *consumor;* and if there is a *deficit,* our delegate will take care of it.

Incidentaly, a *summary* of our report will be sent to you. Please keep its contents in complete confidence.

Sincerely yours,

Cumulative Test. Your teacher will now dictate 40 words chosen from Units 1 through 5 of Part 2. These words will test your retention of the correct spelling of the words in these units. Spell carefully and write plainly.

Checking Your Tests. Your teacher will give you directions for checking the unit test, the proofreading test, and the cumulative test.

Error Analysis. Classify the errors that you made by noting the type of error beside each word that you misspelled.

Review. Use the appropriate attack procedures for studying the words that you misspelled on the unit test, on the proofreading test, and on the cumulative test.

Retest. The retest will tell you if you have mastered the words in Units 1 through 5 of Part 2 and Unit 1 of Part 3. If you misspelled words on the retest, continue your attack procedures until you are sure that you can spell all the words correctly.

Unit 2 Meaning Words

Meaning is the key to the correct spelling of the words in this unit. Spend a few moments reviewing "Spotting Meaning Errors," beginning on page 6, and then begin your study of Lessons 1-4 of this unit, applying the following procedures:

Preview. Your teacher will dictate a list of general-business-vocabulary words. Number a sheet of paper from 1 to 75. Spell as many of the words as you can, but attempt only the words that you are quite sure you know how to spell. If you do not know the spelling of a word, place a question mark (?) beside the number.

Checking Performance. Compare your spellings with the words in the appropriate lesson. Place an *X* beside each word that you misspelled. To the right of any misspelled or omitted word, write the correct spelling. If you are not certain of the correct meaning of the word, study the definition and then use the word in a sentence.

Error Analysis. Classify the errors that you made by noting the type of error beside each word that you misspelled. For instance, if an error was caused by confusion of similar words, write "similar words" beside the word. Refer to Section One if you need to be reminded of the types of errors.

Attack Procedures. Attack procedures for meaning-type errors were presented in Section One, beginning on page 16. Review the corrective technique recommended for each type of error.

Learning to Spell New Words. The pretest words that you did not know how to spell now appear on your answer sheet preceded by a question mark. Use a separate sheet of paper to practice those words, following the SEE, SAY, SPELL, and WRITE routine (see pages 39-41). Hand in the drill paper to your instructor.

Lesson 1

1. adverse	ăd·vûrs′	ad-verse	Opposing; unfavorable.
2. averse	á·vûrs′	a-verse	Disliking; unwilling.
3. anecdote	ăn′ĕk·dōt	an-ec-dote	A brief story about an amusing event.
4. antidote	ăn′tĭ·dōt	an-ti-dote	A remedy to counteract the effects of a poison.
5. appraise	ă·prāz′	ap-praise	To place a value on.
6. apprise	ă·prīz′	ap-prise	To give notice to; to inform.

7. assay	ă·sā′	as-say	To subject to analysis; to attempt.
8. essay	ĕs′ā	es-say	A literary composition; an attempt; a trial.
9. boarder	bōr′dĕr	board-er	One who receives food with his lodging.
10. border	bôr′dĕr	bor-der	n. The outer edge; the margin. v. To touch at the edge or boundary.
11. bouillon	bōō′yôN′	bouil-lon	A clear soup.
12. bullion	bŏŏl′yŭn	bul-lion	Gold or silver metal.
13. calendar	kăl′ĕn·dĕr	cal-en-dar	A record of time.
14. calender	kăl′ĕn·dĕr	cal-en-der	n. A finishing machine used in the manufacture of paper or cloth. v. To press paper or cloth between rollers to make it glossy.
15. casual	kăzh′û·ăl	cas-u-al	Incidental; happening by chance.
16. causal	kôz′ăl	caus-al	Pertaining to a cause; expressing a cause.
17. coma	kō′mà	co-ma	A state of unconsciousness.
18. comma	kŏm′à	com-ma	A mark of punctuation.
19. costume	kŏs′tūm	cos-tume	Dress, including hair style and ornaments worn.
20. custom	kŭs′tŭm	cus-tom	Habit; the usual way of doing things.
21. courtesy	kûr′tĕ·sĭ	cour-te-sy	Politeness.
22. curtsy	kûrt′sĭ	curt-sy	A gesture of respect.
23. decease	dĕ·sēs′	de-cease	n. Death. v. To die.
24. disease	dĭ·zēz′	dis-ease	Sickness; illness.
25. decree	dĕ·krē′	de-cree	An order; a law; an edict.
▶ 26. degree	dĕ·grē′	de-gree	A grade; a step.
27. depraved	dĕ·prāvd′	de-praved	Morally debased.
28. deprived	dĕ·prīvd′	de-prived	Taken away from.
29. desolate	dĕs′ŏ·lĭt	des-o-late	Destitute; lonely.
30. dissolute	dĭs′ŏ·lūt	dis-so-lute	Loose in morals or conduct.
31. dew	dū	dew	Condensed moisture appearing in small drops.
32. due	dū	due	Payable immediately; owed.
33. divers	dī′vĕrz	di-vers	Several; sundry.
34. diverse	dī·vûrs′	di-verse	Different; distinct.
35. equable	ĕk′wà·b′l	eq-ua-ble	Even; uniform.
36. equitable	ĕk′wĭ·tà·b′l	eq-ui-ta-ble	Just; fair; valid in equity.
37. erasable	ē·rās′à·b′l	e-ras-a-ble	Capable of being erased.
38. irascible	ī·răs′ĭ·b′l	i-ras-ci-ble	Quick-tempered; touchy; cranky.
39. expand	ĕks·pănd′	ex-pand	To spread out; to enlarge.
40. expend	ĕks·pĕnd′	ex-pend	To spend; to disburse; to use up.
41. extant	ĕks′tănt	ex-tant	Still existing; not destroyed.
42. extent	ĕks·tĕnt′	ex-tent	Size; length; degree; measure.
43. facetious	fà·sē′shŭs	fa-ce-tious	Amusing; witty; humorous.
44. factitious	făk·tĭsh′ŭs	fac-ti-tious	Artificial; sham; unnatural.
45. fictitious	fĭk·tĭsh′ŭs	fic-ti-tious	Imaginary; like fiction.
46. faze	fāz	faze	To disturb; to worry.
47. phase	fāz	phase	A state of development or change.
48. flew	flōō	flew	Past tense of fly.
49. flue	flōō	flue	Part of a chimney; light down, or fluff.
50. flu	flōō	flu	Colloquial form of influenza.

▶

51. feat	fēt	feat	An act of skill; a deed of courage.
52. feet	fēt	feet	Plural of *foot*.
53. for	fôr	for	A preposition.
54. fore	fōr	fore	*n.* The front. *adj.* Advanced.
55. four	fōr	four	Cardinal number, following *three*.
56. indict	ĭn·dīt′	in-dict	To accuse a person of crime.
57. indite	ĭn·dīt′	in-dite	To compose and write.
58. lath	lăth	lath	A strip of wood.
59. lathe	lāth	lathe	A machine for shaping material.
60. lie	lī	lie	To tell an untruth; to recline.
61. lye	lī	lye	A strong alkaline solution or powder.
62. loan	lōn	loan	That which is lent or borrowed.
63. lone	lōn	lone	Solitary; single.
64. magnate	măg′nāt	mag-nate	An influential or powerful person.
65. magnet	măg′nĕt	mag-net	A body that attracts iron.
66. marital	măr′ĭ·tăl	mar-i-tal	Pertaining to marriage.
67. martial	mär′shăl	mar-tial	Pertaining to war; military.
68. mode	mōd	mode	Fashion; method.
69. mood	mōōd	mood	Disposition; feeling.
70. naught	nôt	naught	In arithmetic, the character *0;* a zero; a cipher.
71. nought	nôt	nought	Nothing; a worthless thing.
72. one	wŭn	one	A single unit.
73. won	wŭn	won	Past tense and past participle of *win*.
74. packed	păkt	packed	Packaged; arranged compactly; crammed.
75. pact	păkt	pact	An agreement.

Lesson 2

1. annual	ăn′ū·ăl	an-nu-al	Yearly.
2. annul	ă·nŭl′	an-nul	To cancel; to make void.
3. assimilate	ă·sĭm′ĭ·lāt	as-sim-i-late	To absorb; to compare.
4. simulate	sĭm′ū·lāt	sim-u-late	To make a pretense of; to imitate.
5. aught	ôt	aught	Anything; any least part. In arithmetic, a cipher.
6. ought	ôt	ought	Should; bound to do something.
7. celery	sĕl′ĕr·ĭ	cel-er-y	A plant of the carrot family, with crisp leafstalks.
8. salary	săl′à·rĭ	sal-a-ry	Wages; payment for services.
9. census	sĕn′sŭs	cen-sus	Statistics of population.
10. senses	sĕns′ĕz	sens-es	Mental faculties.
11. clothes	klōthz	clothes	Garments; wearing apparel.
12. cloths	klôthz	cloths	Fabrics of woven cotton, woolen, silk, rayon, or linen fiber.
13. commence	kŏ·mĕns′	com-mence	To begin.
14. comments	kŏm′ĕnts	com-ments	Remarks.
15. confidant	kŏn′fĭ·dănt′	con-fi-dant	A confidential friend (*masc.*).
16. confident	kŏn′fĭ·dĕnt	con-fi-dent	Sure; positive; self-reliant.

17. decent	dē′sĕnt	de-cent	Proper; right; appropriate.
18. dissent	dĭ·sĕnt′	dis-sent	To differ in opinion; to disagree.
19. disseminate	dĭ·sĕm′ĭ·nāt	dis-sem-i-nate	To spread widely.
20. dissimulate	dĭ·sĭm′ū·lāt	dis-sim-u-late	To conceal the real feeling by pretense; to feign.
21. elicit	ė·lĭs′ĭt	e-lic-it	To draw out; to evoke.
22. illicit	ĭl·lĭs′ĭt	il-lic-it	Unlawful.
23. emanate	ĕm′ȧ·nāt	em-a-nate	To originate from; to spring forth from a source.
24. eminent	ĕm′ĭ·nĕnt	em-i-nent	Distinguished; outstanding; high in rank or reputation.
25. imminent	ĭm′ĭ·nĕnt	im-mi-nent	Threatening to happen immediately.
►			
26. emerge	ė·mûrj′	e-merge	To rise out of; to come into view.
27. immerge	ĭ·mûrj′	im-merge	To sink into; to immerse.
28. facilitate	fȧ·sĭl′ĭ·tāt	fa-cil-i-tate	To make easy.
29. felicitate	fė·lĭs′ĭ·tāt	fe-lic-i-tate	To congratulate.
30. incite	ĭn·sīt′	in-cite	To prompt to action; to urge on.
31. insight	ĭn′sīt′	in-sight	An inner knowledge; keen understanding; intuition.
32. pain	pān	pain	Bodily suffering; distress.
33. pane	pān	pane	A sheet of glass in a window, door, etc.
34. perpetrate	pûr′pė·trāt	per-pe-trate	To commit, as an offense.
35. perpetuate	pēr·pĕt′ū·āt	per-pet-u-ate	To make everlasting.
36. perquisite	pûr′kwĭ·zĭt	per-qui-site	A gain or profit over and above fixed income; an added privilege.
37. prerequisite	prė·rĕk′wĭ·zĭt	pre-req-ui-site	Something required before.
38. physic	fĭz′ĭk	phys-ic	A medicine.
39. physique	fĭ·zēk′	phy-sique	Bodily structure.
40. psychic	sī′kĭk	psy-chic	Pertaining to the mind or spirit.
41. precedence	prė·sēd′ĕns	pre-ced-ence	Act of going before; priority in time, importance, rank.
42. precedents	prĕs′ė·dĕnts	prec-e-dents	Authoritative examples; judicial decisions establishing rules for future decisions.
43. presentiment	prė·zĕn′tĭ·mĕnt	pre-sen-ti-ment	A feeling that something will happen.
44. presentment	prė·zent′mĕnt	pre-sent-ment	A setting forth for exhibition; presentation.
45. pretend	prė·tĕnd′	pre-tend	To make believe; to feign.
46. portend	pōr·tĕnd′	por-tend	To give an advance warning of; to predict; to forecast; to foreshadow.
47. preposition	prĕp′ō·zĭsh′ŭn	prep-o-si-tion	A part of speech.
48. proposition	prŏp′ō·zĭsh′ŭn	prop-o-si-tion	An offer; a business proposal.
49. raise	rāz	raise	To lift up; to erect.
50. rays	rāz	rays	Beams of light.
►			
51. raze	rāz	raze	To tear down; to demolish.

52. read	rēd	read	To go over and gather the meaning of something written.
53. reed	rēd	reed	A plant; bamboolike grass; a musical instrument.
54. remediable	rĕ·mē′dĭ·à·b'l	re-me-di-a-ble	Capable of being remedied.
55. remedial	rĕ·mē′dĭ·ăl	re-me-di-al	Providing a remedy; curing.
56. respectably	rĕ·spĕk′tà·blĭ	re-spect-a-bly	In a conventionally correct manner.
57. respectively	rĕ·spĕk′tĭv·lĭ	re-spec-tive-ly	Each to each in the order designated; as relating to each.
58. sail	sāl	sail	*n.* A sheet of canvas on a ship arranged to catch the wind that propels the ship. *v.* To travel on a sailing vessel.
59. sale	sāl	sale	Act of selling; a contract by which the ownership of property is transferred from one person to another for a sum of money.
60. spacious	spā′shŭs	spa-cious	Roomy; expansive.
61. specious	spē′shŭs	spe-cious	Apparently, but not actually, fair or just; plausible.
62. staid	stād	staid	Sedate; grave.
63. stayed	stād	stayed	Past tense of *stay.*
64. suit	sūt	suit	*n.* A garment, usually consisting of two pieces; a legal action. *v.* To please; to accommodate.
65. suite	swēt	suite	A connected series of things; a retinue.
66. tare	târ	tare	The allowance made for the weight of a container; a deduction from the gross weight to allow for the wrapping.
67. tear	târ	tear	To pull apart by force; to rend.
68. topography	tŏ·pŏg′rà·fĭ	to-pog-ra-phy	The geographical or surface features of a region.
69. typography	tĭ·pŏg′rà·fĭ	ty-pog-ra-phy	The arrangement of matter printed from type; art of printing with type.
70. trail	trāl	trail	*v.* To follow; to draw or drag along behind. *n.* A marked path.
71. trial	trī′ăl	tri-al	The examination of the facts in a law case to determine the innocence or guilt of an accused person; an experiment.
72. vain	vān	vain	Conceited; proud.
73. vein	vān	vein	A tubular vessel that carries the blood back to the heart; a narrow opening in rock filled by mineral matter.
74. ware	wâr	ware	An article of merchandise.
75. wear	wâr	wear	To carry upon the person, as an article of clothing; to exhaust the strength of.

Lesson 3

1. abandon	ȧ·băn′dŭn	a-ban-don	To give up or surrender utterly.
2. discontinue	dĭs′kŏn·tĭn′ū	dis-con-tin-ue	To interrupt the continuance of; to terminate.
3. advise	ăd·vīz′	ad-vise	To give advice to.
4. caution	kô′shŭn	cau-tion	To warn of danger.
5. aggravate	ăg′rȧ·vāt	ag-gra-vate	To make worse; to make more offensive.
6. exasperate	ĕg·zăs′pēr·āt	ex-as-per-ate	To provoke to intense anger; to infuriate.
7. amateur	ăm′ȧ·tûr′	am-a-teur	One who cultivates an activity for personal pleasure instead of for financial gain; a nonprofessional.
8. novice	nŏv′ĭs	nov-ice	One who is new in any business, profession, or calling; one who is unskilled.
9. announce	ȧ·nouns′	an-nounce	To make known publicly; to state the presence of.
10. declare	dĕ·klâr′	de-clare	To make known explicitly and plainly.
11. proclaim	prŏ·klām′	pro-claim	To make known with the widest publicity.
12. apt	ăpt	apt	Suitable; habitually tending; inclined.
13. liable	lī′ȧ·b'l	li-a-ble	Answerable; exposed to some danger or casualty.
14. likely	līk′lĭ	like-ly	Probable; appearing like truth.
15. astonish	ăs·tŏn′ĭsh	as-ton-ish	To strike with sudden wonder; to surprise greatly.
16. surprise	sĕr·prīz′	sur-prise	To amaze; to come upon one unexpectedly.
17. aware	ȧ·wâr′	a-ware	Informed; cognizant; showing vigilance in observing, hearing, etc.
18. conscious	kŏn′shŭs	con-scious	Mentally awake or active; having awareness of something when one allows it to enter the mind and focuses attention on it.
19. balance	băl′ăns	bal-ance	The difference between two sides of an account.
20. rest	rĕst	rest	With the word *the*, any portion, large or small, left over.
21. begin	bĕ·gĭn′	be-gin	To start (less formal and more frequently used than *commence*).
22. commence	kŏ·mĕns′	com-mence	To start; to begin (restricted to a form of action).
23. blunder	blŭn′dĕr	blun-der	An act resulting from ignorance or awkwardness.

24. error	ĕr'ĕr	er-ror	A departure from the truth or from accuracy.
25. bound ▶	bound	bound	Morally or legally constrained or compelled.
26. obliged	ȯ·blījd'	o-bliged	Bound by necessity or favor.
27. celebrated	sĕl'ĕ·brāt'ĕd	cel-e-brat-ed	Famed.
28. renowned	rĕ·nound'	re-nowned	The state of being widely known for one's great achievements of merit.
29. censure	sĕn'shĕr	cen-sure	To find fault with; to blame; to express disapproval of.
30. criticize	krĭt'ĭ·sīz	crit-i-cize	To examine or judge the merits of, as a critic; to find fault with.
31. cite	sīt	cite	To mention a person or passage as an authority.
32. quote	kwōt	quote	To repeat the exact words used by another.
33. colleague	kŏl'ēg	col-league	An associate in a profession or a civil office (not used of partners in business).
34. partner	pärt'nĕr	part-ner	An associate or joint owner in business.
35. compensate	kŏm'pĕn·sāt	com-pen-sate	To make up for; to recompense.
36. remunerate	rĕ·mū'nĕr·āt	re-mu-ner-ate	To pay an equivalent for any service rendered or expense sustained; to reward for work done.
37. contrary	kŏn'trĕr·ĭ	con-tra-ry	Opposed; perverse; unfavorable.
38. opposite	ŏp'ȯ·zĭt	op-po-site	Opposed or hostile; facing.
39. defamation	dĕf'ȧ·mā'shŭn	def-a-ma-tion	Act of casting aspersion on the reputation of another.
40. slander	slăn'dĕr	slan-der	The malicious dissemination or spreading abroad by speech of false tales to the injury of another.
41. defect	dĕ·fĕkt'	de-fect	Want of something necessary for completeness or perfection.
42. blemish	blĕm'ĭsh	blem-ish	A mark of deformity; a flaw.
43. detained	dĕ·tānd'	de-tained	Held back or restrained from proceeding; delayed.
44. hindered	hĭn'dĕrd	hin-dered	Impeded; obstructed.
45. discredit	dĭs·krĕd'ĭt	dis-cred-it	To destroy confidence in a person.
46. disparage	dĭs·păr'ĭj	dis-par-age	To lower in rank or to dishonor by comparison with what is inferior; to undervalue.
47. dispute	dĭs·pūt'	dis-pute	To argue pro and con; to debate; to attempt to overthrow.
48. quarrel	kwŏr'ĕl	quar-rel	To dispute angrily or violently.
49. energetic	ĕn'ĕr·jĕt'ĭk	en-er-get-ic	Having bustling energy; forcible.
50. vigorous ▶	vĭg'ĕr·ŭs	vig-or-ous	Full of physical or mental strength or force.

51. exclusive	ĕks·klōō′sĭv	ex-clu-sive	Chosen by a fastidious or snob-bish group; inclined to exclude others.
52. select	sĕ·lĕkt′	se-lect	Picked by preference; chosen from a number of the same kind as a result of discrimination.
53. glory	glō′rĭ	glo-ry	Praise; reputation; fame.
54. honor	ŏn′ĕr	hon-or	High esteem due for reputation or behavior; integrity.
55. hackneyed	hăk′nĭd	hack-neyed	Worn out by constant use.
56. trite	trīt	trite	Lacking in novelty or interest due to overuse.
57. impossible	ĭm·pŏs′ĭ·b'l	im-pos-si-ble	Not possible; hopeless.
58. impracticable	ĭm·prăk′tĭ·ká·b'l	im-prac-ti-ca-ble	Not possible under existing con-ditions; unmanageable.
59. investigation	ĭn·vĕs′tĭ·gā′shŭn	in-ves-ti-ga-tion	A searching inquiry; an exami-nation of the facts.
60. scrutiny	skrōō′tĭ·nĭ	scru-ti-ny	Minute and critical inspection; close search.
61. join	join	join	To connect; to unite in associa-tion; to unite in effort, action, etc.
62. unite	û·nīt′	u-nite	To put together so as to make one; to combine; to join by treaty.
63. majority	má·jŏr′ĭ·tĭ	ma-jor-i-ty	The number more than half; superiority.
64. plurality	plōō·răl′ĭ·tĭ	plu-ral-i-ty	A multitude; an excess of votes over those for any other candi-date for the same office, espe-cially over the next opponent.
65. mutual	mū′tụ̄·ăl	mu-tu-al	Having joint interest or owner-ship in the same thing or person.
66. reciprocal	rĕ·sĭp′rŏ·kăl	re-cip-ro-cal	Given or felt by both sides; in-terchangeable.
67. number	nŭm′bĕr	num-ber	A figure or group of figures; the amount of units.
68. quantity	kwŏn′tĭ·tĭ	quan-ti-ty	Amount or portion; extent; size.
69. ostensible	ŏs·tĕn′sĭ·b'l	os-ten-si-ble	Given out as such; professed; ap-parent.
70. plausible	plô′zĭ·b'l	plau-si-ble	Apparently reasonable; not quite convincing of the truth.
71. part	părt	part	A fraction of the whole; a por-tion of the whole.
72. portion	pōr′shŭn	por-tion	A share; some rightfully as-signed part of the whole.
73. speak	spēk	speak	To utter words; to converse; to deliver a speech.
74. speech	spēch	speech	A formal public discourse.
75. talk	tôk	talk	v. To exchange ideas by means of spoken words. n. An informal speech; conversation.

Lesson 4

1. **ability**	a·bĭl′ĭ·tĭ	a-bil-i-ty	Skill or competence in an occupation; power to perform; capacity.
2. **weakness**	wēk′nĕs	weak-ness	Feebleness; a fault or defect in a person's ability or character.
3. **abstract**	ăb′străkt	ab-stract	Considered apart from matter and from special cases; theoretical.
4. **concrete**	kŏn′krēt	con-crete	Actual or real; concerned with actual instances.
5. **adopt**	a·dŏpt′	a-dopt	To select or to choose for oneself; to accept.
6. **reject**	rē·jĕkt′	re-ject	To refuse to recognize; to refuse to accept a person or thing.
7. **ample**	ăm′p'l	am-ple	Enough or more than enough to satisfy.
8. **inadequate**	ĭn·ăd′ē·kwĭt	in-ad-e-quate	Not enough; insufficient; incomplete.
9. **arrogant**	ăr′ŏ·gănt	ar-ro-gant	Overbearing; assuming to superior importance; haughty.
10. **meek**	mēk	meek	Patient; submissive; spiritless; tame.
11. **beneficial**	bĕn′ē·fĭsh′ăl	ben-e-fi-cial	Advantageous; conferring benefit; being of help; promoting well-being.
12. **harmful**	härm′fŏŏl	harm-ful	Detrimental; hurtful.
13. **brilliant**	brĭl′yănt	bril-liant	Very bright; lustrous; sparkling.
14. **dull**	dŭl	dull	Not bright; slow of understanding; not intense or clear.
15. **collect**	kŏ·lĕkt′	col-lect	To gather into one place; to assemble.
16. **scatter**	skăt′ēr	scat-ter	To throw about loosely; to disperse.
17. **commend**	kŏ·mĕnd′	com-mend	To recommend; to mention as worthy of confidence.
18. **disapprove**	dĭs′ă·prōōv′	dis-ap-prove	To censure or condemn; to decline to give approval to.
19. **confusion**	kŏn·fū′zhŭn	con-fu-sion	State of being confused; state of disorder.
20. **order**	ôr′dēr	or-der	A condition in which everything is in its proper place.
21. **conservative**	kŏn·sûr′vá·tĭv	con-serv-a-tive	Cautious or moderate; having a tendency to conserve.
22. **radical**	răd′ĭ·kăl	rad-i-cal	Extreme; favoring drastic reforms.
23. **contract**	kŏn·trăkt′	con-tract	To shorten; to narrow; to shrink.
24. **expand**	ĕks·pănd′	ex-pand	To enlarge; to spread out; to distend.
25. **create** ▶	krē·āt′	cre-ate	To cause to exist; to produce.
26. **destroy**	dē·stroi′	de-stroy	To ruin; to demolish.
27. **defective**	dē·fĕk′tĭv	de-fec-tive	Having a defect; being imperfect.
28. **perfect**	pûr′fĕkt	per-fect	Complete; without a blemish; faultless; correct in every detail.
29. **deficiency**	dē·fĭsh′ĕn·sĭ	de-fi-cien-cy	A lacking in something necessary for completeness; a deficit.

30. surplus	sûr′plŭs	sur-plus	The excess of assets over liabilities; the amount in excess of what is required.
31. definite	dĕf′ĭ·nĭt	def-i-nite	Clearly defined; not vague or general.
32. vague	vāg	vague	Not clearly defined; not definite in meaning; not definitely known.
33. discontent	dĭs′kŏn·tĕnt′	dis-con-tent	Dissatisfaction; uneasiness of mind.
34. satisfaction	săt′ĭs·făk′shŭn	sat-is-fac-tion	State of being satisfied; the cause of being contented.
35. exciting	ĕk·sīt′ĭng	ex-cit-ing	Producing excitement; stimulating.
36. tedious	tē′dĭ·ŭs	te-di-ous	Tiresome; wearisome; irksome.
37. exclude	ĕks·klōōd′	ex-clude	To keep out; to shut out.
38. include	ĭn·klōōd′	in-clude	To contain as a part or a member; to embrace; to enclose.
39. exposed	ĕks·pōzd′	ex-posed	Exhibited; unconcealed; disclosed; unmasked.
40. hidden	hĭd′′n	hid-den	Concealed; obscure; kept from view.
41. exterior	ĕks·tĕr′ĭ·ēr	ex-te-ri-or	Being or situated on the outside.
42. interior	ĭn·tĕr′ĭ·ēr	in-te-ri-or	Pertaining to that which is inside.
43. fictitious	fĭk·tĭsh′ŭs	fic-ti-tious	False; not genuine; imaginary.
44. real	rē′ăl	re-al	True; existing rather than fictitious; genuine.
45. fixed	fĭkst	fixed	Made fast or firm; definitely and permanently placed.
46. changeable	chān′ já·b'l	change-a-ble	Liable to change; variable; movable.
47. inferior	ĭn·fēr′ĭ·ēr	in-fe-ri-or	Lower in rank or grade; of poor quality.
48. superior	sŭ·pēr′ĭ·ēr	su-pe-ri-or	Higher in rank or dignity; of top quality.
49. introductory	ĭn′trō·dŭk′tŏ·rĭ	in-tro-duc-to-ry	Preliminary; used to introduce or at the beginning.
▶ 50. concluding	kŏn·klōōd′ĭng	con-clud-ing	Terminating; closing; ending.
51. introvert	ĭn′trō·vûrt′	in-tro-vert	A person strongly inclined to direct the mind, thoughts, or efforts within himself.
52. extrovert	ĕks′trō·vûrt	ex-tro-vert	A person concerned chiefly with external objects and actions.
53. lenient	lē′nĭ·ĕnt	le-ni-ent	Mild; merciful; gentle.
54. strict	strĭkt	strict	Exacting in requirements; precise.
55. local	lō′kăl	lo-cal	Pertaining to a particular place; referring to a small district; not widespread.
56. universal	ū′nĭ·vûr′săl	u-ni-ver-sal	Pertaining to the universe; unlimited.
57. often	ôf′ĕn	of-ten	Many times; frequently.
58. seldom	sĕl′dŭm	sel-dom	Infrequently; not often.
59. oppose	ŏ·pōz′	op-pose	To hinder; to work against.
60. support	sŭ·pōrt′	sup-port	To uphold a person, cause, or policy.

61. optimistic	ŏp'tĭ·mĭs'tĭk	op-ti-mis-tic	Having a tendency to look on the bright side of things.
62. pessimistic	pĕs'ĭ·mĭs'tĭk	pes-si-mis-tic	Having a tendency to look on the gloomiest possible side of things.
63. permit	pẽr·mĭt'	per-mit	To allow a person to do something.
64. prohibit	prō·hĭb'ĭt	pro-hib-it	To forbid a person to do something.
65. pertinent	pûr'tĭ·nĕnt	per-ti-nent	Related to the matter in hand.
66. unrelated	ŭn'rē·lāt'ĕd	un-re-lat-ed	Not connected to the matter in hand.
67. previous	prē'vĭ·ŭs	pre-vi-ous	Occurring before something else; going before; preceding.
68. subsequent	sŭb'sē·kwĕnt	sub-se-quent	Following in order; succeeding.
69. reduce	rē·dūs'	re-duce	To diminish; to lower.
70. enlarge	ĕn·lärj'	en-large	To make larger; to increase in size.
71. shame	shām	shame	A painful feeling of guilt; dishonor; disgrace.
72. fame	fām	fame	Widespread reputation of a favorable character; renown.
73. pride	prīd	pride	High opinion of one's own importance; self-esteem.
74. thrifty	thrĭf'tĭ	thrift-y	Manifesting thrift; saving.
75. wasteful	wāst'fŏol	waste-ful	Characterized by useless expenditure; grossly extravagant.

Lesson 5 Check-Up

Unit Test. Your teacher will dictate 50 words chosen from the lessons in Unit 2 of Part 3. These words are selected to test your mastery of the new words in this unit. Listen closely as each word is dictated, spell the word carefully, and write plainly to assure yourself of a fair test.

Proofreading Test. In the following letter, some of the italicized words are misspelled. Copy the entire letter, making whatever corrections are necessary in the spelling of the words.

Dear Mr. Rock:

According to our *calender*, it is time for our company to *reduse* its *serplus* by increasing the *salaries* of the workers. This is done on an *annual* basis. The increases will be based on the *abilty* and attitude of the worker.

We have *eleminated* many *waistful* practices; *defectiv* parts have been *distroyed;* and *discontend* and *confuson* have been eliminated.

Our workers have expressed satisfaction with the new *exteror* and *interor* painting job at the plant. This is one *contrak* that was not *oposed.* There has been no *averse* criticism to our plan to expand our business *anually.* Our committee is now looking for property that will *boarder* on our present boundaries.

Respectfully yours,

Cumulative Test. Your teacher will now dictate 40 words chosen from Unit 1 of Part 3. These words will test your retention of the correct spelling of words in this unit. Spell carefully, determine the correct meaning, and write plainly.

Checking Your Tests. Your teacher will give you directions for checking the unit test, the proofreading test, and the cumulative test.

Error Analysis. Classify the errors that you made by noting the type of error beside each word that you misspelled.

Review. Use the appropriate attack procedures for studying the words that you misspelled on the unit test, on the proofreading test, and on the cumulative test. Remember that the cumulative test contained sound words.

Retest. The retest will tell you if you have mastered the words in Units 1 and 2 of Part 3. If you misspelled words on the retest, continue your attack procedures until you are sure that you can spell all the words correctly.

Unit 3 Sound Words

Sound is the key to the correct spelling of the words in this unit. Spend a few moments reviewing "Spotting Sound Errors," beginning on page 3, and then begin your study of Lessons 1-4 of this unit, applying the following procedures:

Preview. Your teacher will dictate a list of 75 general-business vocabulary words. Number a sheet of paper from 1 to 75. Spell as many of the words as you can, but attempt only the words that you are quite sure you know how to spell. If you do not know the spelling of a word, place a question mark (?) beside the number.

Checking Performance. Compare your spellings with the words given in the appropriate lesson. Place an X beside each word that you misspelled. To the right of any misspelled or omitted word, write the correct spelling.

Error Analysis. Classify the errors that you made by noting the type of error beside each word that you misspelled. For instance, if an error was caused by adding unnecessary letters, write "addition" beside the word. Refer to Section One if you need to be reminded of the types of errors.

Attack Procedures. Attack procedures for sound-type errors were presented in Section One, beginning on page 7. Review the corrective technique recommended for each type of error.

Learning to Spell New Words. The pretest words that you did not know how to spell now appear on your answer sheet preceded by a question mark. Use a separate sheet of paper to practice those words, following the SEE, SAY, SPELL, and WRITE routine (see pages 39-41). Hand in the drill paper to your instructor.

Lesson 1

1. accrual	ă·krōō′ăl	ac-cru-al	A sum that accumulates gradually.
2. affirmative	ă·fûr′mà·tĭv	af-firm-a-tive	*adj.* Giving a "yes" answer to a question. *n.* A positive proposition.
3. alias	ā′lĭ·ăs	a-li-as	An assumed name.
4. ambiguity	ăm′bĭ·gū′ĭ·tĭ	am-bi-gu-i-ty	That which is not clear in statement or meaning.

5. analogy	ȧ·năl′ŏ·jĭ	a-nal-o-gy	A likeness in one or more ways between things unlike in other ways; similarity.
6. applicable	ăp′lĭ·kȧ·b'l	ap-pli-ca-ble	Suitable; relevant.
7. aspirant	ăs·pīr′ănt	as-pir-ant	A person who seeks advancement or high honors.
8. camphor	kăm′fẽr	cam-phor	A whitish, crystalline substance used in medicine.
9. carnival	kär′nĭ·văl	car-ni-val	A traveling amusement show.
10. chaperon	shăp′ẽr·ōn	chap-er-on	A mature person who is responsible for the good conduct of young people at a social event.
11. clearance	klẽr′ăns	clear-ance	Act of clearing; the passage of checks through a clearing-house.
12. complicate	kŏm′plĭ·kāt	com-pli-cate	To make difficult or complex.
13. correlation	kŏr′ĕ·lā′shŭn	cor-re-la-tion	Mutual relation of two or more things; the establishing of an orderly connection.
14. demonstrative	dĕ·mŏn′strȧ·tĭv	de-mon-stra-tive	Given to exhibiting or expressing feelings; serving to illustrate, demonstrate, or explain.
15. depositor	dĕ·pŏz′ĭ·tẽr	de-pos-i-tor	One who deposits money in a bank.
16. discriminate	dĭs·krĭm′ĭ·nāt	dis-crim-i-nate	To make a distinction in favor of or against a person or a thing.
17. dismissal	dĭs·mĭs′ăl	dis-miss-al	Act of dismissing; state of being discharged or dismissed.
18. dissatisfied	dĭs·săt′ĭs·fīd	dis-sat-is-fied	Displeased; discontented; offended.
19. donor	dō′nẽr	do-nor	One who gives or donates.
20. downtown	doun′toun′	down-town	Toward or in the business section of a town.
21. dutiful	dū′tĭ·fŏŏl	du-ti-ful	Performing the required duties; obedient.
22. economize	ĕ·kŏn′ŏ·mīz	e-con-o-mize	To use sparingly or economically; to manage to the best advantage.
23. ethical	ĕth′ĭ·kăl	eth-i-cal	Pertaining to moral duties and conduct; professionally correct.
24. explicit	ĕks·plĭs′ĭt	ex-plic-it	Clear; clearly expressed.
25. fascinating	făs′ĭ·nāt′ĭng	fas-ci-nat-ing	Charming; enchanting.
▶			
26. flagrant	flā′grănt	fla-grant	Glaring; conspicuously bad.
27. gratuitous	grȧ·tū′ĭ·tŭs	gra-tu-i-tous	Given freely without regard for merit; given without receiving any value in return.
28. hazardous	hăz′ẽr·dŭs	haz-ard-ous	Risky; perilous.

29. honorary	ŏn'ẽr·ẽr'ĭ	hon-or-ar-y	Given for honor only, without the usual duties or services.
30. immaterial	ĭm'má·tẽr'ĭ·ăl	im-ma-te-ri-al	Unimportant; of no real consequence.
31. immature	ĭm'á·tūr'	im-ma-ture	Not mature; not fully developed; not ripe.
32. implacable	ĭm·plā'ká·b'l	im-pla-ca-ble	Not to be appeased or pacified.
33. inconsistent	ĭn'kŏn·sĭs'tĕnt	in-con-sist-ent	Lacking in agreement; not compatible; illogical in thought.
34. indestructible	ĭn'dĕ·strŭk'tĭ·b'l	in-de-struct-i-ble	Incapable of being destroyed.
35. infamous	ĭn'fá·mŭs	in-fa-mous	Of evil fame; scandalous.
36. interrogate	ĭn·tẽr'ŏ·gāt	in-ter-ro-gate	To examine by asking questions.
37. intoxicate	ĭn·tŏk'sĭ·kāt	in-tox-i-cate	To affect temporary loss or control of physical and mental powers by means of a drug or alcohol.
38. itinerary	ī·tĭn'ẽr·ẽr'ĭ	i-tin-er-ar-y	A record of a journey; a route of a planned trip.
39. janitor	jăn'ĭ·tẽr	jan-i-tor	One who takes care of a building, offices, etc.
40. jeopardize	jĕp'ẽr·dīz	jeop-ard-ize	To put into a position of risk or injury; to expose to loss.
41. journalist	jûr'năl·ĭst	jour-nal-ist	One who is engaged in writing for a newspaper or magazine.
42. leniency	lē'nĭ·ĕn·sĭ	le-ni-en-cy	Quality of being lenient.
43. lifelike	līf'līk'	life-like	Resembling real life.
44. lubrication	lū'brĭ·kā'shŭn	lu-bri-ca-tion	Act of applying oil or grease or other substance in order to diminish friction.
45. matrimony	măt'rĭ·mō'nĭ	mat-ri-mo-ny	The married state; the ceremony of marriage.
46. memorandums	mĕm'ô·răn'dŭmz	mem-o-ran-dums	The plural of *memorandum;* informal records of something.
47. mentality	mĕn·tăl'ĭ·tĭ	men-tal-i-ty	Mental capacity; intellectuality.
48. mercantile	mûr'kăn·tīl	mer-can-tile	Pertaining to merchants or to trade; engaged in trade or commerce.
49. molecular	mô·lĕk'û·lẽr	mo-lec-u-lar	Consisting of molecules.
50. monopolize	mô·nŏp'ô·līz	mo-nop-o-lize	To acquire exclusive possession of.
51. neurotic	nû·rŏt'ĭk	neu-rot-ic	Pertaining to the nerves; nervous.
52. optional	ŏp'shŭn·ăl	op-tion-al	Left to one's choice; not compulsory.
53. perforated	pûr'fô·rāt'ĕd	per-fo-rat-ed	Pierced with a hole or holes.
54. precarious	prê·kâr'ĭ·ŭs	pre-car-i-ous	Uncertain; dangerous; insecure.

55. **prohibitive**	prŏ·hĭb′ĭ·tĭv	pro-hib-i-tive	That which forbids something; serving to prevent the use of.
56. **promissory**	prŏm′ĭ·sō′rĭ	prom-is-so-ry	Implying a promise.
57. **quarterly**	kwôr′tĕr·lĭ	quar-ter-ly	*adj*. Recurring during, or at the end of, every three months, or a quarter of a year. *n*. A magazine issued every three months.
58. **recuperate**	rĕ·kū′pēr·āt	re-cu-per-ate	To regain health, strength, or from losses.
59. **regional**	rē′jŭn·ăl	re-gion-al	Pertaining to a particular district, region, or area.
60. **rental**	rĕn′tăl	rent-al	An amount received or paid as rent.
61. **rhythmical**	rĭth′mĭ·kăl	rhyth-mi-cal	Having a flowing rhythm.
62. **seasonal**	sē′z′n·ăl	sea-son-al	Pertaining to the seasons of the year or to some particular season.
63. **semester**	sĕ·mĕs′tĕr	se-mes-ter	A division of the school year, usually half of the school year.
64. **stencil**	stĕn′sĭl	sten-cil	A piece of material perforated so that desired patterns or writing can be reproduced when color or ink is applied.
65. **supposition**	sŭp′ŏ·zĭsh′ŭn	sup-po-si-tion	Act of supposing; an assumption.
66. **surgical**	sûr′jĭ·kăl	sur-gi-cal	Pertaining to surgery.
67. **tepid**	tĕp′ĭd	tep-id	Lukewarm.
68. **testimonial**	tĕs′tĭ·mō′nĭ·ăl	tes-ti-mo-ni-al	A written statement of recommendation; something given or done as an expression of esteem.
69. **ultimatum**	ŭl′tĭ·mā′tŭm	ul-ti-ma-tum	A final proposal or statement of conditions.
70. **valid**	văl′ĭd	val-id	Sound; well-founded; authoritative; having legal strength.
71. **ventilate**	vĕn′tĭ·lāt	ven-ti-late	To provide fresh air.
72. **versus**	vûr′săs	ver-sus	Against (used in contests, legal actions, debates, etc.).
73. **vigilant**	vĭj′ĭ·lănt	vig-i-lant	Alert to detect danger; watchful.
74. **visual**	vĭzh′û·ăl	vis-u-al	Pertaining to sight; visible.
75. **vivacious**	vī·vā′shăs	vi-va-cious	Lively.

Lesson 2

1. **acumen**	ă·kū′mĕn	a-cu-men	Mental acuteness; keenness of insight.
2. **adolescence**	ăd′ŏ·lĕs′ĕns	ad-o-les-cence	Youth; the period of growth between childhood and manhood or womanhood.

3. allegation	ăl′ĕ·gā′shŭn	al-le-ga-tion	A statement offered as an excuse, or a justification; that which is asserted.
4. apricot	ā′prĭ·kŏt	a-pri-cot	The small orange-colored fruit resembling both peach and plum in flavor.
5. apropos	ăp′rŏ·pō′	ap-ro-pos	With reference or regard; in respect.
6. assassin	ă·săs′ĭn	as-sas-sin	A hired murderer who kills by surprise assault.
7. athlete	ăth′lēt	ath-lete	One who is trained to perform physical exercises requiring strength and agility.
8. attest	ă·tĕst′	at-test	To declare to be correct or true; to certify.
9. aviation	ā′vĭ·ā′shŭn	a-vi-a-tion	The art of flying an aircraft.
10. baptize	băp·tīz′	bap-tize	To cleanse spiritually; to christen; to initiate.
11. biography	bī·ŏg′rá·fĭ	bi-og-ra-phy	A written account of a person's life.
12. bother	bŏth′ẽr	both-er	To give trouble; to confuse; to pester; to worry.
13. boycott	boi′kŏt	boy-cott	An action to prevent dealing in a commodity or with a person or a group.
14. category	kăt′ĕ·gō′rĭ	cat-e-go-ry	A class; any general or comprehensive division.
15. certified	sûr′tĭ·fīd	cer-ti-fied	Proved by a certificate; guaranteed.
16. citation	sī·tā′shŭn	ci-ta-tion	Act of citing or quoting a passage from a book; a summons to appear, as in court; mention by way of praising discourse in military dispatches.
17. coincide	kō′ĭn·sīd′	co-in-cide	To correspond exactly in nature or character; to agree; to occur in the same period of time.
18. competence	kŏm′pĕ·tĕns	com-pe-tence	Sufficiency; quality or position of being legally competent; ability.
19. defendant	dĕ·fĕn′dănt	de-fend-ant	One who must make answer in a legal action.
20. depository	dĕ·pŏz′ĭ·tō′rĭ	de-pos-i-to-ry	A place where things may be stored for safekeeping.
21. depreciation	dĕ·prē′shĭ·ā′shŭn	de-pre-ci-a-tion	A decrease in value due to wear and tear or to disuse.
22. descriptive	dĕ·skrĭp′tĭv	de-scrip-tive	Characterized by description.
23. detrimental	dĕt′rĭ·mĕn′tăl	det-ri-men-tal	Injurious; harmful; prejudicial.
24. eccentric	ĕk·sĕn′trĭk	ec-cen-tric	Deviating from the usual pattern of behavior; irregular.
25. eczema	ĕk′sĕ·má	ec-ze-ma	A disease of the skin.

►

26. edifice	ĕd'ĭ·fĭs	ed-i-fice	A large building, such as a palace or a church.
27. egotism	ē'gō·tĭz'm	e-go-tism	The habit of boasting about oneself; self-conceit.
28. election	ê·lĕk'shŭn	e-lec-tion	The process of selecting a person or persons for an office by a vote of the people.
29. elite	à·lēt'	e-lite	The select or choice part.
30. encounter	ĕn·koun'tẽr	en-coun-ter	To engage in conflict; to meet face to face.
31. encumbrance	ĕn·kŭm'brăns	en-cum-brance	A claim, a lien, or another factor that in some respect qualifies the absolute owner-ship of real estate.
32. expiration	ĕk'spĭ·rā'shŭn	ex-pi-ra-tion	A coming to an end; that which is expired.
33. extended	ĕks·tĕn'dĕd	ex-tend-ed	Stretched or spread out.
34. forum	fō'rŭm	fo-rum	A tribunal; a public meeting place for open discussion.
35. franchise	frăn'chīz	fran-chise	A particular privilege conferred by a government; a constitu-tional right, as the right to vote.
36. freeze	frēz	freeze	To change from a liquid form into ice.
37. habitual	hà·bĭt'û·ăl	ha-bit-u-al	Fixed by or resulting from habit.
38. incapacitate	ĭn'kà·păs'ĭ·tāt	in-ca-pac-i-tate	To disqualify; to make inca-pable or unfit.
39. incognito	ĭn·kŏg'nĭ·tō	in-cog-ni-to	Having one's identity con-cealed to avoid notice or atten-tion.
40. indictment	ĭn·dīt'mĕnt	in-dict-ment	An accusation usually pre-sented by a grand jury.
41. inflation	ĭn·flā'shŭn	in-fla-tion	Unsound expansion, especially of currency.
42. invoice	ĭn'vois	in-voice	An itemized statement listing goods sent to a purchaser and including prices, quantities, and charges.
43. irrigate	ĭr'ĭ·gāt	ir-ri-gate	To supply land with water in order to promote vegetation.
44. knell	nĕl	knell	The sound of a bell, as when tolled at a funeral; a mournful sound.
45. maintain	mān·tān'	main-tain	To keep in existence; to pre-serve; to retain.
46. manipulate	mà·nĭp'û·lāt	ma-nip-u-late	To handle skillfully.
47. meager	mē'gẽr	mea-ger	Thin; lacking in quality or quantity; having little money, strength, or the like.
48. negligent	nĕg'lĭ·jĕnt	neg-li-gent	Guilty of neglect; careless.

49. negotiate	nē·gō′shĭ·āt	ne-go-ti-ate	To try to effect an agreement; to effect a valid transfer of a negotiable instrument.
50. objective ▶	ŏb·jĕk′tĭv	ob-jec-tive	The goal toward which one directs his efforts.
51. obligatory	ŏb·lĭg′a·tō′rĭ	ob-lig-a-to-ry	Binding legally or morally.
52. ounce	ouns	ounce	A weight, sixteenth part of a pound.
53. partially	pär′shăl·lĭ	par-tial-ly	Not generally or totally.
54. penalize	pē′năl·īz	pe-nal-ize	To subject to a penalty.
55. pending	pĕn′dĭng	pend-ing	*adj.* Hanging; awaiting a decision. *prep.* During; until.
56. phenomenal	fē·nŏm′ē·năl	phe-nom-e-nal	Extraordinary; unusual.
57. photogenic	fō′tŏ·jĕn′ĭk	pho-to-gen-ic	Suitable for being photographed.
58. priority	prī·ŏr′ĭ·tĭ	pri-or-i-ty	Superiority in rank, position, privilege; precedence.
59. pronunciation	prō·nŭn′sĭ·ā′shŭn	pro-nun-ci-a-tion	Manner of pronouncing words; distinct vocal expression.
60. punctual	pŭngk′tụ̆·ăl	punc-tu-al	Prompt.
61. renegotiate	rē′nē·gō′shĭ·āt	re-ne-go-ti-ate	To readjust a contract (applies particularly to government contracts); to confer again concerning a basis of agreement.
62. reprove	rē·prōōv′	re-prove	To express disapproval of; to rebuke; to blame.
63. rheumatism	rōō′má·tĭz′m	rheu-ma-tism	A disease of the joints or muscles.
64. sanitary	săn′ĭ·tĕr′ĭ	san-i-tar-y	Pertaining to health, with a special reference to cleanliness; free from dirt and germs.
65. saturation	săt′ụ·rā′shŭn	sat-u-ra-tion	The process of saturating.
66. sixty	sĭks′tĭ	six-ty	A cardinal number, following *fifty-nine*.
67. solicitation	sŏ·lĭs′ĭ·tā′shŭn	so-lic-i-ta-tion	The act of soliciting; an entreaty.
68. spontaneous	spŏn·tā′nē·ŭs	spon-ta-ne-ous	Natural and unconstrained; proceeding without effort.
69. status	stā′tŭs	sta-tus	State; condition of a person for legal purposes.
70. suspicious	sŭs·pĭsh′ŭs	sus-pi-cious	Questionable; distrustful.
71. sympathize	sĭm′pá·thīz	sym-pa-thize	To express sympathy; to condole with.
72. systematic	sĭs′tĕm·ăt′ĭk	sys-tem-at-ic	Having a system or a method; having an orderly plan.
73. television	tĕl′ē·vĭzh′ŭn	tel-e-vi-sion	The transmission and reproduction of a scene or setting by any apparatus that converts light waves into electrical waves and then converts them back into visible light rays.

| 74. transparent | trăns·pâr′ĕnt | trans-par-ent | Easily seen through; readily understood. |
| 75. urgent | ûr′jĕnt | ur-gent | Requiring immediate action or attention; pressing. |

Lesson 3

1. abeyance	á·bā′ăns	a-bey-ance	Temporary suspension; a state of waiting.
2. adjournment	ă·jûrn′mĕnt	ad-journ-ment	The act of adjourning or suspending, as a meeting or a session of court.
3. alignment	á·līn′mĕnt	a-lign-ment	Act of arranging in a line; formation in line.
4. amenable	á·mē′ná·b'l	a-me-na-ble	Answerable; ready to yield, or submit without objection; legally responsible.
5. antecedent	ăn′tē·sēd′ĕnt	an-te-ced-ent	Going before in time; preceding.
6. businessman	bĭz′nĕs·măn′	busi-ness-man	A man engaged in business.
7. cerebral	sĕr′ĕ·brăl	cer-e-bral	Pertaining to the brain; having appeal to one's intellectual appreciation.
8. concerted	kŏn·sûr′tĕd	con-cert-ed	Planned or arranged by agreement; prearranged.
9. concise	kŏn·sīs′	con-cise	Brief; comprehensive.
10. convene	kŏn·vēn′	con-vene	To come together; to assemble, usually in a public place.
11. democracy	dē·mŏk′rá·sĭ	de-moc-ra-cy	Government by the people; a state of society that is characterized by equal rights.
12. denunciate	dē·nŭn′shĭ·āt	de-nun-ci-ate	To accuse; to condemn openly; to invoke hostile criticism on.
13. deteriorate	dē·tēr′ĭ·ō·rāt	de-te-ri-o-rate	To become worse; to become lower in character or quality.
14. dexterous	dĕk′stĕr·ŭs	dex-ter-ous	Skillful in using the hands; expert; adroit.
15. encyclopedia	ĕn·sī′klŏ·pē′dĭ·á	en-cy-clo-pe-di-a	A work treating various topics of knowledge; a work treating one art or science completely.
16. expediency	ĕks·pē′dĭ·ĕn·sĭ	ex-pe-di-en-cy	Quality of being expedient; fitness; use of means adopted to get results, often with no regard to fairness or rightness of means.
17. flammable	flăm′á·b'l	flam-ma-ble	May be easily ignited.
18. gist	jĭst	gist	The substance of a matter; the essential point of a question.

19. graphic	grăf′ĭk	graph-ic	Vividly described; pertaining to representation by use of diagrams or graphs.
20. icicle	ĭ′sĭk·′l	i-ci-cle	A tapering mass of ice formed by the freezing of dripping water.
21. impromptu	ĭm·prŏmp′tū	im-promp-tu	Made or done suddenly or hastily.
22. incipient	ĭn·sĭp′ĭ·ĕnt	in-cip-i-ent	Commencing; beginning to be.
23. indiscreet	ĭn′dĭs·krēt′	in-dis-creet	Lacking in discretion; lacking in good judgment.
24. inherent	ĭn·hẹ̆r′ĕnt	in-her-ent	Existing in something as an inseparable quality; belonging by nature.
▶ 25. initiate	ĭ·nĭsh′ĭ·āt	in-i-ti-ate	To begin; to originate.
26. insertion	ĭn·sûr′shŭn	in-ser-tion	Something inserted; act of inserting.
27. intangible	ĭn·tăn′jĭ·b′l	in-tan-gi-ble	Incapable of being touched; not material or physical.
28. integrated	ĭn′tĕ·grāt·ĕd	in-te-grat-ed	Brought together into a whole; made up as a unit.
29. intentionally	ĭn·tĕn′shŭn·ăl·lĭ	in-ten-tion-al-ly	Done purposely.
30. intercede	ĭn′tẽr·sēd′	in-ter-cede	To intervene in behalf of one in trouble; to mediate.
31. interim	ĭn′tẽr·ĭm	in-ter-im	Intervening time; an interval in time.
32. irreparable	ĭ·rĕp′à·rà·b′l	ir-rep-a-ra-ble	Incapable of being remedied.
33. machine	mà·shēn′	ma-chine	An apparatus consisting of related mechanical parts used to perform some special kind of work.
34. merge	mûrj	merge	To cause to be absorbed in something else; to lose identity by combination with something else.
35. method	mĕth′ŭd	meth-od	An orderly or systematic mode of procedure.
36. misinterpreted	mĭs′ĭn·tûr′prĕt·ĕd	mis-in-ter-pret-ed	Misunderstood.
37. naive	nä·ēv′	na-ive	Showing natural simplicity; unsophisticated.
38. nation	nā′shŭn	na-tion	A body of people, generally speaking the same language, occupying a particular territory, and united under a single independent government.
39. nee	nā	nee	Born (placed after the name of a married woman to introduce her maiden name).
40. oscillate	ŏs′ĭ·lāt	os-cil-late	To swing to and fro like a pendulum; to fluctuate between opposing opinions.

41. pecuniary	pė·kū′nĭ·ĕr′ĭ	pe-cu-ni-ar-y	Pertaining to money.
42. peremptory	pĕr·ĕmp′tȯ·rĭ	per-emp-to-ry	Positive; dogmatic; leaving no opportunity for denial or refusal.
43. prelude	prĕl′ūd	prel-ude	Preliminary action or remarks.
44. proficient	prȯ·fĭsh′ĕnt	pro-fi-cient	Skilled in any art, science, or subject.
45. protégé	prō′tĕ·zhā	pro-te-ge	One who is under the care and protection of another.
46. quandary	kwŏn′dȧ·rĭ	quan-da-ry	A dilemma; a state of perplexity or uncertainty.
47. quota	kwō′tȧ	quo-ta	A proportional part or share.
48. realistic	rē′ăl·ĭs′tĭk	re-al-is-tic	Pertaining to what is real or practical.
49. rebate	rē′bāt	re-bate	*n.* A return of part of the original amount. *v.* To deduct as a discount.
▶ 50. refund	rė·fŭnd′	re-fund	To repay; to return money in restitution, reimbursement, etc.
51. reserve	rė·zûrv′	re-serve	To save for future use; to set aside for a particular use.
52. resource	rė·sōrs′	re-source	A reserve source of supply or support.
53. retail	rē′tāl	re-tail	The sale of commodities in small quantities, usually to a householder.
54. scholastic	skȯ·lăs′tĭk	scho-las-tic	Pertaining to schools or scholars.
55. scrupulous	skrōō′pů·lŭs	scru-pu-lous	Precise or exact; having strict regard for what is right or fitting.
56. senile	sē′nĭl	se-nile	Characteristic of old age.
57. spurious	spū′rĭ·ŭs	spu-ri-ous	Not genuine or true; counterfeit.
58. stabilization	stā′bĭ·lĭ·zā′shŭn	sta-bi-li-za-tion	The prevention of fluctuations, as in prices; act of making stable or firm.
59. stringent	strĭn′jĕnt	strin-gent	Strict or severe; tight.
60. subcontract	sŭb·kŏn′trăkt	sub-con-tract	A contract subordinate to a previous contract; a contract that provides services for another contract.
61. submerge	sŭb·mûrj′	sub-merge	To sink below the surface of the water.
62. subsidiary	sŭb·sĭd′ĭ·ĕr′ĭ	sub-sid-i-ar-y	Auxiliary; secondary.
63. substantiate	sŭb·stăn′shĭ·āt	sub-stan-ti-ate	To verify; to establish by proof.
64. succinct	sŭk·sĭngkt′	suc-cinct	Brief; concise; expressed in a few words.

65.	sufficiency	sŭ·fĭsh'ĕn·sĭ	suf-fi-cien-cy	Adequacy; sufficient provision for comfortable living.
66.	susceptible	sŭ·sĕp'tĭ·b'l	sus-cep-ti-ble	Yielding; sensitive; easily affected; prone.
67.	tacit	tăs'ĭt	tacit	Silent; unspoken; implied but not spoken or expressed.
68.	temerity	tĕ·mĕr'ĭ·tĭ	te-mer-i-ty	Boldness; rashness; recklessness.
69.	tenacious	tĕ·nā'shŭs	te-na-cious	Holding fast or keeping a firm hold; retentive.
70.	tricycle	trī'sĭk·'l	tri-cy-cle	A small three-wheeled vehicle.
71.	usury	ū'zhŏŏ·rĭ	u-sury	Interest at a higher rate than is allowed by law.
72.	verdict	vûr'dĭkt	ver-dict	The decision of a jury.
73.	vice versa	vī'sĕ vûr'sá	vi-ce ver-sa	Conversely; in reverse order.
74.	vindictive	vĭn·dĭk'tĭv	vin-dic-tive	Prompted by revenge.
75.	vitamin	vī'tá·mĭn	vi-ta-min	Any of a group of food elements essential to maintain life.

Lesson 4

1.	abbreviation	ă·brē'vĭ·ā'shŭn	ab-bre-vi-a-tion	A shortened form of a word or phrase.
2.	abettor	á·bĕt'ẽr	a-bet-tor	One who encourages or countenances, especially a legal offender or offense.
3.	abridgment	á·brĭj'mĕnt	a-bridg-ment	A condensed form of a work, still keeping the sense and unity of the original.
4.	accountant	ă·koun'tănt	ac-count-ant	A person who keeps, inspects, or adjusts accounts.
5.	accredited	ă·krĕd'ĭt·ĕd	ac-cred-it-ed	Certified as of a prescribed standard.
6.	acquittal	ă·kwĭt'ăl	ac-quit-tal	A setting free by legal process.
7.	activity	ăk·tĭv'ĭ·tĭ	ac-tiv-i-ty	State of action; physical motion.
8.	admittance	ăd·mĭt'ăns	ad-mit-tance	Act of admitting; entrance by permission.
9.	affluent	ăf'lŭ·ĕnt	af-flu-ent	Rich in material possessions; abundant; flowing abundantly.
10.	allergic	ă·lûr'jĭk	al-ler-gic	Affected with an allergy.
11.	alleviate	ă·lē'vĭ·āt	al-le-vi-ate	To make easier to endure; to lighten.
12.	allocate	ăl'ŏ·kāt	al-lo-cate	To assign; to allot; to distribute as a share.
13.	alumnae	á·lŭm'nē	a-lum-nae	Women graduates of a school or college.
14.	annotate	ăn'ŏ·tāt	an-no-tate	To furnish with critical or explanatory notes.

15. announcer	ă·noun′sĕr	an-nounc-er	One who announces, especially on radio or on television.
16. antagonist	ăn·tăg′ŏ·nĭst	an-tag-o-nist	One who opposes another; an adversary.
17. assessment	ă·sĕs′mĕnt	as-sess-ment	The value assigned or assessed to taxable property.
18. auditorium	ô′dĭ·tō′rĭ·ŭm	au-di-to-ri-um	The space in a church, theater, or other public building assigned to the audience.
19. autograph	ô′tŏ·grăf	au-to-graph	A person's own signature or hand-writing.
20. bidder	bĭd′ĕr	bid-der	One who has made a bid or offered a price.
21. blatant	blā′tănt	bla-tant	Offensively noisy; coarse; vulgarly showy.
22. commendable	kŏ·mĕn′dá·b'l	com-mend-a-ble	Praiseworthy; laudable; recommendable.
23. communism	kŏm′û·nĭz'm	com-mu-nism	Any system of social organization based on holding all goods in common, actual ownership being ascribed to the state.
24. condolence	kŏn·dō′lĕns	con-do-lence	An expression of sympathy.
25. confidential	kŏn′fĭ·dĕn′shăl	con-fi-den-tial	Written or spoken in confidence; secret.
26. culinary	kū′lĭ·nĕr′ĭ	cu-li-nar-y	Pertaining to the kitchen or cookery.
27. denunciation	dĕ·nŭn′sĭ·ā′shŭn	de-nun-ci-a-tion	A denouncing; public accusation.
28. disability	dĭs′á·bĭl′ĭ·tĭ	dis-a-bil-i-ty	Lack of competent physical, intellectual, or moral fitness; legal disqualification.
29. district	dĭs′trĭkt	dis-trict	A division of a territory marked off for administrative or other purposes.
30. duress	dū′rĕs	du-ress	Application of force or pressure.
31. embark	ĕm·bärk′	em-bark	To put or go on board a ship; to invest in a business venture.
32. epidemic	ĕp′ĭ·dĕm′ĭk	ep-i-dem-ic	A disease that is spreading rapidly and attacking many people.
33. evaluation	ĕ·văl′û·ā′shŭn	e-val-u-a-tion	The appraised valuation.
34. express	ĕks·prĕs′	ex-press	To put thought into words; to show; to reveal.
35. hesitancy	hĕz′ĭ·tăn·sĭ	hes-i-tan-cy	Hesitation; indecision.
36. ill-mannered	ĭl′măn′ĕrd	ill-man-nered	Having bad manners; impolite; rude.
37. increase	ĭn·krēs′	in-crease	To make greater; to add to; to make more numerous.
38. intermittent	ĭn′tĕr·mĭt′ĕnt	in-ter-mit-tent	Alternately stopping and going again; periodic.
39. intimidation	ĭn·tĭm′ĭ·dā′shŭn	in-tim-i-da-tion	Act of inspiring with fear.
40. irradiate	ĭ·rā′dĭ·āt	ir-ra-di-ate	To enlighten intellectually; to illuminate.

41.	irrespective	ĭr'rĕ·spĕk'tĭv	ir-re-spec-tive	Without regard for persons, conditions, or consequences.
42.	justification	jŭs'tĭ·fĭ·kā'shŭn	jus-ti-fi-ca-tion	Act of justifying; act of showing lawful reason for an action.
43.	kingdom	kĭng'dŭm	king-dom	A state or monarchy having a king or queen as its ruler.
44.	loathsome	lōth'sŭm	loath-some	Hateful; disgusting.
45.	middleman	mĭd'ʼl·măn'	mid-dle-man	Any agent dealing in goods in any of the steps between producer and consumer.
46.	mindful	mīnd'fŏŏl	mind-ful	Keeping or bearing in mind; regardful; attentive.
47.	misrepresent	mĭs'rĕp·rĕ·zĕnt'	mis-rep-re-sent	To represent incorrectly.
48.	nervousness	nûr'vŭs·nĕs	nerv-ous-ness	State of acute uneasiness or apprehension.
49.	newsstand	nūz'stănd'	news-stand	A place where newspapers, magazines, etc., are sold.
50.	nonessential	nŏn'ĕ·sĕn'shăl	non-es-sen-tial	Unnecessary; not essential.
▶ 51.	nostalgia	nŏs·tăl'jĭ·à	nos-tal-gi-a	A wishful or sentimental yearning for return to the things of the past; homesickness.
52.	occupancy	ŏk'û·păn·sĭ	oc-cu-pan-cy	Act of taking possession; occupation.
53.	parchment	pärch'mĕnt	parch-ment	The skin of sheep or goats, prepared for use as writing material.
54.	passport	pás'pōrt	pass-port	A document authorizing a person to leave a country and requesting protection for him abroad.
55.	peculiar	pĕ·kūl'yĕr	pe-cul-iar	Strange; odd; uncommon.
56.	penmanship	pĕn'măn·shĭp	pen-man-ship	The art of handwriting.
57.	penurious	pĕ·nū'rĭ·ŭs	pe-nu-ri-ous	Stingy; miserly.
58.	petroleum	pĕ·trō'lĕ·ŭm	pe-tro-le-um	An oily, dark-colored liquid processed into gasoline, kerosene, etc.
59.	portfolio	pōrt·fō'lĭ·ō	port-fo-li-o	A portable case for holding documents, papers, etc.; a list of securities owned.
60.	possessive	pŏ·zĕs'ĭv	pos-ses-sive	Pertaining to ownership; showing desire to possess or own.
61.	promulgate	prŏ·mŭl'gāt	pro-mul-gate	To publish abroad; to proclaim; to teach a doctrine publicly.
62.	quarantine	kwŏr'ăn·tēn	quar-an-tine	A condition of isolation designed to prevent the spread of a disease.
63.	rearrange	rē'à·rānj'	re-ar-range	To arrange again; to readjust.
64.	recorder	rĕ·kôr'dĕr	re-cord-er	One who records, especially as an official duty; a device for recording words and other sounds.
65.	recurrence	rĕ·kûr'ĕns	re-cur-rence	A returning or reappearing regularly or frequently.
66.	reputable	rĕp'û·tà·b'l	rep-u-ta-ble	Enjoying a good reputation; honorable; respectable.

67. subscriber	sŭb·skrĭb'ĕr	sub-scrib-er	One who promises to give a contribution; one who contracts for the purchase of something, as stock, a magazine, etc.
68. subterfuge	sŭb'tĕr·fūj	sub-ter-fuge	A plan or scheme used to escape the force of an argument, censure, etc.; a device to avoid unfavorable consequences; an evasion.
69. tabulating	tăb'ů·lāt'ĭng	tab-u-la-ting	Arranging or putting items into the form of a table.
70. tenure	tĕn'ûr	ten-ure	The holding of anything; the period for which something is possessed and enjoyed.
71. underrate	ŭn'dĕr·rāt'	un-der-rate	To rate too low.
72. vacillate	văs'ĭ·lāt	vac-il-late	To sway unsteadily; to fluctuate.
73. vagary	vȧ·gâr'ĭ	va-gar-y	A fantastic idea or notion; a whim.
74. validity	vȧ·lĭd'ĭ·tĭ	va-lid-i-ty	Soundness; state of being valid.
75. zipper	zĭp'ĕr	zip-per	Any slide fastener consisting of an interlocking device operated by a pull-tab.

Lesson 5 Check-Up

Unit Test. Your teacher will dictate 50 words chosen from the lessons in Unit 3 of Part 3. These words are selected to test your mastery of the new words in this unit. Listen closely as each word is dictated, recall the "type" of word it is, spell the word carefully, and write plainly to assure yourself of a fair test.

Proofreading Test. In the following letter, some of the italicized words are misspelled. Copy the entire letter, making any corrections necessary in the spelling of the words.

Dear Mr. Jackson:

We have just received a letter from our *accountent* in which he *espresed* his approval of the *quarterly* statement. He noted that the *acrual* figure had been increased during the last fiscal year. There was *justifcation* for the *reelistic* and *systemetic methed* of *aligning* the figures in the tables.

The *corelation* between the monthly *rentel* and the *seaconal* income was *vallid*. The *subsidery* account had been set up as an *intangable* asset.

We are enclosing a report that was duplicated on a *copeing mashine*. You may have more copies if you wish.

Cordially yours,

Cumulative Test. Your teacher will now dictate 40 words chosen from Units 1 and 2 of Part 3. These words will test your retention of the correct spelling of words in these units. Spell carefully and write plainly.

Checking Your Tests. Your teacher will give you directions for checking the unit test, the proofreading test, and the cumulative test.

Error Analysis. Classify the errors that you made by noting the type of error beside each word that you misspelled.

Review. Use the appropriate attack procedures for studying the words that you misspelled on the unit test, on the proofreading test, and on the cumulative test. Remember that both "sound" and "meaning" words are included.

Retest. The retest will tell you if you have mastered the words in Units 1 through 3 of Part 3. If you misspelled words on the retest, continue your attack procedures until you are sure that you can spell all the words correctly.

Unit 4 Rule Words

Spelling rules are the key to the correct spelling of the business words in this unit. Review briefly the spelling rules discussed on pages 20-29, giving particular attention to those rules that are most troublesome for you; then begin your study of Lessons 1-4 of this unit, applying the following procedures:

Preview. Your teacher will dictate a list of 75 general-business-vocabulary words. Number a sheet of paper from 1 to 75. Spell as many of the words as you can, but attempt only the words that you are quite sure you know how to spell. If you do not know the spelling of a word, place a question mark (?) beside the number.

Checking Performance. Compare your spellings with the words given in the appropriate lesson. Place an *X* beside each word that you misspelled. To the right of any misspelled or omitted word, write the correct spelling.

Error Analysis. Classify the errors that you made by noting the type of error beside each word that you misspelled. For instance, if an error was caused by failure to double a final consonant when adding a suffix, write "final consonant" beside the word. Refer to pages 20-29 if you have forgotten the types of rule errors.

Attack Procedures. Attack procedures for rule-type errors were presented in Section One, beginning on page 32. Review the corrective technique recommended for each type of error.

Learning to Spell New Words. The pretest words that you did not know how to spell now appear on your answer sheet preceded by a question mark. Use a separate sheet of paper to practice those words, following the SEE, SAY, SPELL, and WRITE routine (see pages 39-41). Hand in the drill paper to your instructor.

Lesson 1

1. abstraction	ăb·străk′shŭn	ab-strac-tion	A visionary notion; something considered by itself.
2. Addressograph	á·drĕs′ō·gráf	Ad-dres-so-graph	A trade-mark of a machine that prints addresses from stencils.
3. adjusted	á·jŭst′ĕd	ad-just-ed	Regulated; put in good working order.
4. advisable	ăd·vīz′á·b'l	ad-vis-a-ble	Proper to be done; expedient; prudent.
5. comparably	kŏm′pá·rá·blĭ	com-pa-ra-bly	To a comparable degree; in a comparable manner.
6. compilation	kŏm′pĭ·lā′shŭn	com-pi-la-tion	Act of compiling or assembling material from other sources, as for a book.

7. computing	kŏm·pūt'ĭng	com-put-ing	Calculating; reckoning.
8. concurred	kŏn·kûrd'	con-curred	Agreed; co-operated; combined.
9. constitutional	kŏn'stĭ·tū'shŭn·ăl	con-sti-tu-tion-al	Pertaining to the constitution of a state; beneficial to the bodily constitution.
10. continuance	kŏn·tĭn'ū·ăns	con-tin-u-ance	A continuation; a sequel.
11. continuity	kŏn'tĭ·nū'ĭ·tĭ	con-ti-nu-i-ty	Quality of being continuous; a connected whole.
12. conversant	kŏn'vēr·sănt	con-ver-sant	Familiar as a result of use or study; versed; acquainted.
13. convertible	kŏn·vûr'tĭ·b'l	con-vert-i-ble	Capable of being converted or changed.
14. dedication	dĕd'ĭ·kā'shŭn	ded-i-ca-tion	An inscription in a book, dedicating it to a person or cause; act of dedicating something for any special purpose.
15. deduction	dē·dŭk'shŭn	de-duc-tion	An amount subtracted; a conclusion.
16. depart	dē·pärt'	de-part	To go away from a place; to turn away; to deviate.
17. detailed	dē·tāld'	de-tailed	Itemized; full of particulars told minutely.
18. diagnosis	dī'ăg·nō'sĭs	di-ag-no-sis	The decision reached after an examination concerning the nature of an illness.
19. dictation	dĭk·tā'shŭn	dic-ta-tion	Act of uttering something to be written down.
20. dictator	dĭk·tā'tĕr	dic-ta-tor	One who dictates something to be written down; one who rules with supreme authority in a state.
21. directory	dĭ·rĕk'tŏ·rĭ	di-rec-to-ry	A book listing the names and addresses of a particular group of people.
22. distributor	dĭs·trĭb'ū·tĕr	dis-trib-u-tor	A person or thing that distributes.
23. eighty	ā'tĭ	eight-y	Cardinal number, following *seventy-nine*.
24. electrician	ē·lĕk'trĭsh'ăn	e-lec-tri-cian	One who works in the construction or repair of electric apparatus.
25. embezzlement ►	ĕm·bĕz'l·mĕnt	em-bez-zle-ment	Appropriation to one's own use of anything belonging to another, as an employer's money.
26. endurable	ĕn·dūr'à·b'l	en-dur-a-ble	Capable of being endured; tolerable.
27. enumeration	ē·nū'mēr·ā'shŭn	e-nu-mer-a-tion	Act of listing one after another; a catalogue.
28. excitable	ĕk·sīt'à·b'l	ex-cit-a-ble	Can be excited easily.

29. **filing**	fīl′ĭng	fil-ing	Act of putting papers, cards, etc., into a file drawer in a systematic order.
30. **furnishing**	fûr′nĭsh·ĭng	fur-nish-ing	Supplying whatever is needed or useful; giving.
31. **harmonious**	här·mō′nĭ·ŭs	har-mo-ni-ous	Having a pleasing arrangement; congenial; having similar ideas.
32. **housing**	houz′ĭng	hous-ing	Act of providing a house, a store, or shelter for people and things.
33. **imposition**	ĭm′pŏ·zĭsh′ŭn	im-po-si-tion	Act of taking advantage of, as a friendship; an excessive burden.
34. **improbable**	ĭm·prŏb′à·b'l	im-prob-a-ble	Not likely to happen.
35. **incomparable**	ĭn·kŏm′pà·rà·b'l	in-com-pa-ra-ble	Unequaled; matchless; unsuitable for comparison.
36. **indisputable**	ĭn·dĭs′pū·tà·b'l	in-dis-pu-ta-ble	Cannot be questioned or doubted.
37. **inflationary**	ĭn·flā′shŭn·ĕr′ĭ	in-fla-tion-ar-y	Causing a disproportionate and sudden increase in the amount of money in circulation.
38. **injurious**	ĭn·jŏŏr′ĭ·ŭs	in-ju-ri-ous	Causing injury; harmful.
39. **insistent**	ĭn·sĭs′tĕnt	in-sist-ent	Persistent; compelling attention.
40. **jobber**	jŏb′ĕr	job-ber	One who buys goods in quantity from producers or importers and sells them to dealers; a middleman.
41. **likable**	līk′à·b'l	lik-a-ble	Can be liked; pleasant; agreeable.
42. **mandatory**	măn′dà·tō′rĭ	man-da-to-ry	Obligatory; commanded; required.
43. **merchandising**	mûr′chăn·dīz·ĭng	mer-chan-dis-ing	Buying and selling objects of commerce; carrying on a trade.
44. **notation**	nŏ·tā′shŭn	no-ta-tion	A note; an annotation; act of noting or setting down in writing.
45. **observance**	ŏb·zûr′văns	ob-serv-ance	Act of noticing something; a ceremony for a particular occasion.
46. **participation**	păr·tĭs′ĭ·pā′shŭn	par-tic-i-pa-tion	Act of taking part with others; sharing in common with others.
47. **prospectus**	prŏ·spĕk′tŭs	pro-spec-tus	A statement giving advance information about a forthcoming literary work, a new enterprise, a security, etc., to gain interest and support.
48. **purchaser**	pûr′chĭs·ĕr	pur-chas-er	A buyer.

49.	regrettable	rĕ·grĕt′à·b'l	re-gret-ta-ble	Unfortunate; distressing.
50. ►	reimbursement	rē′ĭm·bûrs′mĕnt	re-im-burse-ment	Repayment of money spent; compensation, as for time lost.
51.	reminder	rē·mīn′dẽr	re-mind-er	That which helps one to remember.
52.	remittable	rē·mĭt′à·b'l	re-mit-ta-ble	Can be remitted or transmitted.
53.	removable	rē·mōōv′à·b'l	re-mov-a-ble	Can be removed or taken away.
54.	replacement	rē·plās′mĕnt	re-place-ment	Act of replacing; a person or thing that takes the place of another.
55.	reputation	rĕp′ů·tā′shŭn	rep-u-ta-tion	What others think of a person; good name.
56.	resourceful	rē·sōrs′fŏŏl	re-source-ful	Able to solve problems or difficulties with available means.
57.	seriousness	sẽr′ĭ·ŭs·nĕs	se-ri-ous-ness	Earnestness; importance.
58.	shippers	shĭp′ẽrs	ship-pers	Those engaged in shipping goods.
59.	simplified	sĭm′plĭ·fīd	sim-pli-fied	Made less complicated.
60.	simulated	sĭm′ů·lā′tĕd	sim-u-lat-ed	Pretended; assumed or had the appearance of.
61.	souvenir	sōō′vē·nẽr	sou-ve-nir	A memento; something as a remembrance.
62.	stewardess	stū′ẽrd·ĕs	stew-ard-ess	A woman employed to attend to the comforts of passengers on an airplane, boat, or bus.
63.	transcript	trăn′skrĭpt	tran-script	A written or typewritten copy of shorthand notes; a copy.
64.	triple	trĭp′′l	tri-ple	Threefold; consisting of three.
65.	unavoidable	ŭn′à·void′à·b'l	un-avoid-a-ble	Cannot be avoided; inevitable.
66.	unconditional	ŭn′kŏn·dĭsh′ŭn·ăl	un-con-di-tion-al	Not limited by conditions; without reservations.
67.	unnecessary	ŭn·nĕs′ĕ·sẽr′ĭ	un-nec-es-sary	Needless; not necessary.
68.	unprecedented	ŭn·prĕs′ĕ·dĕn′tĕd	un-prec-e-dent-ed	Without precedent; novel; never known before.
69.	unprofitable	ŭn·prŏf′ĭt·à·b'l	un-prof-it-a-ble	Yielding no profit or gain.
70.	usable	ūz′à·b'l	us-a-ble	Can be used; available for use.
71.	venturesome	vĕn′t̞ûr·sŭm	ven-ture-some	Showing an inclination to take risks; daring.
72.	vitality	vī·tăl′ĭ·tĭ	vi-tal-i-ty	Physical strength or condition; liveliness; vigor.
73.	waiver	wāv′ẽr	waiv-er	A written statement relinquishing some right, interest, claim, or privilege.

| 74. wrench | rĕnch | wrench | v. To overstrain or injure by twisting a part of the body. n. A tool for turning or twisting a nut, bolt, etc. |
| 75. wrestle | rĕs''l | wres-tle | To engage in wrestling; to grapple. |

Lesson 2

1. acceptable	ăk·sĕp′tȧ·b'l	ac-cept-a-ble	Capable of being accepted; having the necessary qualifications.
2. accidentally	ăk′sĭ·dĕn′tăl·ĭ	ac-ci-den-tal-ly	Unexpectedly; unintentionally.
3. aggressive	ȧ·grĕs′ĭv	ag-gres-sive	Tending to be self-assertive; pushing; forward.
4. almighty	ôl·mīt′ĭ	al-mighty	Having unlimited power, strength; overpowering.
5. almond	ä′mŭnd	al-mond	A small tree of the peach family; the stone of the fruit of the almond tree.
6. approachable	ȧ·prōch′ȧ·b'l	ap-proach-a-ble	Capable of being approached; accessible.
7. authoritatively	ô·thŏr′ĭ·tā′tĭv·lĭ	au-thor-i-ta-tive-ly	In a manner whereby one is entitled to obedience or acceptance; dictatorially.
8. biscuit	bĭs′kĭt	bis-cuit	A kind of unleavened bread formed into a small cake and baked hard.
9. character	kăr′ăk·tēr	char-ac-ter	The sum of the qualities that distinguish one person or thing from another; individuality.
10. claimant	klām′ănt	claim-ant	One who makes a claim.
11. confirmation	kŏn′fēr·mā′shŭn	con-fir-ma-tion	Verification; proof.
12. consigned	kŏn·sīnd′	con-signed	Forwarded or delivered to someone to be sold; entrusted.
13. consistent	kŏn·sĭs′tĕnt	con-sist-ent	Agreeing; possessing firmness; not self-contradictory.
14. constructive	kŏn·strŭk′tĭv	con-struc-tive	Tending to construct; pertaining to the nature of construction.
15. contractor	kŏn·trăk′tēr	con-trac-tor	One of the parties to a written agreement; one who supplies or constructs on a large scale for a stated sum.
16. cordially	kôr′jăl·lĭ	cor-dial-ly	In a friendly or sincere manner.
17. cupboard	kŭb′ērd	cup-board	A closet with shelves for dishes, food, etc.

18. deductible	dĕ·dŭkt′ĭ·b'l	de-duct-i-ble	Can be deducted or sub-tracted.
19. discourse	dĭs·kōrs′	dis-course	Talk; conversation.
20. discovery	dĭs·kŭv′ĕr·ĭ	dis-cov-er-y	That which is found for the first time; a disclosure; a revelation.
21. dreary	drẽr′ĭ	drear-y	Causing gloom; dismal; dull.
22. emersed	ĕ·mûrst′	e-mersed	Rising or standing out of a surface, as water.
23. enrollment	ĕn·rōl′mĕnt	en-roll-ment	The process of being en-rolled; the number of people enrolled.
24. excel	ĕk·sĕl′	ex-cel	To be superior; to surpass.
▶ 25. exceptional	ĕk·sĕp′shŭn·ăl	ex-cep-tion-al	Unusual; extraordinary.
26. exempt	ĕg·zĕmpt′	ex-empt	Free from some burden or limitation to which other persons or things are sub-ject.
27. exhilaration	ĕg·zĭl′a·rā′shŭn	ex-hil-a-ra-tion	Animation; condition of being exhilarated.
28. expansion	ĕks·păn′shŭn	ex-pan-sion	Process of expanding; that which is spread out.
29. expatiate	ĕks·pā′shĭ·āt	ex-pa-ti-ate	To enlarge in discourse or writing; to talk or write at length.
30. expiate	ĕks′pĭ·āt	ex-pi-ate	To atone for; to make amends.
31. furlough	fûr′lō	fur-lough	A leave of absence granted to a soldier.
32. gauge	gāj	gauge	To appraise; to estimate; to judge.
33. helpful	hĕlp′fŏŏl	help-ful	Giving help; useful.
34. hypochondriac	hī′pŏ·kŏn′drĭ·ăk	hy-po-chon-dri-ac	A person affected with mor-bid concern about his health.
35. illiterate	ĭl·lĭt′ĕr·ĭt	il-lit-er-ate	Unable to read and write; uneducated.
36. immersed	ĭ·mûrst′	im-mersed	Plunged into a liquid.
37. improbably	ĭm·prŏb′a·blĭ	im-prob-a-bly	Not very likely.
38. inability	ĭn′·a·bĭl′ĭ·tĭ	in-a-bil-i-ty	Lack of ability or power.
39. inaccessible	ĭn′ăk·sĕs′ĭ·b'l	in-ac-ces-si-ble	Not accessible; not obtain-able.
40. indefinitely	ĭn·dĕf′ĭ·nĭt·lĭ	in-def-i-nite-ly	Vaguely; generally; ob-scurely.
41. infallible	ĭn·făl′ĭ·b'l	in-fal-li-ble	Incapable of error; certain.
42. inveigle	ĭn·vē′g'l	in-vei-gle	To acquire or win by artful inducements.
43. inventor	ĭn·vĕn′tẽr	in-ven-tor	One who invents or devises some new process; one who makes new machines or in-ventions.

44. inventory	ĭn′vĕn·tō′rĭ	in-ven-to-ry	A detailed list of articles, with quantity and estimated value of each; a periodic account of stock taken in a business.
45. investor	ĭn·vĕs′tẽr	in-ves-tor	One who lays out money or capital in business with a view of obtaining an income or profit.
46. invigorate	ĭn·vĭg′ẽr·āt	in-vig-or-ate	To fill with life and energy·
47. judicial	jōō·dĭsh′ăl	ju-di-cial	Pertaining to the administration of justice.
48. loathe	lōth	loathe	To hate; to abhor; to detest; to dislike intensely.
49. mislead	mĭs·lēd′	mis-lead	To lead astray; to lead into error.
50. misunderstand ►	mĭs′ŭn·dẽr·stănd′	mis-un-der-stand	To fail to understand.
51. mollify	mŏl′ĭ·fī	mol-li-fy	To pacify; to calm; to appease.
52. nationally	năsh′ŭn·ăl·ĭ	na-tion-al-ly	Patriotically; over an entire country; widely.
53. nonexistent	nŏn′ĕg·zĭs′tĕnt	non-ex-ist-ent	Not existing.
54. obnoxious	ŏb·nŏk′shŭs	ob-nox-ious	Objectionable; offensive.
55. pension	pĕn′shŭn	pen-sion	A fixed, regular payment given for past services or for an injury or loss sustained.
56. portable	pŏr′tȧ·b′l	port-a-ble	Can be carried in the hand; easily conveyed.
57. prescribe	prĕ·skrīb′	pre-scribe	To lay down as a rule, guide, or course; to designate remedies or treatment to be used.
58. presume	prĕ·zūm′	pre-sume	To take for granted; to assume as true.
59. presumption	prĕ·zŭmp′shŭn	pre-sump-tion	Act of assuming something as true.
60. procure	prŏ·kūr′	pro-cure	To obtain or get by special means.
61. prosperous	prŏs′pĕr·ŭs	pros-per-ous	Having continued good fortune; successful.
62. rascal	răs′kăl	ras-cal	A dishonest person; a rogue.
63. reconnoiter	rĕk′ŏ·noi′tẽr	rec-on-noi-ter	To make a preliminary survey in order to gain information, as for military or engineering operations.
64. refining	rĕ·fīn′ĭng	re-fin-ing	Bringing to a fine or pure state.
65. reluctant	rĕ·lŭk′tănt	re-luc-tant	Unwilling; disinclined; hesitant.
66. simultaneous	sī′mŭl·tā′nĕ·ŭs	si-mul-ta-ne-ous	Occurring or functioning at the same time.

67. sociable	sō′sha·b′l	so-cia-ble	Friendly; agreeable with others.
68. submission	sŭb·mĭsh′ŭn	sub-mis-sion	Act of submitting; obedience; compliance.
69. subscription	sŭb·skrĭp′shŭn	sub-scrip-tion	The amount subscribed toward some cause; a signed paper.
70. transcription	trăn·skrĭp′shŭn	tran-scrip-tion	The act of transcribing; a transcript; a copy.
71. transmission	trăns·mĭsh′ŭn	trans-mis-sion	That which is transmitted; a device for transferring motive force.
72. trying	trī′ĭng	try-ing	Annoying; distressing.
73. vehicle	vē′ĭ·k′l	ve-hi-cle	A receptacle in which something is carried or moved; a means of conveyance.
74. vicious	vĭsh′ŭs	vi-cious	Depraved; disposed to evil; spiteful.
75. waitress	wāt′rĕs	wait-ress	A woman who waits on table.

Lesson 3

1. advertise	ăd′vĕr·tīz	ad-ver-tise	To call public attention to goods for sale to encourage the public to buy.
2. ambiguous	ăm·bĭg′û·ŭs	am-big-u-ous	Can be understood in two or more ways; uncertain; of doubtful nature.
3. ambulance	ăm′bû·lăns	am-bu-lance	A vehicle equipped for carrying the sick or injured.
4. antedate	ăn′tĕ·dāt′	an-te-date	To date earlier than the actual time; to assign to an earlier date.
5. anticipation	ăn·tĭs′ĭ·pā′shŭn	an-tic-i-pa-tion	Expectation; foretaste.
6. antihistamine	ăn′tĭ·hĭs′ta·mēn	an-ti-his-ta-mine	Any of several substances used to relieve the symptoms of hay fever and the common cold.
7. antipathy	ăn·tĭp′a·thĭ	an-tip-a-thy	A fixed dislike; an aversion.
8. antitrust	ăn′tĭ·trŭst′	an-ti-trust	Against trusts or large combinations formed to control industries, trade, etc.
9. beneficiary	bĕn′ĕ·fĭsh′ĭ·ĕr′ĭ	ben-e-fi-ci-ar-y	One who receives benefits, profits, or advantages.
10. bimonthly	bī·mŭnth′lĭ	bi-month-ly	Occurring once in every two months.

11. cautious	kô′shŭs	cau-tious	Very careful; showing caution or prudence to avoid danger.
12. classroom	klás′rōōm′	class-room	A room in a school or college where classes meet.
13. clemency	klĕm′ĕn·sĭ	clem-en-cy	Compassion; mercy; leniency.
14. combustible	kŏm·bŭs′tĭ·b'l	com-bus-ti-ble	Inflammable; capable of easily catching fire and burning.
15. compatible	kŏm·păt′ĭ·b'l	com-pat-i-ble	Capable of existing together in harmony.
16. consume	kŏn·sūm′	con-sume	To use up; to eat up; to destroy, as by fire.
17. contact	kŏn′tăkt	con-tact	A touching of bodies; close association.
18. containers	kŏn·tān′ĕrs	con-tain-ers	Any receptacle, as a box, carton, crate, etc., used for holding goods.
19. conventional	kŏn·vĕn′shŭn·ăl	con-ven-tion-al	Conforming to accepted standards of conduct; pertaining to general agreement.
20. coolly	kōōl′lĭ	cool-ly	In a cool manner.
21. despicable	dĕs′pĭ·kà·b'l	des-pi-ca-ble	Contemptible; should be despised.
22. dimension	dĭ·mĕn′shŭn	di-men-sion	Measure; extent; size.
23. disbursement	dĭs·bûrs′mĕnt	dis-burse-ment	Act of disbursing; money expended.
24. discrepancy	dĭs·krĕp′ăn·sĭ	dis-crep-an-cy	A disagreement; a variance; a difference.
25. diversion	dĭ·vûr′shŭn	di-ver-sion	Act of turning aside; distraction from business; recreation; entertainment.
26. enjoyable	ĕn·joi′à·b'l	en-joy-a-ble	Can be enjoyed; affording enjoyment.
27. en route	än rōōt′	en route	On the way; along the way.
28. envious	ĕn′vĭ·ŭs	en-vi-ous	Full of envy; expressing a feeling of envy.
29. eventually	ê·vĕn′tụ̆·ăl·lĭ	e-ven-tu-al-ly	Finally; ultimately.
30. excursion	ĕks·kûr′zhŭn	ex-cur-sion	A short journey or trip usually for recreation; a trip on a train or a boat at a reduced rate.
31. exert	ĕg·zûrt′	ex-ert	To put forth into vigorous action; to use one's efforts.
32. exertion	ĕg·zûr′shŭn	ex-er-tion	Vigorous action or effort; struggle.
33. flexible	flĕk′sĭ·b'l	flex-i-ble	Easily bent; adaptable.

34. forecast	fōr′kȧst′	fore-cast	To predict, as the weather; to plan ahead.
35. foregoing	fōr·gō′ĭng	fore-go-ing	Going before; preceding.
36. foreman	fōr′măn	fore-man	One in charge of a group of workers; chief man of a jury.
37. forfeit	fôr′fĭt	for-feit	A fine; a penalty.
38. formulae	fôr′mū·lē	for-mu-lae	A plural form of *formula*, the other being *formulas*. A conventional method; a set form of words for use in ceremonies.
39. hereby	hẹr·bī′	here-by	By means of this.
40. herein	hẹr·ĭn′	here-in	In or into this.
41. hereto	hẹr·tōō′	hereto	To this; hereunto.
42. herewith	hẹr·wĭth′	here-with	With this.
43. hospitable	hŏs′pĭ·tȧ·b'l	hos-pi-ta-ble	Affording or giving a generous welcome to guests or strangers.
44. hypercritical	hī′pēr·krĭt′ĭ·kȧl	hy-per-crit-i-cal	Overcritical.
45. imitator	ĭm′ĭ·tā′tēr	im-i-ta-tor	One who imitates or copies.
46. impartial	ĭm·pär′shȧl	im-par-tial	Unbiased; just.
47. impatient	ĭm·pā′shĕnt	im-pa-tient	Lacking in patience; uneasy.
48. impervious	ĭm·pûr′vĭ·ŭs	im-per-vi-ous	Cannot be penetrated, as by light rays, moisture, etc.; not affected or influenced by.
49. imprint	ĭm′prĭnt	im-print	A mark or a figure impressed or printed on something.
▶ 50. improvise	ĭm′prŏ·vīz	im-pro-vise	To prepare, do, or provide offhand. To recite, sing, act, etc., extemporaneously.
51. inconclusive	ĭn′kŏn·klōō′sĭv	in-con-clu-sive	Not conclusive; coming to no definite result or conclusion.
52. increasingly	ĭn·krēs′ĭng·lĭ	in-creas-ing-ly	To an ever-increasing degree.
53. infection	ĭn·fĕk′shŭn	in-fec-tion	Act of infecting; state of being infected.
54. infectious	ĭn·fĕk′shŭs	in-fec-tious	Causing infection; tending to infect from one to another.
55. influence	ĭn′flōō·ĕns	in-flu-ence	The act of producing effects on persons or things without apparent force or authority; a person or thing that exerts influence.

56. influential	ĭn'flōō·ĕn'shăl	in-flu-en-tial	Having or exerting influence.
57. inoculate	ĭn·ŏk'ū·lāt	in-oc-u-late	To inject an immunizing serum or vaccine into, to prevent a disease.
58. insolvent	ĭn·sŏl'vĕnt	in-sol-vent	Unable to pay one's debts as they become due; bankrupt.
59. intercept	ĭn'tĕr·sĕpt'	in-ter-cept	To seize on the way to a destination; to stop the natural course of.
60. interdependence	ĭn'tĕr·dĕ·pĕn'dĕns	in-ter-de-pend-ence	Dependence on each other; mutual dependence.
61. interoffice	ĭn'tĕr·ŏf'ĭs	in-ter-of-fice	Between one office and another office.
62. lacerate	lăs'ĕr·āt	lac-er-ate	To tear; to mangle.
63. litigation	lĭt'ĭ·gā'shŭn	lit-i-ga-tion	A suit at law; a legal contest in a court of justice.
64. microphone	mī'krŏ·fōn	mi-cro-phone	An instrument for transmitting sounds.
65. movers	mōōv'ĕrs	mov-ers	Persons engaged in the business of moving things, as furniture, equipment, etc.
66. parentheses	pȧ·rĕn'thĕ·sēz	pa-ren-the-ses	Plural of *parenthesis;* marks () used to enclose a parenthetical word or phrase.
67. postscript	pōst'skrĭpt	post-script	That which is added to a completed letter, book, etc., usually as an afterthought.
68. prescription	prĕ·skrĭp'shŭn	pre-scrip-tion	A written direction by a doctor for medicine to be used to combat an illness; act of prescribing.
69. pro rata	prō rā'tȧ	pro-ra-ta	Proportionately; according to share.
70. resemblance	rĕ·zĕm'blăns	re-sem-blance	Similarity; likeness.
71. semicircle	sĕm'ĭ·sûr'k'l	sem-i-cir-cle	The half of a circle.
72. substantially	sŭb·stăn'shăl·lĭ	sub-stan-tial-ly	In a substantial manner; solidly; firmly; with strength.
73. thereabouts	thâr'ȧ·bouts'	there-a-bouts	Close to that place; close to that number, degree, or quantity.
74. thereby	thâr·bī'	there-by	By means of that.
75. whereas	hwâr·ăz'	where-as	While on the contrary; it being the case; considering that.

Lesson 4

1. accrue	ă·krōō′	ac-crue	To be added by regular growth over a period of time, as interest.
2. allocation	ăl′ō·kā′shŭn	al-lo-ca-tion	Apportionment, as of funds.
3. allotment	ă·lŏt′měnt	al-lot-ment	A share or part granted or distributed.
4. analyst	ăn′à·lĭst	an-a-lyst	One who examines closely and critically; one skilled in making analyses.
5. arbitrage	är′bĭ·trĭj	ar-bi-trage	Buying securities or commodities for immediate resale in another market at a higher price.
6. authorization	ô′thĕr·ĭ·zā′shŭn	au-thor-i-za-tion	Act of authorizing; permission from one in authority.
7. bankrupt	băngk′rŭpt	bank-rupt	One who is unable to pay his bills or settle just debts.
8. bequeath	bē·kwēth′	be-queath	To give property, usually personal property, by will; to hand down.
9. breakage	brāk′ĭj	break-age	An allowance made by a shipper for loss due to the destruction of merchandise.
10. brokerage	brō′kĕr·ĭj	bro-ker-age	The commission paid to a broker for buying or selling securities.
11. compartments	kŏm·pärt′měnts	com-part-ments	Separate divisions or rooms; separate sections.
12. compete	kŏm·pēt′	com-pete	To engage in a contest for a prize; to contend in rivalry, as in business or in sports.
13. competent	kŏm′pē·tĕnt	com-pe-tent	Fit, suitable, or adequate for the purpose; properly qualified.
14. comptroller	kŏn·trōl′ĕr	comp-trol-ler	A controller; the official who supervises all phases of accounting procedure.
15. conductor	kŏn·dŭk′tĕr	con-duc-tor	A leader; a guide; a director; one in charge of a train.

16. consignor	kŏn·sīn′ĕr	con-sign-or	One who sends goods to another.
17. consumption	kŏn·sŭmp′shŭn	con-sump-tion	Act of consuming; destruction by use; the using up of something, as goods, strength, etc.
18. corporate	kôr′pŏ·rĭt	cor-po-rate	Incorporated; united; belonging to a corporation.
19. corruption	kŏ·rŭp′shŭn	cor-rup-tion	Act of corrupting; dishonest proceedings.
20. countersign	koun′tĕr·sīn′	coun-ter-sign	A signature added to another signature to prove its authenticity.
21. cycle	sī′k'l	cy-cle	A recurring succession of business conditions.
22. depression	dē·prĕsh′ŭn	de-pres-sion	A period of reduction in business activity.
23. devaluation	dē·văl′û·ā′shŭn	de-val-u-a-tion	The process of reducing the value of money.
24. dishonest	dĭs·ŏn′ĕst	dis-hon-est	Not honest; fraudulent.
▶ 25. diversification	dĭ·vûr′sĭ·fĭ·kā′shŭn	di-ver-si-fi-ca-tion	Variation; distribution among different types of securities.
26. diversity	dĭ·vûr′sĭ·tĭ	di-ver-si-ty	Variety; unlikeness.
27. economist	ē·kŏn′ŏ·mĭst	e-con-o-mist	One who is versed in the science of economics; a thrifty manager of affairs.
28. embassy	ĕm′bă·sĭ	em-bas-sy	The function or position of an ambassador; the residence or office of an ambassador.
29. embezzle	ĕm·bĕz′′l	em-bez-zle	To misappropriate fraudulently money or property entrusted to one's care.
30. employment	ĕm·ploi′mĕnt	em-ploy-ment	State of being employed; occupation; business.
31. equalization	ē′kwăl·ĭ·zā′shŭn	e-qual-i-za-tion	The process of making anything equal, uniform, or constant.
32. executive	ĕg·zĕk′û·tĭv	ex-ec-u-tive	A person assigned administrative work.
33. exemption	ĕg·zĕmp′shŭn	ex-emp-tion	Act of exempting; immunity.
34. flexibility	flĕk′sĭ·bĭl′ĭ·tĭ	flex-i-bil-i-ty	State of being adaptable; quality of being flexible.

35.	fluctuation	flŭk'tū·ā'shŭn	fluc-tu-a-tion	Act of changing continually from one position or condition to another; a wavering.
36.	hypothecation	hī·pŏth'ē·kā'shŭn	hy-poth-e-ca-tion	The pledging of a security for the payment of a loan.
37.	import	ĭm·pōrt'	im-port	To bring merchandise in from a foreign country.
38.	incorporated	ĭn·kôr'pŏ·rāt'ĕd	in-cor-po-rat-ed	Forming a legal corporation.
39.	inherit	ĭn·hĕr'ĭt	in-her-it	To receive by law as the heir of the former owner.
40.	investment	ĭn·vĕst'mĕnt	in-vest-ment	Money expended for any kind of property purchased for income; also, the property so purchased.
41.	liquidate	lĭk'wĭ·dāt	liq-ui-date	To settle or pay, as a debt; to settle the accounts and distribute the assets of a business or estate.
42.	marketing	mär'kĕt·ĭng	mar-ket-ing	The combined effort involved in moving goods from producer to consumer, including the entire process of supplying market information.
43.	merger	mûr'jĕr	merg-er	Act of merging two or more business enterprises into a single enterprise.
44.	monetary	mŏn'ē·tĕr'ĭ	mon-e-tar-y	Pertaining to money or to the currency of a country.
45.	negotiable	nē·gō'shĭ·a·b'l	ne-go-ti-a-ble	Transferable by delivery with or without endorsement; capable of being negotiated.
46.	occupation	ŏk'ū·pā'shŭn	oc-cu-pa-tion	One's business, trade, or calling.
47.	preferential	prĕf'ēr·ĕn'shăl	pref-er-en-tial	Showing or giving preference.
48.	pretentious	prē·tĕn'shŭs	pre-ten-tious	Full of exaggerated importance; ostentatious.
49.	protested	prŏ·tĕst'ĕd	pro-test-ed	Acted to fix the liability for a dishonored note or check.

50. radiogram ▶	rā′dĭ·ȯ·grăm′	ra-di-o-gram	A message transmitted by radiotelegraphy.
51. readjustment	rē′ȧ·jŭst′mĕnt	re-ad-just-ment	Important changes in the structure of a corporation.
52. recapitalization	rē·kăp′ĭ·tăl·ĭ·zā′shŭn	re-cap-i-tal-i-za-tion	A revision of a corporation's capital arrangement by an exchange of securities.
53. redeemable	rē·dēm′ȧ·b′l	re-deem-a-ble	Capable of being redeemed by payment of amount due.
54. redeposit	rē′dē·pŏz′ĭt	re-de-pos-it	To deposit again.
55. reorganization	rē′ôr·găn·ĭ·zā′shŭn	re-or-gan-i-za-tion	Act of reorganizing; a drastic reconstruction of a business corporation.
56. revocation	rĕv′ȯ·kā′shŭn	rev-o-ca-tion	Act of annulment; the withdrawal of an offer to contract.
57. shareholder	shâr′hōl′dĕr	share-hold-er	One who owns a share of stock in a corporation.
58. specialization	spĕsh′ăl·ĭ·zā′shŭn	spe-cial-i-za-tion	Act of pursuing some special line of study or work.
59. speculators	spĕk′ū·lā′tĕrz	spec-u-la-tors	Those who engage in an operation with a view to quick profits due to a favorable turn in prices or events.
60. standards	stăn′dĕrds	stand-ards	Those things that are set up by popular consent as a rule for measuring or as a basis of comparison; approved models.
61. statistical	stȧ·tĭs′tĭ·kăl	sta-tis-ti-cal	Dealing with statistics, such as numerical facts and data.
62. stockholder	stŏk′hōl′dĕr	stock-hold-er	The holder or the owner of a share of stock.
63. stockyard	stŏk′yärd′	stock-yard	A yard with pens, sheds, etc., for the temporary shelter of livestock before being shipped to market.
64. storekeeper	stōr′kēp′ĕr	store-keep-er	A person who has charge of a store.
65. subsidy	sŭb′sĭ·dĭ	sub-si-dy	A grant or contribution of money.

66. supermarket	sū′pẽr·mär′kĕt	su-per-mar-ket	A large store operated on a self-service plan.
67. surtax	sûr′tăks′	sur-tax	An additional tax on something that is already taxed.
68. telegraph	tĕl′ĕ·gráf	tel-e-graph	An apparatus for transmitting messages by means of an electrical device.
69. timetable	tīm′tā′b′l	time-ta-ble	A schedule that shows the arrival and departure times of trains, airplanes, etc.; a schedule of events.
70. transact	trăns·ăkt′	trans-act	To conduct, as business.
71. transpire	trăn·spīr′	tran-spire	To take place.
72. transport	trăns·pōrt′	trans-port	To carry from one place to another.
73. unmarketable	ŭn·mär′kĕt·á·b′l	un-mar-ket-a-ble	Not capable of being sold.
74. voidable	void′á·b′l	void-a-ble	Capable of being adjudged invalid.
75. walkout	wôk′out′	walk-out	A walking out or leaving; a labor strike.

Lesson 5 Check-Up

Unit Test. Your teacher will dictate 50 words chosen from the lessons in Unit 4 of Part 3. These words are selected to test your mastery of the new words in this unit. Listen closely as each word is dictated, spell the word carefully, and write plainly to assure yourself of a fair test.

Proofreading Test. In the following letter, some of the italicized words are misspelled. Copy the entire letter, making whatever corrections are necessary in the spelling of the words.

Dear Mr. Streeter:

On June 20 there will be a meeting of the *stockholdrs* of the Union Corporation. Some of the points to be discussed at this meeting are:

1. The *disbursments* recommended by the *economist*.
2. The *eighty houzing* projects that the *contracters* have ready for bids. It is *avisable* that the bids be opened at this meeting.
3. The *re-organization* of the *directery* that is sent to the *share holders*.
4. The date of the next *bi-monthly* meeting.
5. The *expantion* of the present *filling* system. We file all correspondence by alphabetic arrangement.

If you cannot be present at this meeting, will you please send a *replasement*.

Very *truely* yours,

Cumulative Test. Your teacher will now dictate 40 words chosen from Units 1 through 3 of Part 3. These words will test your retention of the correct spelling of words in these units. Spell carefully and write plainly.

Checking Your Tests. Your teacher will give you directions for checking the unit test, the proofreading test, and the cumulative test.

Error Analysis. Classify the errors that you made by noting the type of error beside each word that you misspelled.

Review. Use the appropriate attack procedures when you study the words that you misspelled on the unit test, on the proofreading test, and on the cumulative test.

Retest. The retest will tell you if you have mastered the words in Units 1 through 4 of Part 3. If you misspelled words on the retest, continue your attack procedures until you are sure that you can spell all the words correctly.

PART ④

WORDS
FOR
YOUR
SPECIALIZED
BUSINESS
VOCABULARY

Unit 1 Business Terms and Expressions

The lessons in this unit cover the specialized vocabularies used in a number of vital areas of business activity. Sound is involved in the correct spelling of some of the words, while meaning, rules, and demons are involved in some of the terms. Brush up on the "spotting" techniques that you learned in Section One and then begin your study of Lessons 1-4 of this unit, applying the following procedures:

Preview. Your teacher will dictate a list of 40 specialized business terms. Number a sheet of paper from 1 to 40. Spell as many of the terms as you can, but attempt only those that you are quite sure you know how to spell. If you do not know how to spell a term, place a question mark (?) beside the number.

Checking Performance. Compare your spellings with the terms in the appropriate lesson. Place an X beside each term that you misspelled. To the right of any misspelled or omitted term, write the correct spelling.

Error Analysis. Classify the errors that you made by noting the type of error beside each term that you misspelled. For instance, if an error was caused by adding unnecessary letters, write "addition" beside the term. Refer to Section One if you need to be reminded of the types of errors.

Attack Procedures. Attack procedures for the various types of errors were presented in Section One, beginning on page 7. Review the corrective technique recommended for each type of error.

Learning to Spell New Words. The pretest terms that you did not know how to spell now appear on your answer sheet preceded by a question mark. Use a separate sheet of paper to practice those terms, following the SEE, SAY, SPELL, and WRITE routine (see pages 39-41). Hand in the drill paper to your instructor.

Lesson 1   Accounting and Banking Terms

1. **accounts payable**	ă·kountz′ pā′ȧ·b'l	ac-counts pay-a-ble	Amounts owing to unsecured creditors.
2. **accounts receivable**	ă·kountz′ rē·sēv′ȧ·b'l	ac-counts re-ceiv-a-ble	Amounts due from customers.
3. **accrued interest**	ă·krōōd′ ĭn′tĕr·ĕst	ac-crued in-ter-est	Interest that is incurred or earned but not actually paid or received until a future period.
4. **balance sheet**	băl′ăns shēt	bal-ance sheet	A statement of the assets, liabilities, and capital of a business.
5. **bank discount**	băngk′ dĭs′kount	bank dis-count	Interest on a loan deducted in advance from the face value of the note.
6. **canceled check** *Cancelled cheque*	kăn′sĕld chĕk	can-celed check	A check paid by the bank and stamped with the proper mark of cancellation—generally, by perforation.
7. **capital stock**	kăp′ĭ·tăl stŏk	cap-i-tal stock	Shares representing ownership in a corporation.
8. **cashier's check**	kăsh·ẽrz′ chĕk	cash-ier's check	A check drawn on a bank by its cashier.
9. **certified check**	sûr′tĭ·fīd chĕk	cer-ti-fied check	A check that has been guaranteed as to payment by the bank on which it is drawn.
10. **contingent liability**	kŏn·tĭn′jĕnt lī′ȧ·bĭl′ĭ·tĭ	con-tin-gent li-a-bil-i-ty	A debt that may have to be paid if certain circumstances occur.
11. **controlling account**	kŏn·trōl′ĭng ȧ·kount′	con-trol-ling ac-count	An account that summarizes the balances in a subsidiary ledger.
12. **current asset**	kûr′ĕnt ăs′ĕt	cur-rent as-set	Cash or any other asset that may be turned into cash within a relatively short period.
13. **cycle billing**	sī′k'l bĭl′ĭng	cy-cle bill-ing	A method of billing customers under which statements are sent throughout the month according to the first letter of customers' last names.
14. **drawing account**	drô′ĭng ȧ·kount′	draw-ing ac-count	A record of withdrawals against anticipated salary or profits.
15. **fiscal year**	fĭs′kăl yẽr	fis-cal year	The year by which accounts are reckoned. It may or may not coincide with the calendar year.

16. fixed charges	fĭkst chärj′ĕz	fixed charg-es	Established claims on the revenue of a concern, as interest on debts, rental, taxes, etc.
17. footing	fo͝ot′ĭng	foot-ing	Act of adding a column of figures; the sum total so obtained.
18. good will	go͝od wĭl	good will	The intangible asset that a business has because of its reputation for fair dealing.
19. goods in process	go͝odz ĭn prŏs′ĕs	goods in proc-ess	In manufacturing establishments, this term refers to merchandise that is partially completed.
▶ 20. imprest fund	ĭm′prĕst fŭnd	im-prest fund	A fund or sum of money earmarked for a specific purpose, as a petty cash fund.
21. journal	jûr′năl	jour-nal	A book of original entry in which a condensed record of each transaction is entered in chronological order.
22. ledger	lĕj′ẽr	ledg-er	A book of final entry to which the sums entered in the journal are transferred under account names.
23. margin of profit	mär′jĭn ŏv prŏf′ĭt	mar-gin of prof-it	The difference between cost and selling price frequently expressed as a percentage of sales.
24. no-par stock	nō′pär′ stŏk	no-par stock	Stock having no face value.
25. nominal account	nŏm′ĭ·năl ă·kount′	nom-i-nal ac-count	An account representing an expense or income that will ultimately be transferred to proprietorship.
26. obsolescence	ŏb′sŏ·lĕs′ĕns	ob-so-les-cence	The decrease in the value of an asset due to technical advances and lessening of usefulness.
27. odd lot	ŏd lŏt	odd lot	A smaller unit of trade than the standard unit on an exchange, such as less than 100 shares of stock.
28. over-the-counter	ō′vẽr thē koun′tẽr	o-ver the coun-ter	A term referring to dealings in securities that are not listed on any stock exchange.
29. par value	pär văl′ū	par val-ue	The face value of a share of stock.

30. passbook	pás'bŏŏk'	pass-book	A deposit book in which a bank enters deposits and withdrawals made by a depositor.
31. promissory note	prŏm'ĭ·sō'rĭ nōt	prom-is-so-ry note	A written agreement by one person to pay another a certain sum of money on demand or at a specified time.
32. protest	prŏ·tĕst'	pro-test	To declare in an affidavit that a note or check was presented for payment and payment was refused.
33. sinking fund	sĭngk'ĭng fŭnd	sink-ing fund	A fund in which payments are made for the purpose of paying a debt or replacing assets.
34. stock dividend	stŏk dĭv'ĭ·dĕnd	stock div-i-dend	A dividend payable by the distribution of additional stock of the company.
35. stock split	stŏk splĭt	stock split	A division of a corporation's capital stock into a greater number of shares.
36. subsidiary ledger	sŭb·sĭd'ĭ·ĕr'ĭ lĕj'ĕr	sub-sid-i-ar-y ledg-er	A ledger containing certain accounts that are summarized by a controlling account in the general ledger.
37. time draft	tīm dráft	time draft	A draft that has a definite period of time to run.
38. trade discount	trād dĭs'kount	trade dis-count	A deduction from the retail or list price, made generally to established dealers in the trade.
39. trial balance	trī'ăl băl'ăns	tri-al bal-ance	A list of the balances of the accounts in a double-entry ledger.
40. voucher check	vouch'ĕr chĕk	vouch-er check	A check bearing upon it, or upon a detachable stub, a notation of the items covered by the check.

Lesson 2 Advertising, Publishing, and Printing Terms

1. addenda	ă·dĕn'dȧ	ad-den-da	Appendixes or other matter added to a book.
2. bibliography	bĭb'lĭ·ŏg'rȧ·fĭ	bib-li-og-ra-phy	A list of books by a particular author or of the literature on a particular subject.

3. **blurb**	blûrb	blurb	A laudatory announcement of a book, often printed on the jacket or outer paper cover (colloquial).
4. **boldface**	bōld'fās'	bold-face	Type in which the lines are very heavy or thick.
5. **broadside**	brôd'sīd'	broad-side	A large sheet of paper, often printed on one side only, giving information on a product.
6. **brochure**	brō·shoŏr'	bro-chure	A pamphlet or booklet, usually above the average in quality of workmanship; a treatise or an article published in pamphlet form.
7. **by-line**	bī'līn'	by-line	The line at the head of an article showing by whom it was written.
8. **caption**	kăp'shŭn	cap-tion	The headline of an item in a newspaper; the heading of a chapter, section, page, or article; the title above an illustration or table.
9. **caret**	kăr'ĕt	car-et	A sign (∧) placed below a line to indicate where new or omitted words or letters are to be inserted.
10. **cartoon**	kär·tōōn'	car-toon	A humorous drawing; a design drawn as a model.
11. **collate**	kŏ·lāt'	col-late	To gather sheets into a set and to examine them to verify the order and number of pages, maps, etc.
12. **copyright**	kŏp'ĭ·rīt'	cop-y-right	The exclusive right to reproduce or publish.
13. **copy writer**	kŏp'ĭ rīt'ĕr	cop-y writ-er	One who writes, and plans the arrangement of, advertising material.
14. **die**	dī	die	A hard metal device for stamping or cutting out an illustration, design, or title.
15. **dummy**	dŭm'ĭ	dum-my	A set of sheets so bound as to represent a projected book, folder, or other unit of printing.
16. **duotone**	dū'ŏ·tōn	du-o-tone	Describes an ink that, when dry, gives the printed page the appearance of having been printed in two colors.
17. **electrotype**	ē·lĕk'trŏ·tīp	e-lec-tro-type	A metal facsimile plate of type or engravings from which printing is done. Commonly called *electro*.
18. **engraving**	ĕn·grāv'ĭng	en-grav-ing	The process of producing designs on wood, metal, or stone; the block so prepared; a picture printed from such a block.
19. **folio**	fō'lĭ·ō	fo-li-o	The page number; a sheet of paper that has been folded once; a book of the largest dimensions—more than 11 inches high.
20. **font**	fŏnt	font	A complete assortment of type of one design and size.

▶

21. form	fôrm	form	The type from which an impression is to be taken, arranged and locked in a metal frame called a *chase*.
22. format	fôr′mă	for-mat	The size, shape, appearance, and style of a book, pamphlet, magazine, or other publication.
23. galley	găl′ĭ	gal-ley	An oblong metal tray to hold type that has been set. The proof of this type is called *galley proof*.
24. halftone	hăf′tōn′	half-tone	A plate for reproducing varying degrees of lights and shadows, as of photographs.
25. layout	lā′out′	lay-out	The act of planning or arranging a book, periodical, or advertisement in detail.
26. leaders	lēd′ẽrz	lead-ers	A row of dots used in tables, etc., to lead the eye across a space to the right word or number.
27. Linotype	līn′ō·tīp	Lin-o-type	A machine for casting type in lines, for printing.
28. lithography	lĭ·thŏg′rȧ·fĭ	li-thog-ra-phy	The process of putting printing or designs on stone or metal and producing printed impressions therefrom.
29. media	mē′dĭ·ȧ	me-di-a	Plural of *medium*. Used to refer to the periodicals in which an advertisement is printed. The term includes radio, billboards, television, etc.
30. offset	ŏf′sĕt′	off-set	A kind of lithography; a smudge or transfer of ink from a freshly printed sheet upon the back of another sheet.
31. page proof	pāj prōof	page proof	A proof of type matter and plates arranged in page form, as they are finally to appear.
32. pica	pī′kȧ	pi-ca	The standard unit of type measurement, equal to 12 points, or about one-sixth of an inch; 12-point type.
33. proofreader	prōof′rēd′ẽr	proof-read-er	One who reads printed matter and indicates corrections by the use of conventional proofreading marks.
34. roman	rō′măn	ro-man	The style of type most commonly used in books and in all classes of ordinary reading matter; it is light-faced and upright, with serifs and shaded strokes.
35. rotogravure	rō′tō·grȧ·vūr′	ro-to-gra-vure	A picture, design, or type matter etched on a cylindrical printing surface and printed by a rotary press; a process of making such an impression.

36. signature	sĭg′nȧ·t͝ur	sig-na-ture	A sheet of a book folded and ready to be sewn. A signature ordinarily consists of 16 pages, but it may go to 32 or 64 pages if the paper permits the additional folding.
37. silk-screen	sĭlk′skrēn′	silk-screen	Describes a method of printing posters by forcing ink through the mesh of a silk cloth that has the design to be reproduced imposed on it.
38. stereotype	stĕr′ĕ·ȯ·tīp′	ster-e-o-type	A plate cast from a matrix in type metal.
39. stet	stĕt	stet	"Let it stand." The proofreader's way of indicating that something previously crossed out is to remain.
40. tear sheet	târ shēt	tear sheet	A sheet torn from a publication and used as a sample.

Lesson **3** Import and Export Terms

1. ad valorem	ăd vȧ·lō′rĕm	ad va-lo-rem	A term applied especially to duty on imports or exports based on the value of the merchandise.
2. buyer's commission	bī′ĕrz kŏ·mĭsh′ŭn	buy-er's com-mis-sion	A percentage payment given to an agent for negotiating the purchase of merchandise.
3. cable address	kā′b'l ȧ·drĕs′	ca-ble ad-dress	A code address used to reduce the expense of a full address on a cablegram.
4. cartel	kär·tĕl′	car-tel	An agreement among foreign business organizations to regulate competition and fix prices.
5. certificate of origin	sĕr·tĭf′ĭ·kĭt ŏv ŏr′ĭ·jĭn	cer-tif-i-cate of or-i-gin	A certificate that is attached to a draft covering shipments of goods, testifying to the origin of the material or labor used in producing the merchandise.
6. consul general	kŏn′sŭl jĕn′ĕr·ăl	con-sul gen-er-al	The top official appointed to a foreign country to facilitate the affairs and trade of the country sending him and to look out for the commercial interests of its citizens.
7. customhouse	kŭs′tŭm·hous′	cus-tom-house	The building where customs and duties are paid and where vessels are cleared.
8. customs inspector	kŭs′tŭmz ĭn·spĕk′tĕr	cus-toms in-spec-tor	The person who inspects vessels coming into his district and reports all violations of neutrality laws to the customs collector of the port.
9. damageable	dăm′ĭj·ȧ·b'l	dam-age-a-ble	Capable of being injured and thus being reduced in value.
10. declarations	dĕk′lȧ·rā′shŭnz	dec-la-ra-tions	Statements giving a full report of goods so that the duty or taxes may be determined.

11. dutiable	dū′tĭ·a̍·b'l	du-ti-a-ble	Subject to import duty.
12. embargo	ĕm·bär′gō	em-bar-go	An order by a government prohibiting the departure or entry of ships at its ports.
13. estimated weight	ĕs′tĭ·māt·ĕd wāt	es-ti-mated weight	The weight of a consignment of goods derived by computation, or by means other than by actually weighing.
14. exchange charge	ĕks·chānj′ chärj	ex-change charge	A bank fee or service charge made for services rendered in the collection of items.
15. exchange rate	ĕks·chānj′ rāt	ex-change rate	The rate at which one unit of currency will buy a given amount of another currency.
16. export quotas	ĕks′pōrt kwō′ta̍z	ex-port quo-tas	Limitations on the amount of domestic goods shipped abroad in a given time period in respect to certain commodities or nations receiving the goods.
17. exporter	ĕks·pōr′tĕr	ex-port-er	A person who exports goods for commercial purposes.
18. fathom	fă̱th′ŭm	fath-om	A nautical measure of 6 feet, used in measuring cordage or for sounding the depth of water.
19. firm offering	fûrm ŏf′ĕr·ĭng	firm of-fer-ing	A valid offer to sell a security at a definite price, either for a brief moment or for a specified period of time.
20. foreign exchange	fŏr′ĭn ĕks·chānj′	for-eign ex-change	The exchange of, or the trading in, foreign currencies.
▶ 21. free on board	frē ŏn bōrd	free on board	Refers to freight placed and/or transported on board a ship, train, or other means of transportation without charge to the purchaser.
22. general average	jĕn′ĕr·a̍l ă̍v′ĕr·ĭj	gen-er-al av-er-age	A principle of maritime law that provides that all involved shall share ratably in a common peril for the purpose of saving part of the venture.
23. gross tonnage	grōs tŭn′ĭj	gross ton-nage	The total capacity of a vessel without any deduction.
24. importer	ĭm·pōrt′ĕr	im-port-er	One who buys wares from foreign markets and resells to domestic stores.
25. kilogram	kĭl′ō·grăm	kil-o-gram	Equal to 2.2046 pounds in the metric system.
26. leakage	lēk′ĭj	leak-age	That which leaks in or out; the percentage allowance for loss by leaking.
27. lighter	līt′ĕr	light-er	A heavily built craft, used in bringing cargo alongside or in transferring it from a vessel.

28. mooring	mŏŏr′ĭng	moor-ing	A cable, a line, or an anchor by which a vessel is secured.
29. net weight	nĕt wāt	net weight	The weight of a quantity of merchandise exclusive of container or wrapper.
30. packing list	păk′ĭng lĭst	pack-ing list	A list of the contents of a package, giving gross weight and net weight, also dimensions of the package.
31. particular average	pĕr·tĭk′ů·lẽr ăv′ẽr·ĭj	par-tic-u-lar av-er-age	Partial loss of cargo or freight falling entirely on the interest concerned.
32. pilotage	pī′lŭt·ĭj	pi-lot-age	The charge made for services of a maritime pilot.
33. port of embarkation	pŏrt ŏv ĕm′bär·kā′shŭn	port of em-bar-ka-tion	A place where people go on shipboard for a voyage; place where troops embark for a foreign land.
34. pro forma	prō fôr′mȧ	pro for-ma	As a matter of form.
35. proviso	prŏ·vī′zō	pro-vi-so	A condition inserted in an agreement declaring that the agreement shall not be effective unless certain terms are complied with.
36. quayage	kē′ĭj	quay-age	A charge for using pier facilities for loading and unloading ships.
37. salvage	săl′vĭj	sal-vage	The award to persons who voluntarily render services to save maritime property from destruction in a wreck, fire, etc.; compensation paid for saving a ship.
38. stowage	stō′ĭj	stow-age	The arranging of a cargo aboard a vessel in such a way that the goods will not be damaged during the voyage.
39. transatlantic	trăns′ăt·lăn′tĭk	trans-at-lan-tic	Crossing the Atlantic Ocean.
40. wharfage	hwôr′fĭj	wharf-age	The fee for using a wharf or pier.

Lesson 4 Legal Terms

1. adjudicate	ȧ·jōō′dĭ·kāt	ad-ju-di-cate	To hear and decide a case in court.
2. administrator	ăd·mĭn′ĭs·trā′tẽr	ad-min-is-tra-tor	One appointed by a court to settle the estate of a person who dies intestate.
3. alimony	ăl′ĭ·mō′nĭ	al-i-mo-ny	The separate maintenance payable to a wife by her husband under court order after commencement of suit for divorce or legal separation.
4. annulment	ȧ·nŭl′mĕnt	an-nul-ment	Act of making void or invalid.
5. attachment	ȧ·tăch′mĕnt	at-tach-ment	A seizure by legal process; the instrument authorizing such seizure.

6. bailee	bāl′ē′	bail-ee	A person who, other than as owner, receives the custody of goods for a specific purpose.
7. chancery	chán′sĕr·ĭ	chan-cer-y	A court of equity.
8. codicil	kŏd′ĭ·sĭl	cod-i-cil	A supplement to a will.
9. decedent	dĕ·sē′dĕnt	de-ce-dent	A deceased person.
10. deponent	dĕ·pō′nĕnt	de-po-nent	One who makes an affidavit or testifies in writing under oath.
11. docket	dŏk′ĕt	dock-et	An abridged entry of legal proceedings; the book or register in which such entries are listed.
12. domicile	dŏm′ĭ·sĭl	dom-i-cile	A person's legal and presumably permanent residence.
13. easement	ēz′mĕnt	ease-ment	Any of several rights that one may have over another's land; as, a right of way.
14. felony	fĕl′ŏ·nĭ	fel-o-ny	Any crime graver than a misdemeanor, as murder, larceny, embezzlement, bribery, arson, etc.
15. garnishee	gär′nĭsh·ē′	gar-nish-ee	To attach the salary, wages, income, or property to pay a debt.
16. impanel	ĭm·păn′ĕl	im-pan-el	To enroll in a panel or list, as for jury duty.
17. indenture	ĭn·dĕn′tûr	in-den-ture	A written agreement under seal.
18. injunction	ĭn·jŭngk′shŭn	in-junc-tion	A court order usually requiring a person to refrain from doing a certain thing.
19. interlocutory	ĭn′tĕr·lŏk′û·tō′rĭ	in-ter-loc-u-to-ry	Not final or definitive; provisional.
▶ 20. intestate	ĭn·tĕs′tăt	in-tes-tate	adj. Not having made a lawful will. n. One who dies without having made a lawful will.
21. jurisprudence	jŏŏr′ĭs·prōō′dĕns	ju-ris-pru-dence	A system of laws of a country.
22. legatee	lĕg′à·tē′	leg-a-tee	One to whom property is given by will.
23. lien	lē′ĕn	li-en	A legal claim or charge on property for the satisfaction of a debt or obligation.
24. malfeasance	măl·fē′zăns	mal-fea-sance	Misconduct, especially the performance of an illegal act by a public official.
25. mandamus	măn·dā′mŭs	man-da-mus	A writ served to compel a person, corporation, or inferior court to perform some official duty.
26. manslaughter	măn′slô′tĕr	man-slaugh-ter	The unlawful killing of a human being without malice.
27. misdemeanor	mĭs′dĕ·mēn′ĕr	mis-de-mean-or	An offense less serious than a felony.
28. mittimus	mĭt′ĭ·mŭs	mit-ti-mus	A warrant of commitment to prison; a writ for removal of records from one court to another.

29.	ordinance	ôr'dĭ·năns	or-di-nance	A local law passed by the government of a municipality.
30.	perjury	pûr'jer·ĭ	pur-ju-ry	The intentional giving of false testimony under oath.
31.	plaintiff	plān'tĭf	plain-tiff	One who brings suit.
32.	probate	prō'bāt	pro-bate	*v.* To prove legally and officially, as a will. *adj.* Having jurisdiction over wills.
33.	prosecute	prŏs'ĕ·kūt	pros-e-cute	To seek to enforce by legal process.
34.	ratification	răt'ĭ·fĭ·kā'shŭn	rat-i-fi-ca-tion	The formal sanctioning of an act, treaty, contract, etc.
35.	residuary	rĕ·zĭd'û·ĕr'ĭ	re-sid-u-ar-y	Pertaining to that which remains of an estate after prior provisions of a will are satisfied.
36.	revert	rĕ·vûrt'	re-vert	To return property to the former owner or his heirs at the termination of a grant.
37.	subpoena	sŭb·pē'nȧ	sub-poe-na	A writ requiring a person to appear in court at a certain time.
38.	subrogation	sŭb'rŏ·gā'shŭn	sub-ro-ga-tion	The substitution of one person for another as a creditor, the former acquiring the rights of the latter.
39.	summons	sŭm'ŭnz	sum-mons	A served written notice to appear in court on a certain day.
40.	surrogate	sûr'ŏ·gȧt	sur-ro-gate	A judge who has jurisdiction over the probate of wills and the administration of estates.

Lesson 5 Check-Up

Unit Test. Your teacher will dictate 50 terms chosen from the lessons in Unit 1 of Part 4. These terms are selected to test your mastery of the new terms in this unit. Listen closely as each term is dictated, spell the term carefully, and write plainly to assure yourself of a fair test.

Proofreading Test. The following paragraphs represent excerpts from business letters and reports. Some of the italicized words are misspelled. Copy each paragraph, making any corrections necessary in the spelling of the words.

At a meeting of the *board* of *directors*, the purchase of *no-par* value *prefered stok* was *authorized*. A check was *issured* to pay for the *acrued interst* on the *securities* when they are purchased.

A *balanse sheat*, showing the *acounts receivable*, *acounts payible*, and *capitol stok*, was mailed to each person recorded on the *leger*. The *fixxed charges* and *contijant liabilitys* were also shown on the statement.

The members of the *board* discussed the authority of the *adminstrater* to *garnishe* the salary of the worker. The worker demanded a *chek* for the work he had completed on the *bibleography* and on the *copy-wright* page.

Cumulative Test. Your teacher will now dictate 40 terms chosen from Units 1 through 4 of Part 3. These terms will test your retention of the correct spelling of terms in these units. Spell carefully, determine the correct meanings, and write plainly.

Checking Your Tests. Your teacher will give you directions for checking the unit test, the proofreading test, and the cumulative test.

Error Analysis. Classify the errors that you made by noting the type of error beside each term that you misspelled.

Review. Use the appropriate attack procedures for studying the terms that you misspelled on the unit test, on the proofreading test, and on the cumulative test. Remember that the cumulative test contained both sound and meaning words.

Retest. The retest will tell you if you have mastered the terms in Units 1 through 4 of Part 3 and Unit 1 of Part 4. If you misspelled any terms on the retest, continue your attack procedures until you are sure that you can spell all the terms correctly.

Unit 2 Business Terms and Expressions

The lessons in this unit cover the specialized vocabularies used in a number of vital areas of business activity. Sound is involved in the correct spelling of some of the words, while meaning, rules, and demons are involved in some of the terms. Brush up on the "spotting" techniques that you learned in Section One and then begin your study of Lessons 1-4 of this unit, applying the following procedures:

Preview. Your teacher will dictate a list of 40 specialized business terms. Number a sheet of paper from 1 to 40. Spell as many of the terms as you can, but attempt only those that you are quite sure you know how to spell. If you do not know a term, place a question mark (?) beside the number.

Checking Performance. Compare your spellings with the terms given in the appropriate lesson. Place an *X* beside each term that you misspelled. To the right of any misspelled or omitted term, write the correct spelling.

Error Analysis. Classify the errors that you made by noting the type of error beside each term that you misspelled. For instance, if an error was caused by adding unnecessary letters, write "addition" beside the term. Refer to Section One if you need to be reminded of the types of errors.

Attack Procedures. Attack procedures for the various types of errors were presented in Section One, beginning on page 7. Review the corrective technique recommended for each type of error.

Learning to Spell New Words. The pretest terms that you did not know how to spell now appear on your answer sheet preceded by a question mark. Use a separate sheet of paper to practice those terms, following the SEE, SAY, SPELL, and WRITE routine (see pages 39-41). Hand in the drill paper to your instructor.

Lesson 1 Terms for the Medical Assistant

1. **anamnesis**	ăn′ăm·nē′sĭs	an-am-ne-sis	The past medical history of a patient.
2. **anesthetist**	ăn·ĕs′thĕ·tĭst	an-es-the-tist	One trained to administer anesthetics.

3.	antibiotic	ăn'tĭ·bī·ŏt'ĭk	an-ti-bi-ot-ic	A substance used to destroy infectious organisms.
4.	antiseptic	ăn'tĭ·sĕp'tĭk	an-ti-sep-tic	A substance used to prevent infection.
5.	aspirator	ăs'pĭ·rā'tẽr	as-pi-ra-tor	An instrument used to remove fluids or gases by suction.
6.	aureomycin	ô'rē·ō·mī'sĭn	au-re-o-my-cin	An antibiotic substance effective against certain diseases.
7.	autoclave	ô'tō·klāv	au-to-clave	An apparatus for sterilizing with steam under pressure.
8.	autopsy	ô'tŏp·sĭ	au-top-sy	The examination of a dead body to determine cause of death, nature and extent of disease, etc.
9.	biopsy	bī'ŏp·sĕ	bi-op-sy	The removal and examination of a piece of living tissue.
10.	centigrade scale	sĕn'tĭ·grād skāl	cen-ti-grade scale	A scale divided into 100 degrees.
11.	disinfectant	dĭs'ĭn·fĕk'tănt	dis-in-fect-ant	A substance used to destroy disease germs.
12.	dosage	dōs'ĭj	dos-age	Act of administering medicine in doses; the amount of medicine in a dose.
13.	electrocardiograph	ē·lĕk'trō·kär'dĭ·ō·gráf'	e-lec-tro-car-di-o-graph	An instrument for measuring the changes of electrical potential during the heartbeat.
14.	electrolysis	ē·lĕk'trŏl'ĭ·sĭs	e-lec-trol-y-sis	Chemical decomposition by use of electric current, as when removing hair.
15.	excavator	ĕks'ká·vā'tẽr	ex-ca-va-tor	A sharp instrument used to clean a dental cavity.
16.	expectorant	ĕks·pĕk'tō·rănt	ex-pec-to-rant	Something that is used to facilitate the ejection of sputum.
17.	fluoroscope	flōō'ō·rō·skōp	flu-o-ro-scope	An instrument used to examine internal structures and organs.
18.	hypnotic	hĭp·nŏt'ĭk	hyp-not-ic	Tending to produce sleep; pertaining to a drug for inducing sleep.
19.	immunity	ĭ·mū'nĭ·tĭ	im-mu-ni-ty	Protection against a particular disease.
20.	intradermal injections	ĭn'trá·dûr'măl ĭn·jĕk'shŭnz	in-tra-der-mal in-jec-tions	Injections made into the upper layer of the skin.
▶ 21.	intramuscular injections	ĭn'trá·mŭs'kŭ·lẽr ĭn·jĕk'shŭnz	in-tra-mus-cu-lar in-jec-tions	Injections made into a muscle directly.
22.	intravenous injections	ĭn'trá·vē'nŭs ĭn·jĕk'shŭnz	in-tra-ve-nous in-jec-tions	Injections made into a vein.
23.	ophthalmoscope	ŏf·thăl'mō·skōp	oph-thal-mo-scope	An instrument used for an eye examination.

24. orthodontia	ôr′thŏ·dŏn′shĭ·á	or-tho-don-ti-a	A branch of dentistry that deals with the correction of abnormal teeth.
25. oscillograph	ŏ·sĭl′ŏ·gráf	os-cil-lo-graph	An instrument used for recording changes in the blood volume.
26. otoscope	ō′tŏ·skōp	o-to-scope	An instrument used in examining the ear.
27. outpatient	out′pā′shĕnt	out-pa-tient	A person who visits a hospital clinic for treatment.
28. penicillin	pĕn′ĭ·sĭl′ĭn	pen-i-cil-lin	A powerful antibiotic agent.
29. photospectrometer	fō′tŏ·spĕk′trŏ-mē′tēr	pho-to-spec-tro-me-ter	An apparatus used for chemical analysis by use of the spectrum.
30. post-mortem	pōst′môr′tĕm	post-mor-tem	An autopsy; an examination after death.
31. prognosis	prŏg·nō′sĭs	prog-no-sis	A prediction of the probable development of a disease.
32. respirator	rĕs′pĭ·rā′tēr	res-pi-ra-tor	An apparatus for artificial respiration.
33. sedation	sĕ·dā′shŭn	se-da-tion	Act of calming a nervous person by the use of sedatives.
34. specimen	spĕs′ĭ·mĕn	spec-i-men	A sample used for an analysis of the bacteria, blood count, sugar count, etc.
35. sterilize	stĕr′ĭ·līz	ster-i-lize	To rid of living microorganisms.
36. stethoscope	stĕth′ŏ·skōp	steth-o-scope	An instrument for listening to the sounds in the body.
37. streptomycin	strĕp′tŏ·mī′sĭn	strep-to-my-cin	An antibiotic substance used to combat certain diseases.
38. subcutaneous injections	sŭb′kû·tā′nê·ŭs ĭn·jĕk′shŭnz	sub-cu-ta-ne-ous in-jec-tions	Injections into the tissue between the skin and the muscle.
39. syringe	sĭr′ĭnj	syr-inge	An instrument used to inject fluids.
40. therapeutics	thĕr′á·pū′tĭks	ther-a-peu-tics	The branch of medicine that deals with the application of remedies for diseases.

Lesson 2 Personnel and Management Terms

1. absentee	ăb′sĕn·tē′	ab-sen-tee	An employee who is absent from work.
2. accession	ăk·sĕsh′ŭn	ac-ces-sion	The hiring of a new worker, or the rehiring of a former employee.
3. admonition	ăd′mŏ·nĭsh′ŭn	ad-mo-ni-tion	Counseling an employee about his faults in a friendly manner.

4. arbitrator	är′bĭ·trā′tĕr	ar-bi-tra-tor	One who is called upon to settle a difference between parties in a dispute.
5. authorization card	ô′thĕr·ĭ·zā′shŭn kärd	au-thor-i-za-tion card	A declaration signed by an employee and giving a union the power to act as his collective bargaining agent.
6. basic points	bās′ĭk pointz	bas-ic points	The point values assigned to the minimum job requirements in job evaluation, and to which all other point values are added.
7. betterment	bĕt′ĕr·mĕnt	bet-ter-ment	Improvement of employee status or working conditions.
8. bidding	bĭd′ĭng	bid-ding	A recruiting device or a system of accepting applications to fill job vacancies on the basis of seniority.
9. brotherhood	brŭth′ĕr·hŏŏd	broth-er-hood	A national or an international union formed as a fraternal or benefit organization.
10. centralization	sĕn′trăl·ĭ·zā′shŭn	cen-tral-i-za-tion	Act of bringing together activities of the same type and combining them into a central unit.
11. check list	chĕk lĭst	check list	An itemized list of facts or information, as attitude, job, or rating check list.
12. conciliator	kŏn·sĭl′ĭ·ā′tĕr	con-cil-i-a-tor	One who attempts to settle a labor dispute by a compromise of the original demands.
13. consultant	kŏn·sŭl′tănt	con-sult-ant	One who acts in an advisory capacity; a specialist in his field.
14. decentralization	dē·sĕn′trăl·ĭ·zā′shŭn	de-cen-tral-i-za-tion	The division and distribution of the same type of work to various areas, usually closer to the source requiring the work. The reverse of *centralization*.
15. expediter	ĕks′pĕ·dĭt′ĕr	ex-pe-dit-er	One who dispatches orders, facilitates production schedules; sometimes called a *troubleshooter*.
16. follow-up	fŏl′ō·ŭp′	fol-low-up	A system of checking work, tests, or materials at certain stages to ensure their being completed on schedule.

17. grouping	grōōp'ĭng	group-ing	The process of evaluating jobs and sorting them into a predetermined number of classes.
18. immobility	ĭm'ō·bĭl'ĭ·tĭ	im-mo-bil-i-ty	Motionlessness; immovableness.
19. impartiality	ĭm'pär·shĭ·ăl'ĭ·tĭ	im-par-ti-al-i-ty	State of freedom from bias or favoritism.
20. incentive wages ▶	ĭn·sĕn'tĭv wāj'ĕz	in-cen-tive wag-es	Bonus payments for higher production above the standard requirements.
21. independent union	ĭn'dĕ·pĕn'dĕnt ūn'yŭn	in-de-pend-ent un-ion	A union that exists within a company or industry but that has neither national nor international affiliation.
22. induction	ĭn·dŭk'shŭn	in-duc-tion	A process of acquainting a new employee with the policies of the company and the duties of his job.
23. inequities	ĭn·ĕk'wĭ·tĭz	in-eq-ui-ties	Wages and working conditions that are greatly different from those in other parts of a plant.
24. informant	ĭn·fôr'mănt	in-form-ant	One who gives information.
25. interpretation	ĭn·tûr'prĕ·tā'shŭn	in-ter-pre-ta-tion	An explanation or clarification of the meaning of some particular action or policy.
26. interview	ĭn'tĕr·vū	in-ter-view	A conversation directed toward learning about a person's abilities, personality, emotional stability.
27. journeyman	jûr'nĭ·măn	jour-ney-man	A worker who has completed his apprenticeship in a skilled trade.
28. learner	lûrn'ẽr	learn-er	A beginner in an occupation who learns through actual work experience and job performance under supervision.
29. longevity pay	lŏn·jĕv'ĭ·tĭ pā	lon-gev-i-ty pay	The wages or bonus compensation determined by and based on length of service.
30. mediation	mē'dĭ·ā'shŭn	me-di-a-tion	A bargaining process in which representatives of the parties attempt to reach a settlement of grievances.
31. methodology	mĕth'ŭd·ŏl'ō·jĭ	meth-od-ol-o-gy	Scientific study that deals with the principles of procedure; the science that describes materials of instruction.

32. morale index	mŏ·rál′ ĭn′dĕks	mo-rale in-dex	The level of worker attitude, as indicated by interviews, toward his employer or his job.
33. motivation	mō′tĭ·vā′shŭn	mo-ti-va-tion	Inducement of individuals, through incentives, to do a better job or to do more work.
34. nominal wages	nŏm′ĭ·năl wāj′ĕz	nom-i-nal wag-es	Money wages.
35. objectivity	ŏb′jĕk·tĭv′ĭ·tĭ	ob-jec-tiv-i-ty	The quality of dealing with facts as presented rather than with thoughts or personal feelings about the facts.
36. orientation	ō′rĭ·ĕn·tā′shŭn	o-ri-en-ta-tion	A process of training designed to acquaint a new employee with company policies, plans, and procedures.
37. performance test	pĕr·fôr′măns tĕst	per-form-ance test	A test that measures what a person does on a job.
38. predetermination	prē′dĕ·tûr′mĭ·nā′-shŭn	pre-de-ter-mi-na-tion	Act of deciding on a course of action before the action happens.
39. recruitment	rĕ·krōōt′mĕnt	re-cruit-ment	The process of attracting suitable and desirable people for employment.
40. seniority	sēn·yŏr′ĭ·tĭ	sen-ior-i-ty	A factor that secures certain rights, promotions, etc., due to length of service in the company.

Lesson 3 Radio and Television Terms

1. acoustics	à·kōōs′tĭks	a-cous-tics	The science of sound, dealing with its production, transmission, reception, and effect.
2. affiliate	ă·fĭl′ĭ·āt	af-fil-i-ate	To connect or associate oneself, as with an organization or a radio station.
3. amplifier	ăm′plĭ·fī′ĕr	am-pli-fi-er	A device to increase electrical voltage or currents.
4. amplitude	ăm′plĭ·tūd	am-pli-tude	A term used to describe the magnitude of a simple wave or simple part of a complex wave.
5. announcement	ă·nouns′mĕnt	an-nounce-ment	A short notification or advertising message in a radio or television broadcast.
6. antenna	ăn·tĕn′à	an-ten-na	A wire or combination of wires, supported in the air, for receiving or transmitting electric waves.

7. audition	ô·dĭsh'ŭn	au-di-tion	A tryout of artists for a program or performance.
8. backdrop	băk'drŏp'	back-drop	The curtain, usually a painted cloth, at the back of a scene or stage.
9. broadcast	brôd'kȧst'	broad-cast	To send a program or message in all directions by way of the radio or television.
10. channel	chăn'ĕl	chan-nel	A narrow band of frequencies of sufficient width for a single radio communication; a band of radio frequencies assigned to a television station.
11. circuit	sûr'kĭt	cir-cuit	A path over which an electric current can flow.
12. coaxial cable	kō·ăk'sĭ·ăl kā'b'l	co-ax-i-al ca-ble	A special metallic cable for transmitting the visible part of a telecast.
13. commentator	kŏm'ĕn·tā'tĕr	com-men-ta-tor	One who makes explanatory remarks about current events or daily news items.
14. condenser	kŏn·dĕn'sĕr	con-dens-er	An instrument for compressing or storing electricity.
15. cyclometer	sī·klŏm'ê·tĕr	cy-clom-e-ter	An instrument that measures arcs of circles.
16. decibel	dĕs'ĭ·bĕl	dec-i-bel	A unit for measuring sound intensities.
17. dialogue	dī'ȧ·lŏg	di-a-logue	A conversation between two persons in a drama.
18. dielectric	dī'ê·lĕk'trĭk	di-e-lec-tric	A nonconducting material; an insulator.
19. distortion	dĭs·tôr'shŭn	dis-tor-tion	Imperfection in the receiving signal, usually resulting from imperfect design of the transmitting or receiving equipment.
20. electronics ▶	ê·lĕk'trŏn'ĭks	e-lec-tron-ics	That branch of physics that treats of the behavior and effect of electrons, especially in vacuum tubes, and the like.
21. frequency	frē'kwĕn·sĭ	fre-quen-cy	The number of complete cycles per second of an alternating current or voltage.
22. heterodyne	hĕt'ĕr·ô·dīn'	het-er-o-dyne	Pertaining to the production of a difference frequency by combining two frequencies.
23. iconoscope	ī·kŏn'ô·skōp	i-con-o-scope	A cathode-ray television pickup tube for use in electronic television cameras.
24. insulator	ĭn'sṻ·lā'tĕr	in-su-la-tor	A nonconducting material used to prevent escape or access of electric current.

25. interference	ĭn′tẽr·fẽr′ĕns	in-ter-fer-ence	A confusion in a received signal due to undesired signals, noises, strays, or other causes.
26. kilocycle	kĭl′ō·sī′k′l	kil-o-cy-cle	Unit of frequency equal to one thousand cycles a second.
27. Kinescope	kĭn′ē·skōp	Kin-e-scope	A trade-mark applied to the television picture tube in which electrical impulses are translated into picture elements at the receiver.
28. loud-speaker	loud′spēk′ẽr	loud-speak-er	A device for converting audio frequency current into sound waves.
29. megacycle	mĕg′à·sī′k′l	meg-a-cy-cle	Unit of frequency equal to one million cycles a second.
30. microphone amplifier	mī′krō·fōn ăm′plĭ·fī′ẽr	mi-cro-phone am-pli-fi-er	An audio amplifier used to raise the output level of a microphone.
31. microwave	mī′krō·wāv′	mi-cro-wave	An electromagnetic wave that has a frequency higher than 300 megacycles.
32. monitor	mŏn′ĭ·tẽr	mon-i-tor	n. A loud-speaker and its associated amplifier used in the control room to listen to a radio or television program. v. To check quality of transmission through use of a receiver.
33. nonconductor	nŏn′kŏn·dŭk′tẽr	non-con-duc-tor	An insulating material.
34. oscillator	ŏs′ĭ·lā′tẽr	os-cil-la-tor	A radio-frequency generator, especially for a nonrotating type; examples are vacuum tubes, sparks, or arc generators.
35. pantomime	păn′tō·mīm	pan-to-mime	A performance in which the actor imitates another, usually without speaking any lines.
36. reverberation	rē·vûr′bẽr·ā′shŭn	re-ver-ber-a-tion	A succession of echoes caused by reflections of sound within an enclosed space.
37. telecast	tĕl′ē·kàst′	tel-e-cast	Act of broadcasting by television.
38. telephoto	tĕl′ē·fō′tō	tel-e-pho-to	Transmission of photographs or other single images over a wire.
39. television camera	tĕl′ē·vĭzh′ŭn kăm′ẽr·à	tel-e-vi-sion cam-er-a	The pickup unit used in a television system.
40. video	vĭd′ē·ō	vid-e-o	Pertaining to the transmission or reception of an image; a Latin expression meaning *I see.*

Lesson 4 Real-Estate and Insurance Terms

1. abstract of title	ăb'străkt ŏv tī't'l	ab-stract of ti-tle	A summary showing the history of the ownership of a piece of real estate and any claims or charges against it.
2. actuarial	ăk'tṳ·âr'ĭ·ăl	ac-tu-ar-i-al	Pertaining to the calculation of insurance risks.
3. adjuster	ă·jŭs'tĕr	ad-just-er	One who determines the amount payable under a policy for a fire loss, shipping loss, etc.
4. appraisal	ă·prāz'ăl	ap-prais-al	An expert's opinion of the value of land, buildings, or personal property.
5. assessed valuation	ă·sĕsd' văl'û·ā'shŭn	as-sess-ed val-u-a-tion	The appraisal of real estate for taxation purposes.
6. attained age	ă·tānd'āj	at-tained age	The age that the insured has reached at a particular birthday.
7. beneficiaries	bĕn'ĕ·fĭsh'ĭ·ĕr'ĭz	ben-e-fi-ci-ar-ies	Persons to whom the value of an insurance policy is paid.
8. cash surrender value	kăsh sŭ·rĕn'dĕr văl'ū	cash sur-ren-der val-ue	The refund that a life insurance policyholder may receive when he cancels his contract.
9. contingency	kŏn·tĭn'jĕn·sĭ	con-tin-gen-cy	A possible event or condition.
10. conveyance	kŏn·vā'ăns	con-vey-ance	Act of transferring real property to another.
11. coverage	kŭv'ĕr·ĭj	cov-er-age	The extent and kind of protection afforded under an insurance policy.
12. ejectment	ē·jĕct'mĕnt	e-ject-ment	The removal of an occupant of real estate, usually under a court order.
13. endowment	ĕn·dou'mĕnt	en-dow-ment	Insurance in which the policy provides for the payment of a fixed sum to the insured at the expiration of a term of years.
14. fiduciary	fĭ·dū'shĭ·ĕr'ĭ	fi-du-ci-ar-y	A person or company entrusted to hold, control, or manage property.

15. floater policy	flōt′ĕr pŏl′ĭ·sĭ	float-er pol-i-cy	A policy to protect property that is moved about from one place to another.
16. foreclosure	fōr·klō′zhĕr	fore-clo-sure	A legal proceeding to compel the sale of real estate to satisfy a financial claim against it.
17. forfeiture	fôr′fĭ·tụr	for-fei-ture	That which is lost by way of penalty.
18. insurable interest	ĭn·shōōr′á·b'l ĭn′tĕr·ĕst	in-sur-a-ble in-ter-est	A person is said to have an insurable interest in a property or in the life of a person if he might suffer financial loss as a result of the event insured against.
19. irrevocable	ĭ·rĕv′ŏ·ká·b'l	ir-rev-o-ca-ble	That may not be repealed or annulled.
▶ 20. lapsed policy	lăpst pŏl′ĭ·sĭ	lapsed pol-i-cy	A policy that became void because of nonpayment of the premium.
21. lease	lēs	lease	An agreement for the use and occupancy of real estate for a definite consideration (called *rent*) for a definite term.
22. leasehold	lēs′hōld′	lease-hold	An interest in real property in the form of a lease for a period of time.
23. maturity date	má·tū′rĭ·tĭ dāt	ma-tu-ri-ty date	The date on which a policy matures or may be paid.
24. metes and bounds	mētz ănd boundz	metes and bounds	The boundary lines of a piece of property.
25. mortality table	môr·tăl′ĭ·tĭ tā′b'l	mor-tal-i-ty ta-ble	A table that shows the life span of people.
26. mortgagee	môr′gĭ·jē′	mort-ga-gee	One who holds a mortgage.
27. notarize	nō′tá·rīz	no-ta-rize	To authenticate, such as a contract, etc.
28. paid-up policy	pād ŭp pŏl′ĭ·sĭ	paid-up pol-i-cy	A policy on which premiums have been paid in full.
29. patio	păt′ĭ·ō	pat-i-o	A paved area close to a house, used especially for recreation.
30. premises	prĕm′ĭs·ĕz	prem-is-es	A stated portion or parcel of real estate conveyed in a deed.

31. realtor	rē'ăl·tẽr	re-al-tor	A member of the National Association of Real Estate Boards; a real estate broker.
32. realty	rē'ăl·tĭ	re-al-ty	Property that is land as distinguished from personal property.
33. reinstate	rē'ĭn·stāt'	re-in-state	To restore to a former position; to reinstall.
34. renewable	rẽ·nū'á·b'l	re-new-a-ble	That may be made effective again, as a policy that may be renewed.
35. rider	rīd'ẽr	rid-er	A clause added to a policy to cover matters that do not form a part of the policy proper.
36. suburban	sŭb·ûr'băn	sub-ur-ban	Pertaining to an outlying district of a city.
37. survivor	sẽr·vī'vẽr	sur-vi-vor	One who outlives another person or lives beyond a certain time or event.
38. underwriter	ŭn'dẽr·rīt'ẽr	un-der-writ-er	One who underwrites policies of insurance or carries on insurance as a business.
39. urban	ûr'băn	ur-ban	Pertaining to a city or town.
40. zoning	zōn'ĭng	zon-ing	Partitioning a city by ordinance into zones reserved for different purposes, as residential, business, etc.

Lesson 5 Check-Up

Unit Test. Your teacher will dictate 50 terms chosen from the lessons in Unit 2 of Part 4. These terms are selected to test your mastery of the new terms in this unit. Listen closely as each term is dictated, spell the term carefully, and write plainly to assure yourself of a fair test.

Proofreading Test. The following paragraphs represent excerpts from business letters and reports. Some of the italicized words are misspelled. Copy each paragraph, making any corrections necessary in the spelling of the words.

In the new hospital there will be an *anestetist* and an *asperater* assigned to each operating room. The *autoclav* will be kept in Room 3. The *electrokardiograf* and *fluoroscop* will be in Room 4.

The *outpatient* department will be *equipped* with a *resparator* and a *stethoscop*. The *antibotic* medicines and all the *anticeptics* will be kept in the refrigerator on the first floor.

The *assessed valuation* of the hospital is low. The insurance *adjustor* recommended the *apraisle* of the land and buildings. He will write a policy for *maximum covrage* of the property.

Both the *urbon* and *suburbon* zoning laws were changed to permit the hospital to serve a greater area.

The *acoustics* of the hall were excellent for the *television* programs. An *anouncment* of the *broadcast* had been mailed to interested *personel*. The *transmission* was completed without *interfrense* and a *Kineskop* copy was made of all the *audisions*.

Cumulative Test. Your teacher will now dictate 40 terms chosen from Unit 1 of Part 4. These terms will test your retention of the correct spelling of the terms in Unit 1. Spell carefully and write plainly.

Checking Your Tests. Your teacher will give you directions for checking the unit test, the proofreading test, and the cumulative test.

Error Analysis. Classify the errors that you made by noting the type of error beside each term that you misspelled.

Review. Use the appropriate attack procedures for studying the terms that you misspelled on the unit test, on the proofreading test, and on the cumulative test. Remember that Unit 1 contained sound and meaning words.

Retest. The retest will tell you if you have mastered the terms in Units 1 and 2. If you misspelled terms on the retest, continue your attack procedures until you are sure that you can spell all the terms correctly.

Fifty Largest Cities of the United States and Canada
In Order of Population

New York, N. Y.
Chicago, Ill.
Philadelphia, Pa.
Los Angeles, Calif.
Detroit, Mich.
Montreal, Que.
Baltimore, Md.
Cleveland, Ohio
St. Louis, Mo.
Washington, D. C.
Boston, Mass.
San Francisco, Calif.
Pittsburgh, Pa.
Toronto, Ont.
Milwaukee, Wis.
Houston, Tex.
Buffalo, N. Y.

New Orleans, La.
Minneapolis, Minn.
Cincinnati, Ohio
Seattle, Wash.
Kansas City, Mo.
Newark, N. J.
Dallas, Tex.
Indianapolis, Ind.
Denver, Colo.
San Antonio, Tex.
Memphis, Tenn.
Oakland, Calif.
Columbus, Ohio
Portland, Oreg.
Louisville, Ky.
Vancouver, B. C.
San Diego, Calif.

Rochester, N. Y.
Atlanta, Ga.
Birmingham, Ala.
St. Paul, Minn.
Toledo, Ohio
Jersey City, N. J.
Fort Worth, Tex.
Akron, Ohio
Omaha, Nebr.
Long Beach, Calif.
Miami, Fla.
Providence, R. I.
Dayton, Ohio
Oklahoma City, Okla.
Winnipeg, Man.
Hamilton, Ont.

Fifty Large Cities of the World (Outside the Western Hemisphere)
In Order of Population

Tokyo, Japan
London (Greater), England
Shanghai, China
Moscow, U.S.S.R.
Peiping, China
Berlin, Germany
Leningrad, U.S.S.R.
Calcutta, India
Tientsin, China
Paris, France
Bombay, India
Jakarta, Indonesia
Cairo, Egypt
Hong Kong, China
Osaka, Japan
Manila, Philippine Islands
Rome, Italy

Sydney, Australia
Vienna, Austria
Hamburg, Germany
Madrid, Spain
Seoul, Korea
Melbourne, Australia
Canton, China
Chungking, China
Tehran, Iran
Madras, India
Barcelona, Spain
Alexandria, Egypt
Nagoya, Japan
Milan, Italy
Bucharest, Rumania
Brussels, Belgium
Singapore, Malaya

Istanbul, Turkey
Kyoto, Japan
Yokohama, Japan
Copenhagen, Denmark
Budapest, Hungary
Karachi, Pakistan
Stockholm, Sweden
Nanking, China
Birmingham, England
Naples, Italy
Hyderabad, India
Johannesburg, Union of
    South Africa
Glasgow, Scotland
Praha (Prague), Czechoslo-
    vakia
Baku, U.S.S.R.
Delhi, India

States of the United States

State	Abbreviation	Capital	State	Abbreviation	Capital
Alabama	Ala.	Montgomery	Georgia	Ga.	Atlanta
Alaska		Juneau	Hawaii		Honolulu
Arizona	Ariz.	Phoenix	Idaho		Boise
Arkansas	Ark.	Little Rock	Illinois	Ill.	Springfield
California	Calif.	Sacramento	Indiana	Ind.	Indianapolis
Colorado	Colo.	Denver	Iowa		Des Moines
Connecticut	Conn.	Hartford	Kansas	Kans.	Topeka
Delaware	Del.	Dover	Kentucky	Ky.	Frankfort
Florida	Fla.	Tallahassee	Louisiana	La.	Baton Rouge

State	Abbreviation	Capital	State	Abbreviation	Capital
Maine		Augusta	Ohio		Columbus
Maryland	Md.	Annapolis	Oklahoma	Okla.	Oklahoma City
Massachusetts	Mass.	Boston	Oregon	Oreg.	Salem
Michigan	Mich.	Lansing	Pennsylvania	Pa.	Harrisburg
Minnesota	Minn.	St. Paul	Rhode Island	R. I.	Providence
Mississippi	Miss.	Jackson	South Carolina	S. C.	Columbia
Missouri	Mo.	Jefferson City	South Dakota	S. Dak.	Pierre
Montana	Mont.	Helena	Tennessee	Tenn.	Nashville
Nebraska	Nebr.	Lincoln	Texas	Tex.	Austin
Nevada	Nev.	Carson City	Utah		Salt Lake City
New Hampshire	N. H.	Concord	Vermont	Vt.	Montpelier
New Jersey	N. J.	Trenton	Virginia	Va.	Richmond
New Mexico	N. Mex.	Santa Fe	Washington	Wash.	Olympia
New York	N. Y.	Albany	West Virginia	W. Va.	Charleston
North Carolina	N. C.	Raleigh	Wisconsin	Wis.	Madison
North Dakota	N. Dak.	Bismarck	Wyoming	Wyo.	Cheyenne

U. S. Dependencies	Abbreviation	Capital
Canal Zone		
Guam		Agaña
Puerto Rico	P. R.	San Juan
American Samoa		Pago Pago, Island of Tutuila
Virgin Islands		Charlotte Amalie on Saint Thomas Island

Canada: Ottawa (Capital)

Province	Abbreviation	Capital	Province	Abbreviation	Capital
Alberta	Alta.	Edmonton	Prince Edward Island	P. E. I.	Charlottetown
British Columbia	B. C.	Victoria	Quebec	Que.	Quebec
Manitoba	Man.	Winnipeg	Saskatchewan	Sask.	Regina
New Brunswick	N. B.	Fredericton	Newfoundland	Nfld.	St. John's
Nova Scotia	N. S.	Halifax			
Ontario	Ont.	Toronto			

Other Western Hemisphere Countries

South America
Buenos Aires, Argentina
La Paz (and) Sucre, Bolivia
Brasilia, Brazil
Santiago, Chile
Bogotá, Colombia
Quito, Ecuador
Asunción, Paraguay
Lima, Peru
Montevideo, Uruguay
Caracas, Venezuela

Central America
Belize, British Honduras
San Jose, Costa Rica
Guatemala City, Guatemala
Tegucigalpa, Honduras
Managua, Nicaragua
San Salvador, Salvador

West Indies
Hamilton, Bermuda
Havana, Cuba
Ciudad Trujillo, Dominican Republic

Port-au-Prince, Haiti
Kingston, Jamaica

Mexico
Mexico City

Northern-Border States
Chihuahua, Chihuahua
Saltillo, Coahuila
Monterrey, Nuevo León
Hermosillo, Sonora
Ciudad Victoria, Tamaulipas

Why Word-Division Rules?

You have long known that, if it becomes necessary to divide a word at the end of a line of typewriting or of print, division may be between syllables only. This rule precludes dividing such long single-syllable words as *strength* and *through*, as well as many words that are still single-syllable words even after *ed* has been added, as *drowned* and *weighed*. Since the dictionary, as well as the lessons in this text, shows the syllable breakdown of words, you may question the necessity of learning rules for dividing words. While division *may* be made between any adjoining syllables, certain points of division are preferable. Why?

I. To Facilitate Readability. A division that will suggest to the reader what the carried-over portion of the word is likely to be is a help in reading. For example, the division *conven-ience* suggests the complete word more readily than does *con-venience;* likewise, *persuasion*, rather than *per-suasion*. Dividing after an accented syllable helps the reader.

II. To Obtain an Attractive Appearance. The unattractiveness of such divisions as the following is sufficient reason for avoiding them: *self-suf-ficient, does-n't, Thomp-son, $750,-000, Atty.-Gen., 185 Broad-way.*

III. To Avoid Misuse of Space. Remembering that a hyphen takes the same space as a letter helps one avoid such divisions as *camer-a, heav-y, absolute-ly.* Always carry at least three strokes to the next line. The third stroke, however, may be a punctuation mark. Remembering that a one-letter syllable at the end of a line not only looks lost, and is thus unattractive, but also is a "silly" use of space helps one avoid such divisions as *o-bedience* or *e-numerate*. With these general aims in mind, now consider the word-division rules that a typist, a proofreader, or a writer should follow.

1. A one-letter syllable, whether at the beginning or at the end of a word, should not be separated from the rest of the word (see examples in Paragraph III).

2. A one-letter syllable *within* a word should not be carried over to a new line; for example, *sepa-rate, medi-cine, deli-cate, regu-lar.* If two one-letter syllables come together within a word, division is made between those syllables; for example, *radi-ator, cre-ative, gradu-ation.*

3. A two-letter final syllable should not be carried over to a new line unless it is followed by a punctuation mark; thus, *satisfy, delighted;* but, *She was delight-ed.*

4. Four- and five-letter words of more than one syllable, as *begin, idea, only*, should not be divided, for such divisions are both unsightly and a poor use of space. However, a five-letter word of more than one syllable followed by a punctuation mark may be divided.

5. Words that begin with a prefix of two or more letters are preferably divided after the prefix; for example, *im-possible, pro-motion, over-influence, super-abundant.*

6. When a word ends with a suffix of three or more letters, division should be before the suffix; as, *consist-ent, deli-cious, proce-dure, nega-tive, tempera-ment, comfort-able, convert-ible.*

However, if division after a prefix or before a suffix would result in a mispronunciation—that is, would not follow the syllabication of the word—division should be at the point of syllabication; for example, *antic-ipate, pref-erence; combus-tible, spar-kling, compe-tence.*

7. When a final consonant is doubled on the addition of a suffix, the division is between the double letters, provided the last part of the word forms a separate syllable; as, *ship-ping, allot-ted;* but, *occurred, inferred, shipped.*

8. When a suffix is added to a word that itself ends in a double letter, however, division is before the suffix; as, *full-est, pass-ing, careless-ness.*

9. Compound words, whether solid or hyphenated, should be divided only between the elements of the word. Hyphenated words: *self-esteem, machine-made;* solid words: *letter-head, business-man.*

10. Do not divide abbreviations, contractions, personal names, numbers (but *very* long numbers may be divided after any comma in the number), dates, addresses (see Paragraph II for illustrations).

Many words do not come under these special rules. For them, follow dictionary divisions.

INDEX TO WORDS

D. C., 210
daily, 48
dairy, 57
Dallas, 210
damageable, 193
damaged, 106
dangerous, 100
data, 136
daughter, 44
daughters-in-law, 34
day labor, 27
days, 53, 96
Dayton, 210
daze, 53
death, 48
debit, 55
debris, 36, 76
debt, 3, 55, 87
debtor, 142
✗debut, 36, 79
decade, 132
decease, 146
deceased, 55
decedent, 196
deceit, 21
deceitful, 32
deceive, 118
decent, 57, 148
decentralization, 201
decibel, 204
decide, 5, 44
decimal, 4
decipher, 5, 35, 81
decision, 70
declaration, 126
declarations, 193
declare, 150
decline, 136
decoration, 126
decrease, 114
decree, 146
dedication, 171
deduct, 33
deductible, 175
deduction, 171
deductions, 11
deface, 132
defamation, 151
default, 136
defeat, 67
defect, 151
defective, 153
defend, 139
defendant, 160
defense, 62
✗defensible, 62, 98
defer, 22, 33
deference, 22
deficiency, 153
deficit, 142

definite, 8, 9, 13, 154
definitely, 13, 114, 118
definition, 136
degree, 146
Del., 210
Delaware, 210
delay, 23, 86
delayed, 86
delaying, 23
delegate, 139
delegation, 136
Delhi, 210
deliberately, 121
delicate, 90
delicious, 115
delight, 67
delinquent, 132
deliver, 86
delivery, 132
democracy, 163
demonstrate, 76
demonstration, 126
demonstrative, 157
Denmark, 210
denomination, 35, 79
dentifrice, 40, 41
denunciate, 163
denunciation, 167
Denver, 210
depart, 171
department, 50
depend, 22
dependable, 22
dependent, 5
deplete, 136
depletion, 9
deponent, 196
depositor, 157
depository, 160
depot, 136
depraved, 146
depreciation, 160
depression, 182
deprived, 146
depth, 73
deputy, 132
derogatory, 40
Des Moines, 210
descend, 14, 70
descendant, 142
descent, 57
describe, 4, 32
described, 48
describing, 48, 98
description, 5, 15, 106
descriptive, 160
desert, 6, 55
deserve, 90

✗desiccate, 36, 79
design, 87
desirable, 126
desire, 22, 32
desolate, 146
despair, 4, 15, 90
desperate, 90
despicable, 178
despise, 112
despite, 109
dessert, 6, 55
destroy, 48, 153
detail, 50
detailed, 50, 98, 171
detained, 151
deteriorate, 163
determination, 126
determined, 139
determining, 50, 73, 98
detract, 29
detrimental, 160
Detroit, 210
devaluation, 182
develop, 15, 23, 33, 64
developing, 100
development, 23, 64, 96
device, 57
devise, 57
dew, 146
dexterous, 163
diagnosis, 171
dialogue, 204
diamond, 50
diary, 57
dictation, 171
dictator, 171
dictionary, 15
die (n.), 191
die (v), 54
dielectric, 204
diet, 109
differ, 22
difference, 14, 19, 44, 96
different, 22, 44, 96
difficulty, 50, 102
digest, 112
digestible, 112
dignified, 4
dignity, 92
dilemma, 30
diligence, 139
dimension, 178
diminish, 115
direct, 33
direction, 96
director, 88, 123

directory, 171
disability, 167
disable, 139
disagreeable, 132
disappear, 86
disappoint, 109
disapprove, 153
disastrous, 13
disburse, 32
disbursement, 178
discerning, 40, 41
disciplinary, 115, 123
discipline, 4
disclose, 32
discontent, 154
discontinue, 150
discourse, 175
discover, 48, 132
discovery, 175
discredit, 151
discrepancy, 178
discriminate, 157
discrimination, 4, 5
discuss, 136
discussion, 5, 15, 92
disease, 146
diseased, 55
diseases, 86, 98
disgrace, 22, 32
disguise, 115
dishonest, 182
disinfectant, 199
dislike, 39
dismissal, 157
disparage, 151
dispatch, 24, 34
dispatches, 24, 37
disposition, 123
dispute, 151
dissatisfaction, 4, 5
dissatisfied, 157
disseminate, 31, 41, 79, 148
dissent, 148
dissimulate, 148
dissipate, 4
dissolute, 146
dissolve, 109
distance, 48
distinction, 127
distortion, 204
distribution, 112, 123
distributor, 171
district, 167
disturb, 88
dittoed, 81
divers, 146
diverse, 146

diversification, 182
diversion, 178
diversity, 182
divide, 44
dividend, 139
division, 48
docket, 196
doctor, 13, 44
doctrine, 106
document, 9
dollar, 44
domicile, 196
dominant, 4, 79
Dominican Republic, 211
donor, 157
domestic, 88
dormitory, 13
dosage, 199
double, 46
doubt, 12, 48
doubtful, 127
Dover, 210
downtown, 157
dozen, 86
drawing account, 188
dreadful, 88
dreary, 175
dress, 24
dresses, 24
drop-off, 34
drown, 109
drowned, 86
drudgery, 36, 76
dry-clean, 27, 28
due, 146
dull, 153
duly, 21
dummy, 191
duodenal, 81
duotone, 191
duplicate, 136
durable, 139
duress, 167
during, 44
dutiable, 194
dutiful, 157
duty, 33
dye, 21, 32, 54
dyeing, 21, 76, 121
dying, 76

each, 62, 73
earlier, 50, 98
earliest, 48, 98
early, 48
earn, 90

earnings, 25, 121
easement, 196
easier, 50, 98
easily, 23, 50, 102
eastern, 50, 100
easy, 23
eccentric, 160
echo, 88
economic, 139
economist, 182
economize, 157
ecstasy, 73, 140
Ecuador, 211
eczema, 160
edifice, 161
edition, 6, 54, 127
editor, 50, 102
Edmonton, 211
education, 88
effect, 18, 55, 86
effective, 109, 127
efficiency, 11, 124
efficient, 21, 127
efficiently, 32
effort, 44
egotism, 161
Egypt, 210
eight, 21
eighteen, 76, 109, 124
eighth, 73
eighty, 32, 76, 171
either, 21, 37, 98
ejectment, 206
elected, 102
election, 161
electric, 88
electrician, 171
electrocardiograph, 199
electrolysis, 199
electronics, 204
electrotype, 191
element, 70
elementary, 140
eleven, 90
elicit, 148
eligible, 4, 13, 15, 35, 59, 81
eliminate, 13
elite, 161
eloquence, 136
elsewhere, 28
elusive, 6
emanate, 148
embargo, 6, 15, 24, 26, 194
embargoes, 24
embark, 167
embarrass, 5, 23

embarrassing, 23
embassy, 182
embezzle, 182
embezzlement, 171
emblem, 140
embrace, 92
embroidery, 73
emerge, 148
emersed, 175
emigrant, 57
eminent, 59, 136, 148
emotion, 106
emperor, 86
employ, 23
employed, 96
employee, 3, 5, 33, 115
employees, 34, 118
employer, 23, 100, 115
employment, 182
emptied, 102
en route, 178
enclose, 21, 32
enclosure, 21
encore, 36, 79
encounter, 161
encourage, 21, 70
encouragement, 21, 127
encumbrance, 161
encyclopedia, 163
endeavor, 92
endowment, 206
endurable, 171
endure, 5, 88
enemies, 24, 45, 73, 98
enemy, 24, 45
energetic, 136, 151
energy, 88
enforce, 21, 22
enforceable, 21, 37, 121
engage, 32, 67
engagement, 118
engineer, 103
England, 210
Englishwomen, 26
Englishwomen's, 26
engraving, 191
enjoy, 23, 33, 45
enjoyable, 23, 33, 178
enjoyed, 33
enjoying, 33
enjoyment, 33
enlarge, 155
enormous, 70

enough, 48
enroll, 23, 33
enrolling, 23, 103
enrollment, 175
ensemble, 76
entered, 96
enterprise, 9, 106, 124
entertain, 118
enthusiasm, 109
entire, 22, 32
entirely, 98
entitled, 112
entrance, 62
enumerate, 140
enumeration, 171
envelop, 57
envelope, 57, 115
envious, 178
environment, 76
epidemic, 167
epitome, 36, 79
equable, 146
equal, 22, 33
equality, 121
equalization, 182
equalize, 22
equally, 86
equipment, 100
equitable, 146
equivalent, 136
erasable, 146
erase, 32
eraser, 59
erasure, 59
err, 140
error, 90, 151
erroneous, 15
escape, 46
Eskimo, 24, 26
Eskimos, 24
especially, 14, 19, 45
essay, 146
essential, 92
established, 103
establishment, 118
estimate, 13, 19, 90
estimated weight, 194
ethical, 157
etiquette, 76
evaluation, 167
Evans, Mr., 24
Evanses, the, 24
evaporate, 140
evening, 46, 96
eventually, 178
every, 46
everyone, 112
everything, 46, 96

illustrated, 88
illustration, 127
image, 107
imagination, 90, 118
imaginative, 142
imagine, 32, 62
imitator, 179
immaterial, 158
immature, 158
immediately, 14, 19, 86, 98
immense, 107
immerge, 148
immersed, 175
immigrant, 57
imminent, 59, 148
immobility, 202
immortal, 112
immovable, 142
immunity, 199
impanel, 196
impartial, 179
impartiality, 202
impatient, 179
impediment, 142
impervious, 179
impious, 77
implacable, 158
implement, 136
import, 183
importance, 64, 103
important, 45, 98
importer, 194
imposition, 172
impossible, 50, 152
impracticable, 152
impression, 86
impressive, 143
imprest fund, 189
imprint, 179
improbable, 172
improbably, 175
impromptu, 164
improve, 63
improvement, 103
improving, 100
improvise, 179
impulse, 112
inability, 175
inaccessible, 175
inadequate, 153
inauguration, 4
incapacitate, 161
incentive, 140
incentive wages, 202
incessant, 140
inches, 124
incident, 109
incidentally, 132
incipient, 164

incite, 148
incline, 88
include, 45, 154
including, 98
incognito, 161
income statement, 27
incomparable, 172
inconclusive, 179
inconsistent, 158
inconvenience, 79
inconvenient, 35, 82
incorporate, 4
incorporated, 183
increase, 167
increasingly, 179
incredible, 133
incriminate, 50
incur, 6
Ind., 210
indebtedness, 36, 80
indefinite, 140
indefinitely, 175
indelible, 4, 35, 82
indenture, 196
independence, 90
independent union, 202
indestructible, 158
India, 210
Indiana, 210
Indianapolis, 210
indicate, 63
indicating, 100
X indict, 36, 77, 147
indictment, 161
indiscreet, 164
indispensable, 5
indisputable, 172
indite, 147
individual, 48
individually, 63
Indonesia, 210
induction, 202
industrial, 121
industries, 100
inequities, 202
inexhaustible, 36, 80
inexplicable, 40, 41
infallible, 175
infamous, 158
infection, 179
infectious, 179
infer, 22, 23
inference, 4, 22
inferior, 154
inflammable, 143
inflation, 161
inflationary, 172
influence, 179

influential, 180
inform, 33
informant, 202
information, 63, 118
informative, 118
ingenious, 4, 59
ingenuity, 143
ingenuous, 59
inhabitant, 107
inherent, 164
inherit, 183
inheritance, 11
X inimitable, 82
initial, 143
initiate, 164
initiative, 143
injunction, 196
injure, 32
injuries, 124
injurious, 172
injury, 33
innocence, 112, 133
innocuous, 36, 80
innuendo, 24
innuendoes, 24
innumerable, 77
inoculate, 31, 80, 180
inquire, 64
inquiries, 115, 127
inquiring, 100
inquiry, 115
inquisitive, 140
insertion, 164
insight, 148
insignificant, 136
insist, 33
insistent, 172
insolvent, 180
inspector, 143
inspiration, 127
install, 23, 31
installment, 23
instance, 82
instances, 103
instant, 86
instants, 82
instinct, 107
institute, 115
institution, 70, 103
instruction, 86, 124
instruments, 88, 119
insulator, 204
insurable interest, 207
insurance, 92, 121
insure, 32
intangible, 164
integral, 35, 82
integrated, 164

integrity, 9
intelligence, 13, 107
intend, 86
intention, 92
intentionally, 164
intercede, 164
intercept, 180
interdependence, 180
interested, 45
interesting, 13, 63
interfere, 32
interference, 127, 205
interim, 164
interior, 154
interlocutory, 196
intermittent, 167
international, 90
interoffice, 180
interpret, 56, 77, 90
interpretation, 202
interrogate, 158
interrupt, 14, 56, 88, 124
interruption, 143
interstate, 59
intervene, 143
interview, 202
intestate, 59, 196
intimate, 112
intimidation, 167
intolerable, 140
intolerant, 29
intoxicate, 158
intradermal injections, 199
intramuscular injections, 199
intrastate, 59
intravenous injections, 199
introduce, 63
introduction, 92
introductory, 48, 154
introvert, 154
invalid, 140
invalidate, 136
inveigle, 21, 32, 36, 80, 175
invention, 88
inventor, 175
inventory, 176
investigating, 127
investigation, 152
investment, 183
investor, 176
invigorate, 176
invisible, 115

mood, 147
mooring, 195
moral, 6, 56, 67
morale, 6, 56
morale index, 203
moreover, 28, 128
morning, 58, 98
mortal, 93
mortality, 137
mortality table, 207
mortgage, 3, 12
mortgagee, 207
Moscow, 210
motivation, 203
motive, 113
motorist, 141
mountain, 74
mourn, 115
mourning, 58
mouse, 25, 34
mouth, 48
movement, 97
movers, 180
multiply, 116
multitude, 109
municipal, 133
murmur, 70
muscle, 12, 93
muscular, 137
museum, 30, 37, 77, 93
music, 6, 51
mutilate, 137
mutual, 152
my, 26
mysterious, 110, 124
mystery, 88

N. B., 211
N. C., 211
N. H., 211
N. J., 210, 211
N. S., 211
N. Y., 210, 211
Nagoya, 210
naive, 164
Nanking, 210
Naples, 210
narrow, 51
Nashville, 211
nation, 93, 164
national, 48, 97
nationally, 176
native, 46
natural, 51
naturally, 48, 101
naught, 147
N. Dak., 211

Nebr., 210, 211
Nebraska, 211
nebulous, 41
necessarily, 77, 128
necessary, 30, 46, 74
necessity, 63, 75
nee, 164
need, 22
needy, 22
needle, 93
negative, 137
neglected, 122
negligence, 137
negligent, 161
negotiable, 183
negotiate, 162
Negro, 24
Negroes, 24, 26, 103
Negroes', 26, 122
neighbor, 20, 46, 98
neighborhood, 86, 119
neither, 21, 37, 46, 97
nervous, 90
nervousness, 168
net weight, 195
neurotic, 158
Nev., 211
Nevada, 211
nevertheless, 28, 97
New Brunswick, 211
New Hampshire, 211
New Jersey, 211
New Mexico, 211
New Orleans, 210
New York, 210, 211
Newark, 210
Newfoundland, 211
newsstand, 168
Nfld., 211
Nicaragua, 211
nickel, 143
niece, 21
ninety, 122
ninety-five, 35
ninety-six hundred-ths, 28
ninth, 15, 21, 101
N. Mex., 211
noble, 67
noise, 22
nominal, 137
nominal account, 189
nominal wages, 203
nominee, 137
nonconductor, 205
nonessential, 168

nonexistent, 176
no-par stock, 189
normal, 90
North Carolina, 211
North Dakota, 211
northern, 70
nostalgia, 168
notaries public, 25
notary public, 25
notarize, 207
notation, 172
notebook, 27
nothing, 51
notice, 21, 22, 32, 45
noticeable, 21, 37
notify, 137
notoriety, 32
notorious, 141
nought, 147
Nova Scotia, 211
novel, 90
novice, 150
nuclear, 31, 59, 82
nucleus, 59, 77
Nuevo León, 211
number, 152
numbered, 98
numerous, 48

Oakland, 210
objective, 162
objectivity, 203
obligation, 116, 124
obligatory, 162
oblige, 86
obliged, 151
obliterate, 41
obnoxious, 176
obscure, 22
observance, 172
observation, 119
observe, 32
obsolescence, 189
obtain, 22, 33
obtainable, 22, 37
obtaining, 97
obvious, 116
occasion, 14, 19, 41, 63
occasionally, 13, 88, 101
occupancy, 168
occupation, 183
occupational, 93, 101
occupy, 88
occur, 22, 23, 63
occurred, 22, 63, 119

occurring, 119
odd lot, 189
offensive, 4
offer, 46
offered, 46, 98
offering, 98
office, 46
officer, 46
offices, 46
official, 51, 63, 101
offset, 124, 192
often, 65, 154
Ohio, 210, 211
Okla., 210, 211
Oklahoma, 211
Oklahoma City, 210, 211
old-fashioned, 98
Olympia, 211
Omaha, 210
omission, 133
omit, 133
one, 147
one-eighth, 28
one hundred forty-seven, 28
one hundred twenty-five, 30
Ont., 210, 211
Ontario, 211
open, 33
opening, 91, 122
operation, 51, 63, 101
ophthalmoscope, 199
opinion, 48
opportunities, 63, 103
opportunity, 14, 34, 63
oppose, 154
opposite, 65, 151
optician, 133
optimistic, 155
option, 33
optional, 158
orbit, 137
order, 153
ordered, 98
ordinance, 4, 82, 197
ordinary, 65
ordinarily, 67
ordnance, 82
Oreg., 210, 211
Oregon, 211
organist, 143
organization, 51, 101
organized, 88, 103, 133

policyholder, 27, 65
political, 51
politician, 113
poll, 82
poorly, 58
poplar, 56
popular, 56
population, 88
port of embarkation, 195
portable, 176
Port-au-Prince, 211
portend, 148
portfolio, 168
portion, 51, 152
Portland, 210
position, 47
possess, 65
possesses, 65, 119
possession, 14, 19, 51, 119
possessive, 168
possibilities, 34, 88, 122
possibility, 14, 88
possible, 47
possibly, 65, 91, 104
postage-free, 35
postal, 137
postdated, 27
✗ posthumous, 82
postmark, 27
post-mortem, 200
postpone, 124
postscript, 180
✗ potato, 24, 65
potatoes, 24, 34, 65, 122
potential, 9, 11
powerful, 65
practicable, 6, 56
practical, 6, 51, 56
practically, 51, 134
practice, 45
Prague, 210
Praha, 210
prairie, 116
pray, 77
prayer, 99, 107
precarious, 158
precede, 18, 32, 56
precedence, 148
precedents, 148
precious, 51
precise, 32
predetermination, 203
✗ predominant, 35, 82, 137
pre-existing, 29

prefer, 22, 65
preferable, 22
preferably, 40, 41
preference, 22, 37
preferential, 183
preferred, 15, 65, 122
preliminary, 80
prelude, 165
premises, 6, 54, 207
premium, 141
prepaid, 5
preparation, 88, 119
prepare, 47
prepay, 27
preponderance, 4
preposition, 148
prerequisite, 148
prerogative, 5, 77
prescribe, 176
prescription, 180
presence, 18, 51, 58
present, 88
presentiment, 148
presentment, 148
presentation, 80
presents (n.), 18, 58
presents (v.), 47, 97, 134
preservation, 80, 110
preserve, 65
president, 47
president-elect, 30
presidents, 47, 59, 97
president's, 59
presume, 176
presumption, 176
presumptuous, 143
pretend, 107, 148
pretense, 143
pretentious, 183
prevail, 91
prevalent, 137
prevention, 143
previous, 107, 155
prey, 77, 110
pride, 155
priest, 124
primary, 116
Prince Edward Island, 211
principal, 16, 18, 51, 65, 77
principle, 16, 18, 40, 41, 51, 77
prior, 33
priority, 162
prisoner, 67
privilege, 15, 30, 107
pro forma, 195
pro rata, 28, 180

pro-American, 30
pro-British, 29
probability, 80
probably, 47, 99
probate, 197
problem, 47
procedure, 5, 15
proceed, 5, 14, 18, 19, 56, 64
process, 67
procession, 15, 110
proclaim, 150
procure, 116, 176
produce, 47
producer, 47
producing, 47, 99
product, 66
production, 66, 119
professional, 107
professor, 66
proficient, 165
profit, 22, 23, 33, 66, 77
profited, 22
prognosis, 200
program, 86
progress, 66
prohibit, 155
prohibitive, 159
project, 91
✗ prominent, 18, 58, 113
promise, 47
promises, 6, 54
promissory, 159
promissory note, 190
promoter, 143
promotional, 124
promptly, 93
promulgate, 168
pronounce, 110
pronunciation, 162
proof, 70, 77
proofreader, 192
propaganda, 134
propel, 6
properly, 91
properties, 67, 119
property, 26, 67
prophecy, 6, 7, 59
prophesy, 6, 7, 59
prophet, 77, 113
proportion, 68, 75
proportionate, 35, 82
proposal, 125
propose, 54
proposed, 68, 104
proposition, 128, 148
proprietorship, 35

prosecute, 6, 7, 59, 197
prospect, 86
prospective, 59
prospectus, 172
prosper, 33
prosperity, 110
prosperous, 116, 128, 176
protect, 66
protected, 68, 119
protection, 86, 125
protégé, 165
protest, 66, 190
protested, 183
protocol, 6
proud, 70
proved, 45, 99
provide, 47
Providence, 210, 211
providing, 47, 99
province, 88
provision, 91
proviso, 195
✗ pseudonym, 83
✗ psychiatry, 40, 41
psychic, 148
psychology, 12
published, 104
Puerto Rico, 211
punctual, 162
punish, 93
punishment, 108
purchasable, 68, 101
purchaser, 172
purchasing, 66, 104
purely, 58
purpose, 32, 47, 54
pursue, 32, 70
pursuing, 70, 104
puzzle, 91

qualification, 141
qualify, 134
qualitative, 30, 41, 59, 83
qualities, 68, 119
quality, 18, 68
quandary, 165
quantitative, 30, 59, 83
quantities, 68, 119
quantity, 13, 18, 68, 152
quarantine, 168
quarrel, 151
quarreled, 68, 104
quarter, 47

waitress, 177
waive, 60
waiver, 173
walkout, 185
want, 56
ware, 149
warrant, 5, 15
warship, 56
Wash., 210, 211
Washington (D. C.), 210
Washington (state), 211
waste, 18, 60
wasteful, 155
wave, 60
waybill, 41
we, 26
weak, 60
weakness, 153
weapon, 91
wear, 149
weather, 18, 56, 71
week, 60

weekday, 24
weekdays, 24
weigh, 20
weighed, 66, 83, 104
weight, 18, 60, 101
weird, 21
welfare, 15
West Virginia, 211
Western, 122
wharfage, 195
whatsoever, 104
whenever, 128
whereas, 180
whether, 18, 56
who, 26, 27
whole, 32, 59, 71
wholesale, 102
wholly, 15, 21, 76, 110, 122
whose, 26, 71, 125
wife, 25
window, 34
Winnipeg, 210, 211
Wis., 210, 211

Wisconsin, 211
withdraw, 35
withdrawal, 122
withdrew, 120
without, 104
witness, 27, 71
wives, 25, 34, 128
woman, 25
women, 25, 49, 99
women's, 49, 120
won, 147
won't, 56
world, 26
world's, 26
worship, 56
would, 87
wouldn't, 87
wrap, 110
wrapping, 83, 123
wrench, 174
wrestle, 174
write, 60, 87
writing, 120
written, 51, 102

wrong, 87
wrote, 75, 87
W. Va., 211
Wyo., 211
Wyoming, 211

year's, 125
yellow, 49
yield, 108, 120
yielded, 120
Yokohama, 210
you, 26, 27
your, 26, 54, 102
you're, 54
yours, 26, 123
yourself, 102

zenith, 51, 144
zipper, 169
zoning, 208